Caste Matters

ADVANCE PRAISE FOR THE BOOK

'A new voice has emerged among the younger generation of Dalits in India. It is impatient with earlier styles of Dalit politics and rejects both ceremonial recognition and opportunist electoral alliances. The new voice is angrier, yet wiser. It promises to learn from the experiences of racially oppressed people elsewhere in the world and offers a more principled strategy of seeking allies. Suraj Yengde has written a book that bubbles with energy and passion. It demands to be read'—Partha Chatterjee, Columbia University, New York

'Suraj Yengde's book is a theoretically sophisticated, anthropologically interesting, historically wide-ranging and morally compelling reflection on caste in India. It is exactly the kind of mirror India needs to look into. It is angry, but takes its anger in a reflective, analytical and productive direction. This book will cement Yengde's reputation as one of the more novel voices confronting the realities of caste in his generation'—Pratap Bhanu Mehta, vice chancellor, Ashoka University

'This book about the menacing prowess of caste is an important addition to the anti-caste armoury. It is a must-read for those who display various degree of caste-blindness, saying caste is a thing of the past. It is useful even for those who acknowledge the existence of caste, but believe it would simply melt away under the pressure of urbanization and modernity. For the Dalits, its worst victims, either nothing has changed or things have only become worse. The continuing practice of untouchability, growing number of atrocities and falling markers of development parameters are the hard evidence. But Dalits are not counted within human pathos, their numbers are embedded and hidden.

Caste Matters is an experiential exposition of the hidden side of caste by a promising young scholar who has risen from the dark alleys of his childhood to the academic dazzle of iconic Harvard. It is replete with reflections over the raw experiences of a poor Dalit child as also with the mature commentary about the changes that befell his universe'—Anand Teltumbde, senior professor and chair, Big Data Analytics, Goa Institute of Management

Caste Matters

Suraj Yengde

PENGUIN
VIKING
An imprint of Penguin Random House

VIKING

USA | Canada | UK | Ireland | Australia
New Zealand | India | South Africa | China

Viking is part of the Penguin Random House group of companies
whose addresses can be found at global.penguinrandomhouse.com

Published by Penguin Random House India Pvt. Ltd
7th Floor, Infinity Tower C, DLF Cyber City,
Gurgaon 122 002, Haryana, India

First published in Viking by Penguin Random House India 2019

Copyright © Suraj Yengde 2019

ISBN 9780670091225

Typeset in Adobe Garamond Pro by Manipal Digital Systems, Manipal
Printed at Replika Press Pvt. Ltd, India

www.penguin.co.in

To aamche papa, Milind Vishwanath Yengde, my man on whose love I continue to build my foundation

And aamchi mummy, Rohini Yengde, for all the love and care she continues to bequeath

The 13 Yengdes:
Chandrabhagabai, Mohan, Sunanda, Deepak, Amrapali, Pavan, Samyak, Nitin, Pranali, Akash, Priyanka, Harsh, Prerana

Contents

Introduction

Caste Souls: Motifs of the Twenty-first Century

Taking me into her cushy arms, my *aai* (paternal grandmother) was reminding me of the importance of my presence in her life. 'My dearest *maajhya baalla*, you are so full of life. You've the best eyes. You've so many qualities that I can barely count them.' Her darkened face and frail skin glow in the night, the cheapest light bulb in the market—known as 'zero-power bulb', which truly was a lightless bulb—the only source of light in the room, was switched off. She was consoling me in the room the size of a Toyota Minibus that I shared with her, my mother, father, sister and brother. I shared the floor space underneath the cot with my sick father and brother. Perpendicular to the cot on nylon mats slept my mother and sister.

Running her palm on my face in circles, Aai started massaging my head. Her soft palm had seen everything—the horrors of untouchability, the traditions of imposed inferiority, and her resolution to labour to build her family's life by working in farms and fields as a landless labourer, a servant at someone's house or in the mill. She represents the traditions of unknown yet so great people. The people made outcastes by the Hindu religious order, deemed despicable, polluted, unworthy of life beings whose mere sight in public would bring a cascade of violence upon the entire community.

1

In India, casteism touches 1.35 billion people. It affects 1 billion people. It affects 800 million people badly. It enslaves the human dignity of 500 million people. It is a measure of destruction, pillage, drudgery, servitude, bondage, unaccounted rape, massacre, arson, incarceration, police brutality and loss of moral virtuosity for 300 million Indian Untouchables.[1]

In school I was humiliated for not paying fees on time. The clerk, Tony, would visit the classroom every quarter and call out my name, asking me to stand up. Once I did, he would read out how many months of fees were pending. The higher the number, the more the embarrassment. My classmates added shame to that embarrassment by quietly staring at me in disgust. This was a regular occurrence. Every time Tony came to class, I wanted to leave school and join the hustlers in my slum; they made money and lived as they wanted, without relying on anyone's disrespect to get through the hustle called life.

I grew up in relative poverty in the early part of my life, until I reached sixth grade. After that my family was downgraded to a level below poverty, officially known as Below Poverty Line (BPL). BPL is a state-determined category that calculates the degrees of deprivation. The Tenth Planning Commission fixed seven 'parameters'. Kerala has nine parameters, while Haryana has five parameters to identify families in regard to ownership of land and access to employment, education level, status of children, sanitation, roof, floor, safe drinking water, transportation, food, ownership of colour TV, fridge and so on. In addition, there is an income cap which varies and is adjusted according to one's non-ownership of the above. In Maharashtra, the BPL numbers are premised on the basis of thirteen factors, identifying 46 lakh people (close to 50 per cent of the total population) below the poverty line in the 1990s and 39 per cent in the 2000s.[2] In the year 2012, a World Bank report calculated 17 per cent of the total population below the poverty line. The report stressed on the rising poverty in the northern and eastern districts of Maharashtra. My district, Nanded, had 18 to 24 per cent of the population below the poverty line.[3] There was, however, no distinction made between families belonging to the Scheduled Caste category and other categories. My family, on the urban fringes, fit into the BPL category perfectly.

Caste is understood through various prisms, thus making it the most misunderstood topic of dialogue on/in India. Caste is thought of as synonymous with reservations, Dalits, Adivasis, manual scavenging, poverty, Dalit capitalism, daily-wage labourers, heinous violence, criminality, imprisonment, Rajputs, Brahmins, Banias, Kayasthas, OBCs, etc. These are some of the many variations that bear witness to the everyday nakedness of caste. However, what remains undiscussed (and therefore invisible) is the multiple forms in which caste maintains its sanctity and pushes its agenda through every aspect of human life in India. Caste plays an important role in every facet and over an unthinkably large domain of public and private life.

So, my family had no agricultural land, colour TV or fridge and our income level was as low as it could be as my father was bedridden (health reasons meant he remained unemployed for most of our lives). He did not own a house. We lived on an inherited property of 30×40 feet, half the size of a basketball court—it was evenly distributed among three families comprising sixteen members in all. Access to sanitation was a struggle as we had only one bathroom and toilet. During the morning hours, cousins and siblings would line up as everyone's school started at around the same time. The education level in my house did not go beyond tenth grade. Rusty, corrugated iron sheets that served as the roof were placed on fragile brick walls, pressed down with heavy stones weighing 10–20 kg so that they didn't fly in the wind. Iron sheets transmit electrical current, and the chances of the stones slipping was greater during the rainy season. Iron sheets also meant that we got the first intimation of any change in weather. They were our live weather reports. Drizzles would alert us about the arrival of rain. We were the first to notice as those drops made thunderous noise. When it was summer the iron sheets would attract harsh sunlight. Whoever sat underneath them on a good summer day would choke as it was difficult to breathe. Due to lack of insulation the winter did not spare us either. We slept in the house bearing the ruthless weather. Our prayers round the clock were to somehow get rid of those iron sheets. Sadly, they were never answered. Whenever I visited my mother's side of the family I would wake up surprised to notice that it had rained the previous night and I didn't get to know—they had a thick roof made of cement which made no announcement of rain. The noise of a downpour in my own house made it difficult to sleep. To survive in such a situation, I volunteered to do odd jobs, desperately looking for temporary relief despite my parents' resistance. Once I thought of joining the boot factory where my friends from the area worked as manual labourers. Another time I worked on groundnut soil in the fertile region of Vidarbha, accompanying my mother's family; I worked as a manager overseeing my father's newspaper; I worked as a helper to a truck driver; I worked in a warehouse, all in my attempt to make ends meet. I did all this before I reached puberty.

My family continued to live in the shared house with one room and a kitchen. Till recently, when my mother decided she could not bear the pain of the broken tin roof any longer. She moved to my uncle's house temporarily. She awaits the government-promised subsidized housing for people in the BPL category. This promise of over six years ago has kept her hopes alive. Each year, she gets happy noticing the visit of government officials to survey the house. And like each year, her hopes vanish. Her faith in the government arises not out of trust but from the hopelessness that she was put under by the state.

I grew up in a Dalit neighbourhood. Like all Dalit neighbourhoods in India, mine too was most neglected and placed on the fringes of power structures. The local government turned a blind eye towards us and our problems. Our area was seen by local authorities as despicable, hence it seldom received services of cleanliness and care. Outside each house was a dirty canal that carried faeces in the open, and flies hovering the dirt would often find their way into our house and kitchen. The canal was uncovered and shallow. More often than not, one of the flies would end up in the food we had to consume. Children would be crawling on the streets while their parents worked, flies hovering around their mouths. It was representation of poverty-stricken India.

Malaria-carrying mosquitos and typhoid-carrying flies had a permanent presence in our lives. The diseases that afflicted us were related to this exposure to viruses, a direct outcome of the lack of care and the negligence accorded to our existence. Weekly, a cleaner from the Mehtar, Mahar or Maang caste (employed by the city corporation through a Brahmin/Bania sub-contractor) would manually clean the canal and put the slime that consisted of people's leftover food, shit, bathwater and all kinds of human and animal waste in the open for two to seven days. It would then harden and be difficult to remove. Crawling babies often ended up playing on this mountain of sewerage.

Many times, our cricket balls would end up in this canal and we had to dip our bare hands into the contaminated, darkened, thick muck, searching for it by going horizontal and navigating through the mess. We would often end up catching the ugliest and filthiest discarded things. Sometimes, it would be human waste, at other times hair, nails and other things the very thought of which brings nausea.

The neighbourhoods near ours were similarly infamous. The one on the west was Ambedkar Nagar and another on the east was

Jai Bhim Nagar. Neither of these areas had a respectable reputation. Alarm bells would ring immediately if someone learned that I came from one of these areas. All kinds of stereotypes and prejudices were hurled against me and others who belonged to this part of the marked town. Whenever asked in school or college I would conveniently mention a neighbouring Brahmin area as mine. But casteists are casteists. They would question me about the house number and my neighbours. My lie would be caught and I would get a spiteful gaze to add to my embarrassment. Because those who lived there were not 'people'. They were identified by their occupations: maids, servants, labourers, factory workers and hotel dishwashers.

These areas did not fit into the modern definition of working-class neighbourhoods even though the majority of people living here were workers—skilled, semi-skilled, unskilled and so on. They never had what one would call a 'job' their entire lives. All they had was enslavement without a guarantee of fair returns. They lived with constant troubles which were not of their own making. Thus, they never enjoyed a protected working-class stature. They were class outcastes who had the bare minimum for survival. They seldom had a stable job or a life. Owing to financial distress, many turned to drugs and crime as refuge as they seemed to be the only avenues open for survival. Fights—verbal and physical—violence, prostitution, sexual abuse, alcohol and drug abuse were common. These were the circumstances I grew up in.

~

After one of my lectures on caste and race in Indian and African university campuses at Yale, I was asked by an Indian-American sophomore, 'How do you identify one's caste?' He paused—a moment of silence followed, and the appalled gaze of his classmates stunned him. He was taken aback in embarrassment. He immediately shot me an apologetic gaze.

At another event in Johannesburg. I was attending a lecture on the subject of race as unbecoming of middle-class privilege. Later, I was asked by my friend from the Indian–South African community, Shenny, 'How do you recognize one's caste?' Everyone surrounding her, including Indian Muslims and Hindus, paused and followed her question with a supportive nod, eager to know my answer.

At Harvard, during a discussion on caste, an African-American law professor invited me to her office to discuss the topic in detail. 'Oh! We did not know this. This is great information and I have learnt a great deal,' affirmed the acclaimed figure on campus.

Caste as a social construct is a deceptive substance, known for its elemental capacity to digress from its primary motive of existence that governs this oldest system of human oppression, subjugation and degradation. Originated in the Hindu social order, it has infiltrated all faiths on the Indian subcontinent. As old as the order of Indic civilization, the phenomenon of controlling human capacity, creativity and labour has been core to its ideological performance secured by strict legal order. Caste in India is an *absolute* sanction—of the dominant class over the dominated. Its strict division into five categorical instances organized in horizontal capacities is an archetype of legitimized apartheid. Caste in India is observed according to one's location in one of these five categories. The conversation on caste is navigated by the respective person's investment in the system.

My life was controlled by my surroundings, which had a defining influence on me. Having no power to demonstrate my equal self, violence and harshness proved to be the only way I could emphasize my presence. Anything other than that would not be acknowledged by the 'Others' of my world—Dalits included.

Injustice and mistreatment animated my life experience. I became bitter when experiences of naked injustice were heaped upon me. As I grew older I became extremely sensitive and was constantly looking for hints of injustice or mockery being hurled at me. As soon as I realized that I had been unjustly treated I would become sad and agitated. Other memories of similar mistreatment would immediately flash in my mind like lightning. This would further cause me anguish and agitate me because of my powerlessness. Despite the academic and professional credentials that I had carefully honed, I was still treated like an uneducated labourer from my area—vulnerable and unprotected. I noticed that people were denying me the bare minimum respect and recognition that I desired as an educated man. I was no one, my credentials and my desire could not shine through. I was forced to adjust within the caricatured stereotype of a Dalit—a violent, undeserving, meritless, criminal being. The strict apartheid based on caste and religion retains absolute sanctity, giving little or no occasion to understand the humanity of the 'lowly', 'polluted' or 'unmeritocratic' Dalit. Thus, Dalits live under constant fear and are feared and their humanity denounced. Dominant-caste parents casually stereotype the Dalit classmates of their children, endorsing the popularly held belief of Dalit criminality as a paramount defence of their casteist attitude.

Due to this, a Dalit individual has to live his/her life in marked isolation or anonymity. Most Dalits living in urban cities who have managed to enter into desired professions continue to live in anonymity. Once, a well-known advertising company owner from Mumbai started pointing out the names of successful advertising giants to me. 'The top three in the industry are Dalits, but they are scared to acknowledge themselves as such. People know it but they still hide it.' A successful management professional working for Reliance Industries confessed to me one day that he was a tribal from Haryana. With much difficulty he admitted his social location in the Indian caste order. He had not availed himself of the benefits accorded to Scheduled Tribes for fear that his colleagues might discover his tribal identity.

The answer to the questions raised by my friend, colleague and professor lies in the fact that those who openly defend or have a defensive justification of the caste system or present their 'naivety' over such a gruesome form of subjugation give historical references for the indefinite perpetuation of the caste system. Those who enjoy the privileges of caste never want to attack an abhorrent system as that would threaten their position of power. They are unwilling to face challenges to the caste privileges that were granted to them without any work. Many in this category offer 'merit' as a justification for this attitude without paying attention to their privileges that add up to the creation of 'merit', which is then considered 'impartial'. Their cultural and social capital becomes 'merit'. And therefore, anyone lacking access to these avenues is judged against their predetermined merit. In a competitive, unjust world, merit becomes an excuse for the historically privileged and dominant groups to rally against welfare measures that are oriented towards addressing inbred social inequalities. To address an unequal system, provisions to improve material conditions are necessities. Such material conditions are based on improving the living conditions of those who are oppressed and deprived. Currently, numerical scores are taken as an arbitrary measure of a person's ability to study further, notwithstanding the fact that merit is an *outcome* and not representative of something. It is an outcome of family (support, care and attention to child's education, extracurricular activities, education and economic condition), surroundings, economic support, teachers and access to quality schooling. Entrance exams are designed in a way to cater to the population which has all or most of the above boxes checked. Therefore, anyone coming from such a background can easily segue into the so-called merit-oriented world.

The networks that become the lingua franca of a capitalist society are nothing but caste-based ties, wherein a person from a specific caste ensures that his fellow caste people are given opportunities. In education and the job market, networks play a primary role. Guidance and mentorship are part of these networks, which are critical for students choosing the future course of action. In businesses and most other careers, caste networks play a significant role. They are nothing but euphemisms for caste nepotism. Many people who have seldom experienced the above don't bother about these issues. By choosing to remain silent, the dominant castes effectively practise a thinly veiled 'caste terrorism' by pleading 'ignorance' over caste issues.

This 'ignorance' is practised, it is intentional to not have to face up to reality and instead continue living in a cocooned world. Therefore, their problems become the rest of the world's problems. The rape of Jyoti Singh Pandey, aka 'Nirbhaya', in Delhi in December 2012 was disgraceful and it deserved the attention it got. However, how does one explain the fact that six years earlier, in 2006, forty-year-old Surekha Bhootmange was mercilessly raped along with her seventeen-year-old daughter Priyanka, a twelfth-grade topper, by the Kunbi-Marathas of Khairlanji village, not far from Nagpur, in broad daylight at the village square? Chilli powder, rods and sticks were forced into their vaginas. They were stripped, battered and then paraded naked— and eventually murdered. In this brutal episode, Surekha's sons Roshan, twenty-one, and Sudhir, nineteen, were also stripped, mercilessly beaten and killed in cold blood.[4] The issue did not get the desired media coverage. Had it not been for Dalit activists and a young American reporter who was then interning at the *Times of India*, it would have been completely buried. Even if it had received enough media attention, one wonders how much public outrage it would have generated. Did we have a national uprising after the Khairlanji massacre was reported? Did we take this act as a moment of national disgrace? On the contrary, the Dalits who tried to fight the injustice were hounded by the police and the state. Many individuals had to flee their hometowns to avoid arrest. How can we continue to be 'ignorant' when 'every day three Dalit women are raped, every hour two Dalits are assaulted, two Dalits are murdered, and two Dalit homes are torched'?[5]

Untouchability remains a lifeline of India's present. As recently as 2015, more than 50 per cent of households in the country admitted to practising or witnessing untouchability in urban capitals such as Delhi. India-wide, 30 per cent of Indians have no hesitation in imposing the worst form of human oppression—untouchability—upon fellow humans.[6] In Tamil Nadu, a study over four years (2014–18) revealed that over 640 villages in twenty districts surveyed practise untouchability.[7] Clearly, untouchability and casteism are not things of the past. They are real and present. They are everyday and personal.

Those who do not know about the above incidents and statistics are the ones who partake in perpetuating violent casteism.

~

This book sets out to present the explosive issues in India's totalitarian caste society. It intends to spark the type of public conversations that most shy away from. It is the issue of Brahmin supremacy, inter alia caste supremacy. The Brahmin as a social category has to be tackled and brought forth in critical conversations. Putting the pioneering dialogues of Phule and Ambedkar in the forefront, this book aims to Socratize the dialogical thinking on caste. This kind of method elevates human desire to a level of critical thinking where hierarchies melt and curiosity takes precedence. It is an open-ended inquiry where questions are commonly owned and a democratic process is deployed to find answers. The purpose of such an exercise is not to gain an upper hand or put anyone down, rather it is an opportunity to dive deep into the domain of one's unfulfilled desire for knowledge. Thus, the book aims to bring forward issues of deep philosophical concern that degrade the human personality, by putting the subject in the mould of a conversational tradition—a tradition that believes in the eternal power of conversation and has resolved to encourage self-criticism.

Indian caste society has willingly embraced its violent and toxic ethos. Deep hatred of the Other is a fuel for survival. India has been unleashing caste terrorism upon 'lesser' defamed bodies since the advent of Vedas-sponsored casteism. Brutal chronicles from the past and the continuing experiences of humiliation and stigma in the present determine our imagination, which means having impunity to physical violence on the bodies of labourers working on sites, maids in houses, servants in offices, peasants in fields, orphaned children on streets, beggars on the peripheries of temples—all of whom invite contempt in today's India. We have discovered new reasons to discredit the precious lives of the marginalized sections of society.

My father, Milind, was educated till ninth grade and my mother, Ranju, till seventh grade. My father was the eldest of three siblings and did odd jobs as a teenager. Having a mill-worker father who indulged in heavy drinking and a mother who worked as a maid put enormous responsibility on his fragile shoulders. So he started delivering milk cans in the morning hours and cleaning the floors of a lodge as a child labourer. He worked long hours and was a social person, often demonstrating interest in matters of the intellectual kind. He was polite and could win people's hearts. On one such occasion, he endeared himself to one of his clients, who was a Muslim banker. The banker offered this floor-cleaning staffer a job of a peon, equivalent to his educational qualifications. Eventually, my father was to establish eight social and cultural organizations, began a school for the underprivileged, was an active member in the Dalit Panther movement and a committed BAMCEF/BSP (the Backward and Minority Communities

Employees Federation/Bahujan Samaj Party) activist. He also went on to edit a daily (colour) newspaper, *Daily Sarvjan,* and a weekly, *Vastunishta Vichar* (Objective Thoughts), both in Marathi.

My mother was forcibly married after her father's death by her tyrant uncle and elder cousin, both of whom she ended up cursing her entire life. There is a nasty misogynistic custom in traditional India where marrying a girl child is the only primary responsibility of the male members. After her father is dead, the girl child has to be married within six months or not marry for another three years. Owing to this bizarre custom, my mother was put on the marriage market when she was barely fourteen. Just having passed seventh grade, she was summoned to a group of people visiting from a neighbouring district, Nanded. Dressed in her teenage attire, she was asked to put on her aunt's saree with a little make-up of powder and eye colour. She served them tea and she was accepted as the bride.

My father resisted the marriage as he was not prepared, but his parents saw marriage as the only way to control his big aspirations. For them, an unmarried life meant that he would not be accountable to anyone, which was the kind of life my father preferred. My mother, who had friends belonging to the Komati, Brahmin and Marwari communities, had thought of getting a good education and a job, just as they would. She aspired to become financially independent and support her poverty-stricken family. But, despite protestations against marriage from both my parents, they were urged to tie the knot by older people in the family who eventually died within a decade or so.

In no time, Ranju was married. In the marriage procession, she sat beside a man she had barely spoken to. People came up to her and gave her wishes for the marriage. But in the photographs, Ranju is seldom looking up. Her eyes are mostly cast downwards, thinking about the world of innocence and the future she had imagined that was all going to be left far behind.

Ranju's mother, Sarubai, saw her young, beautiful daughter getting married to a man nine years older than her. Sarubai had tried to prevent it from happening, but the elder male members of the family did not listen to her. Having lost her husband, Sarubai did not matter to the family, let alone her opinion.

Having married at such a young age, Ranju's first child was born when she was fifteen. As is the custom in India, the bride goes to live with the groom's family after marriage. The woman, or in this case, the girl, is alone, exposed and vulnerable, and has yet to acclimatize to the new family's rules, tastes, wishes, dialects, daily schedules, in-laws' commands, new neighbours and so on. Everything must be fully understood and managed by the new bride. She has to make huge efforts to change her mode of behaviour and attitude in order to fit into the new house because that is where she will live her entire life until her death. Walking on this thin thread is her sole responsibility.

Ranju was trying to adjust into the new world that was far and distant from her own—physically as well as emotionally. In this entire process, she braved all the odds. Bearing a child is perhaps the happiest moment for a bride as her fertility is valued in the entire household. And the new baby is her way of winning more respect.

But Ranju's first child died prematurely. She was yet to fully comprehend the experience of bearing a child. It had happened to her when she was not in complete control. She was a passive observer of this calamity. When the baby that suckled at her breast for a day and a half was suddenly gone, Ranju was tormented. She suffered a shock. As days passed, the loss began to sink in. She cried hoarsely at not being able to see her young baby. She was still lactating and the milk had to be released as it caused her pain. She suffered for another month, releasing her milk in a bag of cotton. She did not receive medical attention and care, which is the common fate of a poor person in India.

When Ranju was five months pregnant, she got pain in her legs. It was so unbearable that she cried out loud for an entire day. No one bothered about her, nor did they inquire about the difficulties she was facing. When her husband returned from work, he took her to the hospital, where it was diagnosed that she has lost water content and she desperately needed saline. For two days she was put on twenty-six saline drips, trying to bring her back to life. Ranju's mother-in-law, Chandrabhagabai (Chandra), treated Ranju as her own daughter and nursed her at the hospital. Ranju survived but her foetus had clearly been affected.

One day in her seventh month, her stomach pain increased suddenly. She was in tremendous pain. Once again, she was not given proper medical attention. When she was rushed to the infection-laden government hospital—that lacked proper medical facilities—she gave birth. The baby boy was weak and required serious care. Having no money to admit him in the intensive care unit, the boy's fate was sealed. The doctors did not furnish any medical reports on the cause of the infant's death. There were theories as to what might have caused the baby's death but no word came from the medical side.

Both my grandmothers suffered the intense pain of patriarchy clubbed with the vicious marks of casteism branded on their resilient skin. Their eyes were as deep as one could imagine, that brought me ashore from my uncharted fears. They worked as house servants or cooks in the households of 'upper-caste' maliks or malkins (literally translated as masters and mistresses). I recall an incident with my maternal grandmother, Sarubai Maay, who was a maid in the house of a Bania. She avoided taking her grandchildren to work for fear of exposing her pitiful life. One day, as a curious ten-year-old, I insisted and followed her to see where she worked. She was mortified upon learning that I was there, watching her clean a toilet. I suddenly got the urge to pee. Initially, she was hesitant for me to use the facility. But seeing a ten-year-old in pain melted her heart. She did the unthinkable. She allowed me to use the bathroom of the maliks that was placed outside their luxurious house for the use of visitors. During the course of my less-than-40-second stay in the bathroom, I could see my grandmother moving side to side in anxiety, as if to caution me to come out before anyone from the house spotted me.

I successfully used the toilet and my grandma almost pulled me outside so that she could flush away the evidence. As she did this, a woman with an eye of suspicion glanced at me from behind the door of the house. Her face turned red—her forehead already had a red bindi on it. I was positive she had not seen me exit the bathroom but she suspected something. Her suspicion turned my grandmother's wrinkled face—where each wrinkle was as fixed and historical as the carved layers of sedimentary rock revealing only pain and fear—pale. Maay stood aghast, staring at the woman and then looking away, as if hoping to avoid the abuse she might have to hear. She hoped that she would not be insulted in front of her grandson who studied at an English-medium school, a fact she was very proud of. The inevitable happened. The malkin cursed my grandma with the kind of contempt one has towards a person who has murdered their family members. I did not understand the nature of the curse words, nor their meaning, but as a ten-year-old I recognized the negativity. The malkin did not stop there but also directed her rage towards me. I felt very vulnerable and insecure. I crouched, trying to hide my face.

This incident brought home to me my beingness as a Dalit. The behaviour of this person who yelled nasty and derogatory comments upon the suspicion that a ten-year-old Dalit boy, the grandson of their maid, had used a bathroom on the fringe of their house was unacceptable. I was lesser than the bathroom that was a receptacle of shit. I did not know what I was to imagine. Is there a lexicon that gathers the experiences of such an unexplainable act? I am yet to find it. It remains the marked tattoo that I carry unwillingly—that is why caste matters.

~

We cannot begin a conversation about India without prominently engaging with the metaphors of caste, society and the intra-relations of culturally similar communities. The idea of difference forms the bedrock of discrimination, and thus, despite the commonality of caste as a defining category—Ambedkar referred to this as a 'cultural unit[y]'[8]—there is a strong sense of grouping amongst the members of each caste, sub-caste and sub-sub-caste.

Our impulse to celebrate the common humanity irrespective of differences has been atrophied owing to the diminishing capacity to love. This catastrophic occurrence is the outcome of what Cornel West aptly describes as a market-oriented 'spiritual blackout'—a relative eclipse of integrity, honesty, decency and courage' in the face of naked violence and deceit.[9]

India is not yet a nation. It is still in an improvisational mode like a jazz band that needs to perform repeatedly together in order to uplift every voice in the chorus. India as a mythical construct on the world map gives everyone a shape of their existence. However, beyond the physicality of the nation state, India is a very loosely knit community. Barring its Constitution, nothing ties its citizens to each other. Groupism combined with casteism produces feelings of hostility among different groups. Ambedkar had presciently observed that each caste is a nation in itself as each caste has its own caste-consciousness that did not help to form a fellowship of national feeling.[10] And due to the caste-nation feeling—a sentiment of self-centred growth overlooking the larger benefit of humanity—caste nationality grows stronger as more insecurities hit society in the form of unemployment, poverty and partisan control over resources. In all these issues, caste plays a central role. For instance, loans to farmers by local moneylenders—usually from the Bania caste, known as *sahukars* in Maharashtra—at exorbitant interest rates are primarily responsible for farmer suicides. Instead of making this a central concern, popular and progressive movements misdirect attention to the abstract nation state—which is in any case used by the ruling class to enjoy the inherited privileges of caste society. Though the state is summoned to bail out some farmers, the prime culprit is the sahukar, who is enjoying his caste nationality as an absolute owner and custodian of wealth. The system through which he operates also needs appropriate attention.

The people enjoying the benefits of their caste always direct the attention of suffering people towards the state, thus diverting from the real reason for their troubles, which is the existence of the caste system. For instance, issues surrounding communalism take precedence over anything else that has to do with the state. The case of the Babri Masjid demolition in Ayodhya in 1992 became a diversion from the issue of reservation for OBCs brought forth by the V.P. Singh government on the recommendations of the Mandal Commission report in 1990. In fact, these are specific caste-nation issues but consensus is created by lies and deceit. And the common citizen who is suffering at the hands of dominant-caste nationalism buys into the false propaganda and effectively becomes the martyr of someone else's national imagination. Due to the obvious divisions, everyone holds on to his/her caste. Such feelings produce hostility and insecurities. Thus, the 'nationalistic' feeling has to be constantly manufactured by the ruling classes to obscure the divisions, often seeking opportunities to display their angst. Due to this, India continues to be a nation of repeated riots and atrocities imposed by one caste nation upon another.

Each incident of violence and rioting exhibits the lack of unity amongst so-called Indians. Societies with divisions continue to witness bloodthirsty civil wars in their nation state. Whereas in the Scandinavian countries, ethnic riots rarely take place. The fact is simple—everyone has agreed to the liberal ethos of democracy, and the grievances of their hostilities are resolved by making society culturally, socially and economically equal. In India, the privileged would protect their free privilege to the death, fearing that a dialogue on equality might lead to questions about their unjust position in society. Communal and casteist expletives are deployed towards distressed, poor, lower-caste, working-class groups. This is how fractured India tries to project itself as a unified diverse India. Such a projection of the country helps the traditional elite to easily assemble a 'caste-neutral' definition of the nation state while on the other hand continuing to hold diehard loyalties to its caste nation. This is visible with the number of their caste folks being incorporated and promoted—through the euphemism of 'networking'—into positions of power in the government, bureaucracy, judiciary, education, film, entertainment, non-government, academia and capitalist enterprises.

In contemporary moments of social upheavals and conscientiousness, the cruel reality of caste remains an overtly ignored phenomenon even among the progressives. Indian democracy is not representative and therefore ends up being almost autocratic in its functioning. Caste India is yet to democratize its institutions. We are set to exclude the oppressed castes which form the corpus of the majority, and promote the minority, which are the historically privileged castes. The institutions of films, academia, theatre, business, religion and bureaucracy remain enamoured with caste pathology, imposing physical and mental harm upon the lower-caste subjects in the graded hierarchy. This affects the ability to understand the Indian problem, which is a caste problem—therefore, caste matters.

This book is an ethnography of the sociality of caste in the moment of social justice and prejudice. The caste question is so badly handled that it needs immediate attention among other important issues in parallel globalized social movements. People know about caste but rarely understand it. This is perhaps one of the reasons we do not have regular active dialogues on caste at the world stage or continuous movements rallying for the rights of subjects living under the caste system. People are now slowly getting hold of what it is and they are willing to explore the foundations of such a system. However, there can be no dialogue on caste without becoming aware of the life of the people who are part of an entire caste ecology. Therefore, we need to place our attention on politics, sociality and the cultural discourse of caste.

This book offers a statement on the beingness of Dalit. What does it mean to be a living Dalit in today's caste-capitalistic India? How do we understand a group that is offered no space to think and live independently without intimidation and fear? Thus, being a Dalit is being now, it is being urgent.

Taking the mantle of liberation from their predecessors, Dalits are excited to join the ranks of becoming liberators of their community. The confidence of carrying the self as a Dalit without the immediate fear of social death, psychic death and spiritual death is a characteristic of being a Dalit. This is the focus of Chapter 1 of the book, 'Being a Dalit'.

A Dalit is robbed of his accurate registers of history, then, his human personality is torn apart, he is degraded to the caricature of slavery, and finally he is not allowed to express a profound critique of Brahminical hegemonic creativity—art and music. Living in the midst of such a delusional optic, the Dalit lives in the present as well as the past; the latter being very strong in its spirit. The character of a Dalit in the present moment is forcibly subsumed into the empty rhetoric of banality.

The society and the Dalit have been juxtaposed to co-opt Dalits into the imperial project of Hindu globalism. It is similar to the proclamation of the US 'empire', where Black slaves were the constituent elements in forming the country. The Dalit is a major feature in the making of a universalist Hindu claim. Persons belonging to castes higher than Dalit draw their human-caste legitimacy by keeping Untouchables below them. Dalits are a lifeline to the otherwise fractured Hindu identity. A religion divided among more than 7000 castes and sub-castes—each in conflict with the other—manages to survive only by ensuring the maintenance of untouchability, and then considers itself superior and stable because of this abhorrent practice. A Brahmin is to an Untouchable what the master is to a slave. The Indian caste habitus is a disunited form of comradely existence. I take up these issues in Chapter 2.

The Dalit movement sees itself as a product of dialectical casteism—of caste-based and class-interfaced struggle. The Dalit position has often been relegated to the dilemma of 'metaphysical futurism', that is, whether Dalits are to live in the future or be permanently fixed to the historical registers of India's past. The unseen future is sold as a promise. The future for the dispossessed acts as hope. The hope for Dalits is not of abundance. Time acts as a perception of the lived reality. Historical records show that their being is not considered as precious as that of others. This has a bearing on the making of the future. The present is a randomly arranged accident for Dalits to imagine themselves through the canon of attackers. The Dalit lives in a *no*-time.

As the German philosopher Martin Heidegger observed, there is no absolute, existential ontology of time.[11] The Dalit 'being' is to be understood in a temporal setting that exhibits the limited ownership of existence or *dasein*—one of the original human experiences of being. 'Time' in the Dalit experience could be understood as a deprivation of privilege where the body politic is facilitating the civic death.

Dalit Creation

Dalit identity is disguised in public, it is hidden and loathed. Many affluent Dalits restrict their coterie to the world of Brahmins and other dominant castes. They spitefully denounce every arrangement of Dalitness. Even if they are benefactors of the Dalit movement, emerging Dalit elites try to wilfully damn the credentials of Dalits. You would notice them identifying as 'no more a Dalit' or as Buddhist, Christian, Sikh or simply atheist in order to fit into the grand schematic of a 'humanist' identity. Dalits ascribing to these meta-identities are anxious about their Dalitness. At times they even refer to the word Dalit as something alien to them, an external or downgraded Other. Oppressed Dalits who have not yet broken out of the caste mould very obediently adhere to the supremacist tendencies of their oppressors. The mimicry of the affluent castes is reproduced at every level. Thus, just as Brahmins find an incentive in discriminating amongst themselves based on sub-caste affiliations, every other caste entangled in the adamant cobweb of the caste system does the same.

But awakened Dalits are extraordinary in their sense of being. This book makes a claim for the position of Dalits in the global rights struggle. In the midst of uprisings against fascist right-wing ideologies, many liberals and socialists alike have joined the tirade against populism. Nationalism of a certain order is being summoned by the protectors of the state. The state here is turned into a monologue and a mono-version of a few despots. Therefore, the book presents the perspective of a first-generation educated Dalit, and how he experiences the changing world of diverse ideologies. It is a confrontational battle of deciding whether to borrow jargon from existing parallel social justice movements or creating a new idiom for transformation.

Is the borrowing really a desperate attempt to include the Dalit experience in others who have been traditionally oppressed or to create an affinity of shared marginality? The book aims to add value to ongoing social justice movements by adding the Dalit narrative to their constitutional terms. The Constitution of India is regarded as the foremost document for Dalit hope. However, does it specify the ingredients for emancipation? How has the Indian state confined the possibilities of its progress on the basis of Dalit hope? Simply put, the hope of the state continues to function adjacent to Dalit hope, both intangible and virtuous. The day Dalit hope ends, the state's hope for Dalits will end. This end is to the peril of the Indian state and all who cohabit in it.

Dalit Life

Dalit Life and Dalit spiritualism have been wounded for ages. Its formation as a resistance to human suffering has been destabilized by anti-human casteist forces. This has made Dalit existence miserable. Offering a hermeneutical reading of rich Dalit spiritualism, this book plunges into the lives of Dalit *chawls* and *bastis*—the ghettos and abodes imagined under the traumatic gaze of state-induced immorality—the vicious circle of police, violence, drugs and socially disgraceful acts of existence. The book also visits the elite circles of Dalit and non-Dalit spaces, trying to make sense of Dalit hope. Spiritual warfare is carried on beyond the religious piety of theisms. The Dalit embodiment of supremacist tendencies has only added to the programmatic fortification of the supremacist project.

Dalit spiritualism exists in variant forms across the Indian subcontinent. The remembrance of ancestors and devotion to their egalitarianism promote the healing of the deeply wounded Dalit community. However, these facets encumber a Dalit to fight back. Dalit spiritualism is an in-practice phenomenon which goes beyond the narrow ideology of state secularism. Dalit spiritualism lives with a hope of the divine. The divine is pierced and cut across as hope. Kancha Ilaiah describes this as a lively culture of gods and goddesses wherein the spiritualism informs the metaphysics of Dalit and Shudra cultural production.[12] For him, oppressed-caste groups have not confined their spiritualism to a priest or a certain edifice that practises exclusion. The gods that are part of the Dalit experience have more rationalized beliefs and do not genuflect to Brahminical parameters—they are mostly ancestral formations that have revolted against Brahmins. The 'common god' concept is an abiding form of group unity. The best example of this is found in the Kuldevata, a common deity worshipped by specific caste-clan groups. Dalit Kuldevatas differ from those of Brahmins and other castes. Every year, a pilgrimage is undertaken to remember and offer respects to the caste gods. Children are inducted into this tradition—their names are given in the presence of the Kuldevata; their hair is offered up as sacrifice and even promises are made in the presence of these caste-clan-specific gods. There is no mediation of a Brahmin priest to order the relationship between the Dalit subject and their collective Kuldevata. There is a Dalit priest who officiates at the religious ceremony. Children are exposed to the independence of offering prayers as they please. No restrictions and codes of prayers animate spiritualism like the complicated Brahminical step-by-step method.

Dalits loathe the pre-eminence of Brahmin gods that takes the form of what Ilaiah describes as 'spiritual fascism'.[13] According to him, this is a manifestation of violence in an anti-democratic set-up. The Hindu religion in principle banks on this concept to advocate violent forms of suppression. Thus, the Dalit spirit is found in the natural obeisance of non-material values.

Dalit Moment

The Dalit community is having its Harlem moment at present. It is now able to articulate loudly and clearly through words and action—becoming more global and more reachable than ever. Sensorial Dalit expression is an experience of revelation of the person and the personal. In the revolutionary age of technologies of communication and new expressions of freedom, Dalits are claiming their rightful position in the armours of justice and democracy. Dalits are the recently 'freed Untouchables', the second generation of constitutionally freed citizenry who are now coming out of their inbred shackles and segregated ghettos to combat the enforced Brahminical societal codes.

But with this comes tougher challenges as the endogamous nature of caste is becoming stricter. Shankar, a twenty-two-year-old Dalit from Tamil Nadu, was hacked to death by the parents of a supposedly higher caste girl in full public view after marrying a woman he deeply loved.[14] Twenty-three-year-old Dalit Pranay Kumar was beheaded in broad daylight when he walked out of hospital with his twenty-one-year-old pregnant, dominant-caste spouse in Telangana.[15]

Many Dalits, young and old, reckon how many times they nearly lost the battle to survive for the mere fact of being a Dalit and exercising their virtue of being human. There has been one Rohith Vemula already.[16] There is perhaps another already in the making, surrounded by casteist forces. Dalit as an identity has existed within a suffocating structure. Recognition and appreciation from other human beings is what this whole movement has been arguing for and is about. Ambedkar's famous reference about refusing to abide by the brutal caste Hindu order remains the order of consciousness among the Dalit class, rural and urban. The mandate is not to reform the Hindu social order, rather it is to claim equality on its own terms.

What was demonstrably proven from the much-publicized Rohith Vemula incident is that the acknowledgement of caste-based violence was palpable in cities. The other aspect was the brazen defence of the institutional murder of a Dalit. The state acted as a partner in caste crime. The vice chancellor of Hyderabad Central University, Appa Rao, a prime accused in the Rohith Vemula case, was rewarded with the Millennium Plaque of Honour Award by Prime Minister Narendra Modi.[17] In deference to the law and to honour the victims of caste crime, Modi should have stayed away from such a felicitation. The Brahminical mindset is fascist; it has become a matter of habit to commit caste crimes without any accountability.

The embrace of Dalit feeling is not merely an academically constructed theory. In the quest to make Dalit and caste part of the grand narrative, this book sets out on an ambitious task: to inform the audience—local and global—about the ghastly order of caste and Brahmin supremacy that appears unwilling to wither away. In their quest to seek universal peace and brotherhood, popular global social movements cannot afford to overlook the suppression of 300 million people in the subcontinent. If the ideals of justice have to be promoted, the commitment to this cause needs to be demonstrated steadfastly. The potential of any progressive movement has to be idealized. Caste and the suppression through it need to be exposed, provocatively challenged and eventually delegitimized ad hominem. Chapter 3 deals with these historical conjunctures viewed through different kinds of Dalitness.

~

I was invited to an upper-middle-class event organized by a bunch of bureaucrats, largely Dalits, in Bangalore. Their teenage children—armed with sophisticated smart watches, iPhones and cosmopolitan ideas—were discussing a school project where they had to imagine life in space. After an arresting discussion and jaw-dropping description by one of the youngsters, his parents, who were hosting that dinner, started discussing the prospect of sending their son to NASA.

I asked the students interested in extraterrestrial life about their opinions on the social deficiencies in India, to which they responded by saying that caste was an issue of the past. Their parents, immediately uncomfortable, shifted in their seats, nodding to their children's response. Dalit middle-class dreams are yet to mature; for now they exist in the mimicry of the oppressor Other. Their elevation from living in penury to being an income-owning class in the span of just one generation has put them in a new world, one that their ancestors had not experienced. This new position in mainstream society has burdened them with the added responsibility of commanding an equal position in everyday interactions, producing an asymmetrical power relation. Their aspirations and goals have undergone various changes, at times producing conflicting viewpoints—political, social, economic and cultural—vis-à-vis the rest of the Dalit community. The Dalit middle class, by virtue of its purchasing power, gets seen and heard more than the struggling working-class Dalit. These issues are covered in Chapter 4 with a description of the existence of the Dalit middle class in the aspirational mode and how it has a social responsibility towards poor Dalits. This class at times complicates its position by assuming leadership of the entire Dalit masses, becoming the default representatives of the community and falling short of expectations.

There has been a strong desire from the state and its neo-liberal agents to push for Dalit capitalism. While the economic system of feudalism has been gradually replaced with a mixed modern-day model of capitalism and state socialism, the social aspect of feudalism is as entrenched as ever. The inherent form of capitalism reproduced with it the age-old structure of oppression. The conditions of working in the field as a landless tiller or working in a factory in modern industrial society were premised on the extraction of labour and exploitation of its productive value. This misuse of power remains at the core of the execution of capitalism.

Capitalism, as Anupama Rao has observed, took Dalit existence' outside the culturalism of caste'.[18] On the other hand, Balmurli Natrajan reassesses the cultural dogma that inhibits the cessation of casteism. His theory purports to revisit caste as a system and caste as a functionality. Natrajan argues that the cultural aestheticism attributed to the caste system is a modernist concept that at times ends up ethnicizing an identity which then comes across as 'positive'. This idea supports the conclusion that since caste is a cultural thing, there is no necessary hierarchy or oppression in place, only a tension of intercultural wars; that it is merely a fundamental part of India's intercultural diversity. This presents to us an untenable 'paradox' of multiple misunderstandings: whether the caste system can be improved within the existing structure or it should be eliminated to achieve the sanctity of a religious society, or if caste is needed to maintain historical identity.

Such sanitized versions of casteism are made all over by various stakeholders—the state, civil society, in sacred and secular, private and public spheres. This attribution of the 'cultural' promotes the value of caste as that which upholds culture. Thus, the caste system becomes something to be preserved and not destroyed. Many public spaces echo these amplified iterations of casteism. The 'difference' that persists in the hierarchical form is renamed so as to tamper with the formations of caste-based hierarchy, thus making '"cultural" casteism . . . the legitimate form of casteism'.[19]

The reinvention of capitalism in the most simplistic terms obfuscates the specifics of its destructive capacity. By denying the specificity of caste universalism and its original experiences, the capital-oriented struggle upholds the virtue of labour over the stigmatized Dalit body.[20] A labourer becomes positive value while a Dalit does not. Dalits are shown a distorted vision of the capitalist nodes of living as something to aspire to. This is the focus of

Chapter 5, weaving together personal narratives and stories from African-American and Dalit experiences of capitalism.

I had gone on a group trip organized by Harvard's outing club. It was a two-day hike in the white mountain range of New Hampshire in winter. Two days of rigorous mental and physical exercise brought the team together. After the usual awkward ice-breaking conversations, a Frenchman curiously and rather hesitantly ventured to ask about Indian prejudices. He was not sure what to ask for fear of being called a racist or an ignorant white European. After guzzling two shots of rum, he dared to raise a question about Hindu religion and its metaphysics. The Frenchman was a doctoral student in physics. He had been educated on Hinduism and Indian culture by his Indian cohorts at Harvard. He was told that social and cultural regressiveness is not part of India. The India that we see and read about in early twentieth-century literature as being a land of snake charmers, people pooping on the street, bias and violence against women and caste discrimination were all concepts of the past. He had been presented with an image of India as the shining model that it used to be before the arrival of the British—a golden goose that the English came to and ground its glory to dust in the 200 years of their rule.

The Frenchman was having a hard time believing fellow Indian cohorts as he had read reports in the *New York Times* and *Le Monde* about gender and caste violence. He also accidentally came across a documentary on YouTube that appeared contrary to the description given by his Indian acquaintances. Thus, he wanted to confirm if the Western media was really not being accurate about India's progress out of simple jealousy. His Indian acquaintances had made it clear that they would not tolerate any comments that would make India look like a parochial outfit. He was firm that any reportage of discrimination was amplified by the West for their personal gains. Any inquiry into this would be taken as an offence and could amount to racial bias against Indians.

There is a plain denial and unashamed conviction that caste does not matter in present times. It is for this very reason that the performance of caste and its mechanics is getting reintroduced every day by getting greater visibility through social media. Brahmins in India are primarily responsible for the existence of the caste system. They created it and worked full-time to keep it operational. Epoch after epoch and generations after generations, Brahmins bequeathed crude strategies to their progeny, who carried out the shameful execution of caste-based divisions without much inquiry or questioning. Brahmins were gladly co-opted with any ruling power in order to retain their exploitative status. However, historical records reveal some courageous Brahmin and 'upper-caste' individuals who braved social orthodoxy to challenge the stupidity of the caste system.

There were radical anti-caste Phuleite and Ambedkarite Brahmins who laid their lives in the service of the upliftment of Dalits and in the project of the annihilation of caste. I uncover these figures in Chapter 6 by analysing what prevents contemporary Brahmins, the progeny of Ambedkarite Brahmins, from taking an active stand against caste-based discrimination. Many liberal Brahmins and 'upper castes' do express their disagreement with casteism but their disapproval of such a system does not change the situation of Dalits. This has to do with passive liberalism rather than the radical humanist position of being a 'cultural suicide bomber' willing to blow up the oldest surviving edifice of discrimination.

International Non-Dalitism

This book builds on the theoretical formations of global struggles by identifying caste as an important element in the making of global solidarities. The solidarities that were created in the post-colonial phase nurtured the Third Worldism that was premised on anti-imperial nationalistic sentiments. It also made a call for solidarities mostly premised on class issues, overlooking the internal strife in newly independent nation states. Due to this, the inheritors of the independent nation state, who were mostly from the upper echelons of social hierarchy, continued their dominance by initiating struggles that did not threaten their unquestioned privilege. The historically poor and oppressed continued to live under depredation and penury. Their suffering did not lead to much of a social revolution. Today, such groups are being pushed further to near-extinction by the stakeholders of neo-liberal capitalism. This again is giving rise to class-based sensibility by withdrawing internal caste-based struggles. To clear historical errors and fix the problem I aim to advance the argument why caste-based global activism is an important intervention in current global problems.

The Dalit diaspora has been active in Western spaces since the 1960s. Post-colonial governmental projects in India focused on organizing governance. The non-government sector concentrated on development issues such as poverty and health care while social justice movements took up the issues of social and economic inequality on a larger scale. In spite of this, why has the Dalit cause not yet become an international concern? Why have popular social and cultural movements not considered the miserable suffering of 300 million unfortunate beings? Why is there no empathy to the burgeoning problems of these outcastes, whose mere presence is considered impure? The plight of Untouchables who decide to exercise their rights as human beings is defined within the curvature of a religio-social edifice. It is an impossible task for lower-caste groups to rebel and get recognized, unlike the great Haitian revolution and other rebellions in Africa, of which tales are told and retold in glorious narratives. The Untouchable's inventory of archival memory is meddled with by Brahminical annals, and thus the radical movement is presented as reformist, reducing its revolutionary zeal to that of being willing to be co-opted into the integrationist model as second-class citizens.

Thus, in the 'diversity' clause of popular movements and Internet-savvy social media activists, the phenomenon of suffering is limited to either mental or the most cognitive level of understanding the suffering of the oppressed. The mental state of suffering is hegemonic in that it privileges the narratives that are most audible and readable. In the instances where blind eyes and deaf ears are directed to address the issue of caste, diversity is absent. What a scandal! Diversity cannot be fulfilled as long as the movement is directed from the metropolis. It will retain its hegemony even if one claims to fight for the Dalit, Black, queer or other socially marginalized groups. The top-down approach has created a somewhat unradical understanding. The 'radical' Black movement in the US and around the world that embraces globalism with love is set on the notion of 'pan-___ism': pan-African, pan-Indian, pan-Southern, etc., which falls seriously short of deeper change. The Dalit movement and the Dalit people have a unique position of experiences to share with global struggles—it is their ability to thrive amidst the state and society's refusal to acknowledge their humanity. The Dalit community's focus on attacking the oldest form of human subjugation by mixing various methods of survival—especially anti-caste religious warfare against the oppressive system—is one such example. By being part of the global rights dialogue, Dalits give our collective failures another chance to reckon with our past. Dalits stand testament to the world's oldest surviving discrimination. Their minds, bodies and views of the world carry enormous repositories of 'fight back, live long and stay strong'.

Through empirical evidence and intellectual argument, I wish to make a case for the actual plight of Dalits by drawing the attention of popular social movements towards this larger yet neglected group. There are five major global issues that are mainstreamed in popular social justice movements: race, gender, climate change, capitalism and indigenous people's rights. Every major activity concerning these issues is fairly reported and gets echoed in international bodies. Unlike race and gender, the issue of caste is not physically distinguishable. Thus, hiding behind this justification, many dominant-caste supremacists continue to inveigle themselves into positions from where they can speak for the oppressed.

Due to access to global culture and spaces, dominant-caste people auction Dalit-related issues to attract the attention of international development agencies. The development-related model reinforces the unequal donor–receiver relationship, thereby permanently putting Dalit people at the receiving end—the lower end. This hierarchical engagement with Dalits sidelines the radical call of Dalits who want to destroy the oppressive system from its root. It instead proposes development-based models tied to the liberal notions of welfarism, wherein project-based instalments of community 'progress' are proposed, undermining the urgent call of the oppressed who want to end and annihilate the echo chamber of their oppression. Such development-based models are under neo-liberal control across the world; they are funded wherever oppressed people have demonstrated dissent. These models, as vehicles of neo-liberal finance capitalism, are deployed to pacify the brimming anger of the oppressed and slow down radical action by bureaucratizing and eventually paralysing a potential revolution. The handlers of such agencies and country/ mission heads are invariably dominant-caste people who are hand in glove with neo-liberal aggression. Perhaps due to this, we do not have any active international anti-caste solidarity work on the United Nations and other important forums. Since the inception of the United Nations in 1945 the United Nations General Assembly has not passed any resolution condemning caste-based violence, let alone recognized its prevalence. If this is indicative of anything, for the world and neo-liberal development institutions, 300 million Dalit lives do not matter.

~

The invisibility of extant caste violence—psychic, bodily and on the group—needs serious consideration. As much as caste is cultural, social, political and economic, caste nurturing is also bio-individualistic. It is a performance of individually managed acts conspired to execute violence upon the 'Otherly' body. This is done to produce pain upon beings who are considered lesser. In this definition, I aim to concentrate on the role of the individual and not allow them to escape culpability under the rhetoric of community-oriented action. In horrific events such as the Holocaust, individualized crime brought in a new dimension. The Holocaust theories upheld individual action as culpable on its own.

Discordance and dissent as part of national duty are yet to be cherished in caste-infested India. There is a desperate ethno-nationalism being forcefully promoted through Dalit constituents. Dalits are nationalized in the grand scheme of 'Indianness'—a la 'Bharat Mata' populism seen in the performative zeal of Republic Day or Independence Day celebrations or in extreme instances as the Babri Masjid demolition or the Godhra riots. Every bit of populist nationalism is an order of the tradition that harbours supremacist hierarchies, producing devious harm on marginalized bodies. This nationalism is sold by the caste-obsessed society, the market-driven greed of capitalism and neo-liberalism, and the Hindu right. This has decayed the national ethos of rich traditions that contained democratic branches of self-criticism.

The darkness of Dalit lives quivers in the anecdotal pages of news media summaries when Dalit deaths are reported. The scandal-hungry Brahminical media strives to find the next horrific story to be presented to the audience. The tragedy of a scholar's death ricochets around the corridors of major universities across the world. An author who writes experiences of the self is celebrated in the book reviews sections of major, world-renowned publications. Tales of Dalits are criss-crossing the world over.

> Dalits are struggling to fight the social boycott imposed by dominant-caste villagers in Karnataka, Tamil Nadu, Maharashtra, Uttar Pradesh, Rajasthan, Punjab, Bihar and Kerala;
> Dalit women are still seeking justice for mass rape;
> the souls of raped and lynched bodies paraded in the middle of streets yearn to seek justice;
> the brandishing of Dalit talent before the childish argument of 'merit' is haunting the doorsteps of educational institutes;
> the autonomous political praxis of Dalit students in college campuses is seen as a negative move;
> the death toll of manual scavengers keeps hitting national newspaper headlines;
> we keep talking about the greatness of India's civilization and culture,
> when the only time a Dalit gets noticed is upon his or her death;
> when the world is trying to find solutions to problems with little success;
> when social movements are gearing up to create new bonds with new comrades;
> when ecological disasters affect the person at the bottom who has no means of employment;
> when the neo-liberal catastrophe is sacrificing the measures of livelihood to the global capital monster;
> when pedagogies are proving inadequate to express the blackout of morality;

when teachers are unable to explain to their students where lies
the unaccountability for the oppression of human beings;

when India is 'shining' and the mass is fighting the darkness;

when banks are ruling and governments are following;

when democracy is being prostituted to the profligacies of the
ruling elite;

when the LGBTIQ movement refuses to actively endorse Dalit
queer and trans bodies;

when academic departments do not detail a course on the Dalit
episteme;

when research institutes do not commit to having detailed
studies of Dalit lives in past and present;

when the mother who cannot stop wiping her eyes at the loss
of her three-year-old;

when the temple priest continues to rape Dalit women for
'religious needs';[21]

when the dominant castes continue to loot the country;

when the international left movement honestly takes hold of
their oppressed comrades in India;

when the solidarities of other groups become the priority;

when prisons continue to get populated with oppressed-caste
people;

when the father who has lost his eighteen-year-old son has to
beg for someone's pittance to gather money to bury him;

when the world's governments and international bodies do not
recognize the lives of the unheard;

when an old woman tries to survive by begging on the streets;

when animals are allowed to sit on people's laps while even the
shadow of a Dalit is forbidden in the house;

when atheists say that religion is the primary problem and not caste;

when Dalit remains Dalit and Brahmin remains Brahmin;

when a son loses his father due to the lack of medical care owing
to poverty and the privatization of the health industry . . .

So,
until the progressives can take a courageous stand by denouncing
and renouncing self-privilege;
until radicals make caste their primary project;
until rationalists do not stop commuting to agraharas to
educate;
until Dalixploitation becomes a concern of the world;
until Dalit scientists are able to organize;
until Dalit cinema is successful in the project of creativity;
until Dalit rap becomes the lingua franca of revolt and is
accepted in the mainstream;
until Dalit achievers are unafraid of revealing their identity for
fear of losing their future;
until #castemustgo is truly embraced and #DalitLivesMatter is
in the list of priorities;
until my mother can sleep with reassurance without worrying
about her son's returning home safely in the caste police regime;
until then, caste matters.

Caste will matter until it is done away with.

When my aai talks about love she is interested in the balancing
act of love, which does not intend to harm others. She continues
to live under the coded pressures of caste violence. Her bravado in
fighting caste-mongers has fortified her children. Her compassion
and love have dissolved our fear of others and made us strong.
Through her life we see hope and she sees in us a brave attempt to
break the shackles of caste. That is why caste matters.

May 2019   Suraj Yengde
                                                Cambridge, MA

1

Being a Dalit

'Let me cut your thick casteist skin with the razor of my rage
That breeding ground of all the things
which were directed against me

I am like the sweet passing air
In the midst of a desert

It belongs to no one

Embrace it, enjoy its touch
And feel it to the core of the soul

It doesn't stay with anyone
It is a passing pleasure.'

—Suraj Yengde

'Tell me how to live if at each moment one dies
. . . I feel a foreigner among the people
Bearing the burden of such a bastard life.'

—Yashwant Manohar, 'Ultimatum'[1]

'One should open the manholes of sewers and throw into them
Plato, Einstein, Archimedes, Socrates,

Marx, Ashoka, Hitler, Camus, Sartre, Kafka,
Baudelaire, Rimbaud, Ezra Pound, Hopkins, Goethe,
Dostoevsky, Mayakovsky, Maxim Gorky,
Edison, Madison, Kalidasa, Tukaram, Vyasa, Shakespeare,
Jnaneshvar,
And keep them rotting there with all their words
One should hang to death the descendents of Jesus, the
Paighamber, the Buddha, and Vishnu
One should crumble up temples, churches, mosques, sculptures,
museums
One should blow with cannonballs all priests
And inscribe epigraphs with cloth soaked in their blood'
                —Namdeo Dhasal, excerpted from *Golpitha*, 1972[2]

I live in a world that is Brahmin and Brahminical. Everywhere
I turn my head, I see Brahmins and Brahminical segments in
positions of power, undeterred and unwilling to acknowledge
their status of privilege that nurtures the unaccountability of
their actions. In every field, be it culture, commerce, art, religion,
politics or knowledge, I see a Brahmin plotting to make my life
look unworthy *every day*. I am not a human, I am a Dalit. I am
not a colleague; I am a Dalit. I am not a friend; I am a Dalit.
I am not a co-maker of the moment; I am a Dalit. A Brahmin
lives to exclude Dalits from his life. Whether in celebrations or in
everyday life, the Dalit has to be kept at bay so that the Brahmin
can truly exercise his Brahminness.

For Brahminical society, I have no agency or free will to live
the way I want to anywhere in the world. I am constantly seen and
judged as the Other. I am forced to live in the world as though I
am secondary, and the Brahmin and his universality are primary. I
am urged to take responsibility for actions that have nothing to do
with me. I have to live a twofold life—one for myself and the other

for Brahmins and their Brahminical world. This cosmological servility is attached to my presence. A particular section of elite Brahmins, in order to control the existential environment, want to subordinate not only Dalits and fellow sub-caste Brahmins, but also expand this subordination to everyone around them.

~

I have subscribed to a Dalit–Adivasi news portal run by activists in Uttar Pradesh. It compiles in a daily digest various news items relating to Dalits. The news that often receives coverage is about death and rape; until five years ago, the number of news items ranged from four to six. Today it is ten to fourteen. These reports have become the archetype of contemporary Dalit identity.

It's 7.45 in the morning. The clouds have been consistently grey for a week, with regular drizzles in the depressing winter of London. I wake up tired, still tied to the bed, cosy under the covers. With my eyes half open I reach out for my phone and laptop to catch up with what's been happening. Calls, messages, Facebook, email—all checked. The message from the daily digest I have subscribed to appears in the group email. As a force of habit, I indulge in reading it. I long to find some positive news, see Dalit merit shine through the darkness of the caste empire, or read about the victory of a civil rights suit filed in court. But it is par for the course by now to start the day with depressing news. I hardly ever finish reading the entire digest if the first three news items report atrocities against Dalits.

One such snippet was a review of a documentary by noted film-maker K. Stalin, titled *India Untouched*. When I watched it, nineteen minutes into the film, I couldn't hold myself together. I sobbed unstoppably; the tears just flowed. I left the room and walked outside. Each step I took, the scenes of the film and the memories it evoked flashed before me. The sobbing continued. I was grossly unprepared to witness the spectacle of our children being cruelly humiliated at a school in Gujarat wherein school-going Dalit girls were forced to clean the premises and bathroom of the school and also had to make tea. The film-maker asks a question to the girls, trying to find out why they do the cleaning. With innocent expressions on their faces, they respond: 'We will be beaten if we don't clean the toilets.' The film-maker questions if all the students are assigned the chores. The response is: 'Except Patels and Shiroya kids.' The film-maker appears baffled and says that he doesn't get it. The girl in an immediate response exclaims with a mix of fear and amusement, 'Yes, you do.'[3] The subtext of this part is to say that it is a caste-based humiliation, and like us the world knows why we are oppressed and assigned such a degrading lifestyle.

As I am walking, the mind is stunted and I am constantly thinking about the repeated assaults on Dalit minds that force them to inferiorize their being. I decide to counter this by disowning the terms 'lower' and 'upper'. In my article 'Why Not Lower Caste?' that I published on the same portal soon after, which later got republished in an online human rights magazine, I argue that like the radical Black movement in the US where colour-coded stereotypes were upended by challenging the cruel White gaze, the Dalit ownership of the self has to be foregrounded by rejecting upper–lower signifiers. I furthermore argue in the piece that such downward-looking hierarchical terms should be completely eliminated, for doing that not only offers psychological independence but also paves the way for rightful Dalit assertion. I am responding to the identity that I have not been involved in creating in the first place; it has been forcibly imposed on me and my community.

Caste is an anti-fellowship institution. It does not encourage the sentiment of commonality, of fellow feeling; rather, it encourages belonging to distinct, individual hierarchical groups. The possibility of building a strong unity among various castes on human terms is severely limited. In this chapter, we will reflect on the questions of caste with human relativity: the otherness, the being, Beingness and love.

In India, the metaphors of human affection and disaffection are surrounded by the caste debate. There is an 'Othering' that is at the core of investigating one's caste position. It is hidden as well as visible. In fact, its visibility may even take a serious, violent turn. Any Dalit who claims their identity or exhibits their caste culture openly often receives a cold shoulder. Many a time, Dalits are marginalized for asserting their equal selves in the common space they inhabit with dominant-caste friends. This is done either by demeaning Dalit culture, food, festivals, language and economic conditions, or simply mocking Dalit politicians. Every opportunity offered to Dalit expression is sidelined by looking down on it.

During my studies in the UK, I would spend time with fellow Indians. We had healthy interactions and even cooked dinners together. In a land far from home, my Indian friends who spoke and ate like me provided endearing comfort. However, two months into these friendships, the same people began to distance themselves.

I used to put up posts on Facebook condemning the caste system for atrocities against Dalits. As soon as my updates started to show up on their timelines, some of them blocked me, while those who were relatively closer to me did not engage with the posts.

One day, I was invited to spend an evening at the house of an Indian friend. As I entered, I sensed hostility in the air. No one wanted to engage with me. They looked away when I spoke, and when they did respond to anything I said it was loud and forceful. I was mobbed with virile attacks on my dignity and community. The community backgrounds of these students ranged from Hindu Bania and Sindhi to Sikh, Brahmin and Jain. None of them could bear my Dalit assertion. They started calling me names, degrading Ambedkar. The Sindhi friend, whom I had considered the closest to me among this group, outrageously referred to Surekha Bhootmange, the murdered Dalit woman in the Khairlanji case, as a 'slut', without having any information on the case. He also continued to defend Brahmins for doing their job and brought up the 'oppression' that people like him allegedly face because of reservations. 'Who is going to take care of the Brahmins and what about the atrocities on them?' he yelled. I was put down by these mobs of Indian students who had surrounded me in the room. I was almost sure that if I tried to leave, they would not allow it and things might turn violent. Seeing no other option, I tried to explain my position as the tension grew.

All this had erupted because I had made a presentation on the subject of 'Caste and Gender within Indian Society' for my international human rights course. One of my Indian classmates, a practising Sikh, had reported it to the group of Indian friends. This encounter left me baffled. A Sindhi person who would never have worshipped Brahmin gods was so defensive of Brahmins. The Sikh girl who had taken offence to my criticisms had no apparent reason to, since Sikhism is devoid of Hindu and Brahmin religious practices. I later recalled the experiences of Ambedkar, who was never welcomed into the private quarters of his dominant-caste friends. In his autobiographical account, *Waiting for a Visa*, Ambedkar describes his experience in Baroda, where he had been offered a job but no accommodation. Since he was having trouble finding a place to stay, Ambedkar reached out to a Hindu friend, 'a noble soul and a great personal friend of mine', and another friend who happened to be a Brahmin-turned-Christian. Neither could accommodate him. Ambedkar then managed to get a place at a Parsi guest house as 'their religion [Zoroastrianism] does not recognise untouchability'. However, he got differential treatment even at the hands of the Parsi owner. Ten days in, Ambedkar was chased out by a 'dozen angry-looking, tall, sturdy Parsis, each armed with a stick'. The 'mob of angry and fanatic Parsis' too could not tolerate an 'Untouchable' in their space, irrespective of their difference from Hindu caste beliefs.

My experience with non-Hindu friends echoed the experience of Ambedkar. This incident proved that a Dalit, anywhere in the world, has to negotiate their identity to the satisfaction of privileged-caste friends and colleagues. Anything else is unwelcome. The mob will ensure that the person dare not expose his or her suffering.

However, Dalits are not a mono-identity, and the perception of them being so creates an additional burden on Dalit Being. There are multiple cultural differences and lived experiences among Dalits. Dalit Being is a broader category of inclusivity as well as exclusivity. It is welcoming as well as exclusionary. Dalits do not often talk about caste; rather, they live their lives in the caste debacle. To experience the Dalit expression of livelihood, one would need to visit the kindled spaces of Dalit ghettos and be part of their social occasions like marriages, festivals and ceremonies. Dalits locate the universal in their surroundings. They not only take stock of Brahminical culture but are also aware of Africa, the Blacks and indigenous populations while consolidating the Bahujan (oppressed majority) identity.

Dalit Love

Before we analyse the Dalit condition and the catastrophe that is the caste system, we need to understand the collective experience of Dalit survival. What has enabled the Dalit community to survive amidst the generations of inferiority imposed upon their minds? What has enabled it to reproduce the next generation and hope for change? What are the important factors to draw such courage to face the powerful without losing hope due to the fear of Brahminical terrorism? The reasons vary.

Having the courage to agree to a dialogue with the oppressor as well as a firm commitment to resolve conflict is integral to Dalit Humanity. The primacy of Dalitness emerges in its innate capacity to cultivate self-love in the bareness of apathy and tragedy. The audacity to hope while locked in darkness testifies to the existence of Dalit Love. It is the unwritten resolution of the community to adhere to this principle of love. From here originate the feelings of compassion in the lives of Dalits. It is Dalit Love that has kept the community alive and guarded it against utter destruction. This continues to be a strong moral force that needs to be carefully understood. By loving the Other and embracing the ignorant for his lack of empathy, the Dalit community has shown how to deep-love and efface the malice that hides beneath. To love in a casteist society is violence and a violation—of the juridical, moral and sexual codes underwritten in the religious dictions that are sold as idealized tradition. Insubordination and defiance form the methodical process of Dalit Love.

Within the clutches of Brahmin ritual and social orders, Dalits have been lynched, raped, tortured and humiliated, without having played any role in creating the orders. Even after chronic episodes, the community manages to get past its historical scars and nurtures younger generations to act with empathy, love and compassion towards others. It privileges reason and puts a premium on rationality. It advances the idea of love and lovability. By mustering the courage to practise love in the face of severe oppression, the Dalit community actualizes the lofty ideals of humanity. Rooted in the traditions of Dalit upbringing, these epochal values are passed on to succeeding generations to carry in their minds and on their bodies.

Dalit Love is what my grandmother practises in her everyday life. Her love for her grandchildren is built on her faith in the movement of love. She bequeaths all the love she has got in her preserve to younger generations. Her love is a fortification against the evils her grandson is going to face in the cruel world. Her love is also a move to find loving kindness in others and spread the value of love in the world. She understands the brutality of the system that we live in and has seen it all. Standing testament to the winds of time, my grandma—*maajhi* aai—an unlettered domestic servant, lives in hope, guided by her enormous audacity to love. Her outright rejection of the foul elements in society and her readiness to fight them come from the sincere love ethic that was passed on to her by her grandma. She belongs to a people who could remain alive only because they never gave up on love. Love fortified them against a system that seemed intent on breaking them. My grandma's purity of love is a continuation of thousands of years of history. Her gentle touch on my face, her palms cupping my cheeks, and her eyes illuminated with tears are a window to my ancestors, whose blood in me is a proof of Dalit Love.

Dalit Love is embodied in moments when someone makes a gesture of kindness towards me and I open myself up—ready to share my spirit, my love, my house with the gentle gesturer. I recall an incident in Geneva. I was outdoors on a fine Swiss summer weekend morning. My colleague and I were playing table tennis and a passing couple requested if they could play doubles with us. We readily agreed. The game lasted for less than an hour, during which we laughed endlessly. It was pure joy as we struggled to keep playing in the blowing wind. We enjoyed the game and later, while we were saying goodbye, I invited them to dinner at my place. They were slightly taken aback upon my invitation and said they had plans and wouldn't be able to come.

My Italian colleague made me aware of my silly forthrightness. She said my invitation was pretty forward and people were not used to receiving such unsolicited dinner invitations to someone's house. I was perplexed because I thought we had all shared a good time and it could have carried on. But my colleague did not find it an appropriate gesture. I thought this was because they were Europeans and they had a different understanding of hosting someone. So I thought it to be an Indian habit. I discussed this incident with my Indian friend and said that we Indians were so open about hosting people and inviting them into our households.

But he also replied in the negative, saying that my invitation was not appropriate and even he would not have behaved so. He said it took time to know anyone and it was better to grow that understanding before becoming friends.

I went back to England and got in touch with the Dalit community there. During my first conversations with them, one of the British Dalits immediately extended an invite to spend a night at their place, which turned out to be an amazing mansion. I ate and slept at their place with due care.

A few years later, I was travelling with a non-Dalit friend in India. Wherever I went, Dalits were opening their hearts and houses to welcome us. Back at my home in Nanded, I often saw people visiting and spending a fair bit of time with my father. My parents also would throw open their doors for any visitor who was kind enough to extend his or her warmth to them. Later, I realized it was specifically my community that was so open-hearted because they understood the value of trust that was built on the conditions of love. So if anyone who gave them even a hint of these qualities, they gave it right back manifold.

Dalit Love needs to be embraced. It has more depth and affection, compassion and dedication than it is given credit for. It has an untasted sense of freedom and liberation for a shackled mind. Dalit Love is not tied to or determined by material things. It is an observation of one's moral sense and more care. Regaining hold of the caring that is lost in the world because of anger and violence is central to this type of worldliness. Dalit Love is a spiritual experience; it is a transcendental feeling. However, to acquire love, one must be in the position of giving love. The giving and receiving are conditional to the acknowledgement of the Other. Who will muster up the courage to love someone who is considered part of a lower 'social condition'—the Dalit forced into the midst of callous insecurities piled on by the dominant culture of the oppressor castes?

Why love a 'despicable' Dalit? Because the Dalit represents a love that remains suppressed in the inner core of one's unexplored self. Dalit Love is a beautiful rendition of pain and joy, healing the past and getting consciously lost in a future of possibilities and faith. Loving oneself through the love of others, seeing oneself through the fears located in one's outside world. Dalit Love is simple and therefore misunderstood. It is a love that every human yearns for but is unable to find. It is meditative and present in the enlightened, liberated self. Love, empathy and trueness inform the logic of one's being. Thus, when we bracket the Dalit within the limits of a nation, we relegate the universal appeal of Dalit Love. The Dalit remains a footnote to our guilty pleasures of superiority and cruel sensibility.

Dalit Love is a juxtacondition of possibilities and deep pain. It is not a negation of unlove, but a movement of possibilities. It is a belief that comes from a singular conviction of loving the unloved. The unloved belong to an under-appreciated and unrecognized segment that determines the suffering of humanity. Dalit Love creates and recreates the belief in their ancestral inheritance of the resilience to survive. It is, in fact, an example of the model of life. It teaches how to breathe life into a moribund kind of love. It thrives on the struggle between life and hope. Dalit Love is the only way to avoid nihilistic tendencies. A community whose agency is snatched, dreams shattered and bodies massacred still finds reason to love. Dalit Love is tender and soft, and light in weight. It is conditionally rooted in pain and simultaneously desires real escape.

India needs to be grateful to Dalit Love. Had it not been for Dalit Love, Dalits would have created their own vengeful organizations. They would have had their own version of Dalit supremacist movements and hate camps against the non-Dalit Indians who continue to perpetuate violence upon them, as if their survival is premised on the altar of dead Dalit bodies. Indian history would have witnessed repetitious episodes of caste violence. The historical struggle of Dalits carries rich legacies of non-violent movements. Their commitment to resolve through dialogue rather than violence is an understated and under-appreciated fact.

No group in India can completely claim the non-violent arena as a form of resistance.

Soulful brother and thinker Cornel West challenges us to self-examine what we are willing to risk our lives for. The Dalit offers an answer to earthly conditions. Willing to offer himself for the larger good of humanity, a Dalit stands as a testament to sacrifice. Dalit struggle teaches to only love and overcome hatred. This aspect needs closer reading as a queering experience. Dalit Love is a soulful ride that evokes the goosebumps of reality, making the body shudder with its force.

Dalit Love is *our* project—a common and harmoniously created experience. It is so powerful that it is an effective antidote to the malady of caste. It is an intense force of fraternity. Dalit Love is the only force in India that can accommodate the ignorant and uphold the virtues of compassion. It can easily offset the negativity of caste bias. Dalit Love is so exceptional that its adaptability to thrive in the midst of annihilation makes it feared by malevolent groups. The fact that we have 'arranged' marriages in India is primarily because of the fear of Dalit Love, which has the ability to inject the ideals of justice, compassion, forgiveness and the cultivation of humanness into closed orthodox minds; hence, it is banished by the prejudiced society. Through arranged marriages, the entire caste society is dispossessed of the unique ability to give and receive love. A kind of love that is not material, temporal or vulgar, but one that is earthly, grounded and dialogical with mutual communication, and one that speaks of possibilities and hope. The potential to understand and learn from each other and bridge gaps is curtailed by the system of arranged marriage.

Love within the confines of caste also limits itself to hetero-normative values. It doesn't open up a space for love as an ultimate human virtue that is beyond the constructed identities of gender, sexuality and caste. As Dhrubo Jyoti, a powerful and genuine voice of the Dalit queer movement, said in an exposé of inter-caste homosexual relationships: 'Caste broke our hearts and love cannot put them back together.'[4] This construction of love puts the locus on the receiver and giver of love, who are not caste blind. Hence, the imposition of caste features prominently even in queer and trans circles in India.

Love, as Cornel West points out, is 'a last attempt at generating a sense of agency among the downtrodden people'.[5] I would add that apolitical love is mere demonstration without demands. Love needs to be supported with a politically charged vision. To love and to grow together in love is resistance. A juxtacondition of needing by one and rejecting by the other plays in the minds of insecure beings. Because Dalit Love offers what one is constantly trying to find in oneself, it is most desired. However, this desire comes with conditions that the caste ecology is unwilling to abandon. This is the reason Dalit Love is most desired and simultaneously hated.

Its capacity to transcend parochial territories and migrate into the audacious terrains of hope comes down heavily on the Brahminical codes of discipline. Therefore, whenever the desired Dalit is embraced by a non-Dalit, Dalit Love is immediately murdered. Piles and piles of slaughtered bodies of young and old Dalits lie bare in the market of flesh-trading casteists. Caste killings go unmentioned and instead 'honour' killings take precedence. Casteist killers are acquitted from the constitutional morality that prohibits untouchability, while society condemns only so-called honour killings that are caste-neutral. The beautiful and precious lives of Pranay Kumar, Shankar, Rekha Kumari, Mridul Kumar, Soni Kumari, Manoj Sharma, Kumar, Amit and Jyoti, Ankit, Rama and many others have been cut short due to the violent refusal to embrace the nurturing qualities of Dalit Love. Among the slaughtered bodies, Dalits do not monopolize the numbers—all castes take the hit.

Psychological distress follows the Dalit child all through his or her life like a mental condition. The childhood violence that children are exposed to eventually creates social outcastes and criminals. Bryan Stevenson, a civil rights lawyer in the US who specializes in counselling prisoners on death row, illuminates how a modern criminal is created in a law-obsessed society. All the death-row criminals he has represented have had a history of mental health problems, which usually stemmed from the childhood trauma they suffered because of exposure to violence or exploitation at the hands of family members and society. These childhood abuses reflected in their later antisocial behaviour. Such actions made the children legally accountable, thus turning them into violent criminals. In addition, being locked up in prison and exposed to its horrendous conditions and the prison ecology further dehumanized them.

Each story about a dangerous criminal narrated in *Just Mercy*[6] had a background of childhood trauma on account of social, economic and racial differences. Apply that logic to the Indian caste system. The situation that Dalits live under is akin to an open prison. They are heavily policed since childhood and their actions are disciplined by caste codes. They face trauma, abuse and exploitation at the hands of the beneficiaries of the caste system. Since childhood, every insult and heckling abuse that comes their way from rabid landlords, teachers, neighbours, coaches, tutors and advisers adds to the creation of a psychological condition. Having no access to mental health support, Dalits carry around these scars and are weighed down by emotional stress. When they grow up, their actions are doubly policed and if they do not 'act' in prescribed ways, they are declared insane or mentally assaulted for being 'unstable'.

In the Dalit basti where I grew up in Nanded, Maharashtra, there were at least three married women who immolated themselves. Many young students, owing to their mental condition, could not cope with the pressures and thus gave up education. Fathers who had a traumatized childhood found refuge in alcohol. The childhood friends with whom I grew up are now counted in the ranks of criminals. The difference between them and me: their parents and the family condition they were in did not accord them the same opportunity that my parents could offer me. Their parents were drunkards, and would constantly beat their children. Amidst such an environment, many turned to drugs at an early age.

One of my friends, Avi, was a cricket star and the captain of my team. People admired him for his sportsmanship. Without any proper coaching or parental support, in no time Avi started playing cricket matches for money and not as a sport. His madness for money turned him into an avid gambler. He played lotteries and other sports dealing with money. Soon, he started smoking ganja and taking pills to get high, and alcohol became his best friend. Today, when I see Avi, he hides from me. He doesn't have the courage to face me. A smart and beautiful Dalit child is now on the verge of being imprisoned. In such catastrophic conditions, the question remains: what keeps the Dalit basti alive and moving? I would argue that it is the protective Dalit Love that has maintained the ethical dimensions of love and the sacrilege of the act of loving. It has protected many, if not all, the children from going astray. Whosoever has achieved something in his or her life has had the intimate touch of Dalit Love and caring. It is to the credit of Dalit Love that many Dalits have been prevented from turning into antisocial elements, despite the constant efforts of society to declare them criminals.[7] Dalit survival comes from accountability to the preserved histories of Dalit Love.

Therefore, love here is not simply a rehashing of the love ethic. It is a love that is spiritually rooted and in conversation with the inner self in a reflective mode. It values the best of others and acknowledges the worst in others as a human fallibility. The self-examination of Dalits, however, is inescapable in accounting for Dalit Love.

~

A group of Dalit and Muslim transgender folk from Nanded once shared with me the experiences of their multilayered beings. The hierarchies of oppression constantly repeated in the social justice circles of Dalits do not include their experiences. They do not feature in the order of oppression. Their leader, a widely known transperson and much loved by queer activists all over the world, is seen as a cocooned activist.

'She is the one responsible for our plight now with the state. We rallied behind her and thought she would speak for us. Instead, she got all the attention she deserved, got loads of money and better housing and future. She never visits our [Dalit transgender] houses. She is a cunning Brahmin,' cried Krupa, a transgender Dalit activist.

Society at large has banished the precious trans- or third-gender narratives. And the ones responsible for their upliftment—their own community that expresses solidarity with all oppression—continue to bluntly overlook their experiences. In fact, at times the queer community itself participates in oppressing Dalit trans and queer people in India.

Historically, the Dalit movement has taken up the cause of transgender people and prostitutes on par with the Dalit struggle. Firebrand leader of the Dalit Panthers, Namdeo Dhasal, organized Dalits, transgender people and prostitutes under the Samatha Morcha. This coalition advocated for the annihilation of caste-based prejudices by making a clear case against it. '*Aarey jaat paat ko hataav rey*' was their collective cry.[8]

However, in contemporary times, such efforts are difficult to see on a national scale. The dissenting Dalit public sphere continues to lament about the specific rights of the binary genders of male and female, which gets echoed in the chambers of hetero-normative, anti-queer and trans-phobic Brahminical spaces. By proffering a reactionary stable space to maintain the Brahminical order, Dalits end up challenging the system without demonstrating the will to destroy it. Thus, the negotiation of rights becomes a way to articulate their freedoms. However, in these conservative negotiations, little or nothing comes to the most oppressed Dalits.

Dalit Humour

A market-driven, greedy world earns tremendous benefits from the retention of the caste system. A Dalit is forced to undergo imperious subjugation under the despicable desires of the oppressors who designate the Dalit as the inferior Other. This manifests in various forms. Dalit beauty, for example, carries no significant recognition as opposed to the *savarna* model of beauty. On television, in cinema and in commercials, there is a monopoly on the 'ideal' of beauty based on a certain Brahminical prototype of colour-coded supremacy. The Dalit character is totally absent from the visuals of appreciation. The immense inferiority injected through popular culture produces what Toni Morrison refers to as 'internal death'.[9]

Dalit orality and articulation too are ignored by most of the world. This alternative genre of the Dalit voice amplifies the declarations of the everyday subaltern. However, because the dominant castes do not view Dalit orality as equal, it is plainly considered devoid of quality. Brahminical culture is ready to discredit the multiple varieties of Dalit expression. The language, protests and expressions of Dalits often go unrecognized. Culture, rituals, festivals, rites, customs and celebrations do not constitute the many meanings of Indian diversity.

Ask any dominant-caste person in India what Dalit culture is, and in all likelihood he or she will be amused with such a question. For, the commonly held belief is that there is no private Dalit sphere or culture. That Dalits are merely by-products that are feeding off the leftovers of Brahminical culture. The rich dialects and performance of life in the Dalit private sphere are not even known, let alone acknowledged.

The resounding double effect of Dalit expression in public and private spheres has resulted in a carrier of alternative traditions of countercultures, preserved and passed on to the next generation as an arm to defend and protect the community's integrity. The private culture is a rich repository of subtle modes of survival. The varying tonality and rhythmic patterns of pronunciation are manifested in all aspects of Dalit lives. It works in articulating their multicoloured patterns.

Variant forms of language, tones, accents and *waadas*—the segregated ghetto's impersonation of the oppressor, the plays and jokes that centre the Brahmin as the culprit—form a part of the Dalit public culture of resistance. Humour is the most valued human expression in Dalit circles.[10] The teasing, joking, picking on each other and passing humorous comments within families, friends and social circles bind Dalits together. Laughter constitutes the moment of bonding, paving a path into Dalit humanity. The emotion of laughing out loud is a creative method of generating the energy of mutuality in Dalit lives. Laughing with someone and laughing at someone has a twofold objective: to ridicule the other and to create a space with synergy for all to contribute and celebrate the moment. Laughter is an important sensorial expression to understand Dalit humanism. It coexists athwart pain. Laughing out loud on the turf of pain is a negotiated act that has enabled the Dalit commoner to embrace the philosophy of life: acknowledge suffering as a given and still find moments to dive into the pleasures of joy through unbounded laughter.

Sigmund Freud distinguishes the relation of laughter into three acts: joking, comedy and humour.[11] Humour as an expressive intonation of spontaneous, witty comments extends over two senses: one where the onlooker also enjoys the process along with the one who is being humorous; the second where one person does not take part in the joke at all but is made an object of that humour. In this process, the acceptability of humour as a set rule offers a liberating elevation to everyone involved. This experience, Freud argues, cannot be obtained from any other intellectual activity. Due to this, humour offers a secure position to the 'ego's invulnerability'. The ego is elated and therefore, seeing no threat, humour becomes 'rebellious'.[12] Rebellion is the ideal purpose of jokes. Through jokes, one can air repressed emotions.[13] Therefore, Dalits who critique Brahmins and the Brahminical order not only express their emotions but also emphasize their individual superiority over the perpetrators of repression. Through this act, they create a shared space of solidarity amongst Dalits who have a similar view of Brahmins. A significant community spirit is created around the humour that contributes to the development of a narrative that views things from the bottom up.

Therefore, jokes among teenagers and grown-ups in a Dalit critique are explicit and do not attempt a disguise to protect the object of humour. The jokes in Marathi are direct and intended to reach the receiver:

'Thuiyaan thuss, ka rey Baamna padla tuch!' (Why, o Brahmin, are you the only one farting.) Farting is equated with the image of pot-bellied, freeloading Brahmins. Thus, if you fart you are a *paadra Baman* (farting Brahmin).

'Bapat hulkat komati telkat' (Pervert Brahmin, oily shopkeeper). This refers to the unattractiveness of the shopkeeper who lazes around all day in the shop.

'Shahukaar taallu varcha loni khato' (The Bania is looking for opportunities to eat the butter placed on the forehead of a dead body—this is part of the final rites among most Hindus).

'Bhatta nibhar khatta' (A Brahmin priest, a stringent man), 'chikat marwadi' (miser Marwari), 'dhabada saavkar' (pot-bellied grocer). These terms are used to deride a person who acts like a Brahmin or a Bania, both infamous for their lack of compassion and empathy. These people are seen as merciless. To make a joke about them and laugh out loud is to protest against them. It is a protest laughter movement. All these repositories of humour of the Dalit world remain excluded from the mainstream Indian experience.

These kinds of everyday protest vocabularies have not yet entered the fortified signifiers of language. Generic language is problematized and its valuation has not yet been quantified. Thus, a Dalit tone where their culture is hidden has not yet been attended to. Thus, the symbolic lexicon of Dalits remains unexplored. In his reference to the English language as a hegemon, Ngugi wa Thiong'o talks about the imperial imposition of language. When one is compelled to use that language while voicing one's concerns, it is a cultural bombardment. The 'cultural bomb' is to 'annihilate a people's belief in their names, in their languages, in their environment, in their heritage of struggle, in their unity, in their capacities and ultimately in themselves'.[14] If the Dalit experience is not acknowledged and studied through its humour and language, the public and private spheres of Dalits face the threat of erasure.

Indian Mainstream Humour No More than Entertainment

In contrast to politically charged Dalit humour as a lived critique, the non-Dalit humorous sphere lacks rebellious content even in apparently 'political' stand-up comedies. The Indian comedy scene largely lacks protest humour. It exists simply to pass the time, and for unreflective entertainment. The Indian stand-up comedy circuit took off on a grand scale during the late twentieth century. Until then, stand-up comedians had been a complementary addition to entertainment shows. Comedians in India mostly had a space in the public performances of music shows, election rallies, netas' birthdays or private ceremonies as in-between acts to entertain for five to fifteen minutes. These stand-up comedians mostly engaged in mimicry and taunts. Given the limited space and time, they had to draw upon the most relevant issues to cater to the temper of the contemporary period. The names that have become the most well known from popular Hindi cinema are Johnny Walker, Mahmood, Kader Khan, Johnny Lever, Keshto Mukherjee, Shakti Kapoor and Govinda. People in both villages and cities enjoyed letting off steam through their simple comedy. Lever was perhaps the only one among them who came from a background of stand-up comedy, which he continued to be part of even after his entry in Hindi cinema.

Then there was a huge wave of professional stand-up comedy in the first decade of the twenty-first century where mainstream cable networks carried entire segments on comedians. Suddenly, stand-up comedy had become prime-time entertainment, and this made people laugh hard every week for a good number of years. The diversity of gender, region and religion were all represented in the space of comedy, which had otherwise become monotonous. The success of this wave of comedy encouraged other regional-language networks to carry vernacular segments. And so it happened: comedy became a central theme for a country that had otherwise found rape, horror, violence and scandals in their daily news feeds. Comedy became widely appreciated and stand-up comedians saw their art being compensated handsomely.

Next was the era of independent comedians, who started occupying the space of the Internet and YouTube in the second decade of the twenty-first century. This fresh set of comedians began creating new content that largely found purchase amongst the young, urban-educated and English-speaking audience. Millions of subscribers started tuning in to discover freshly baked puns that were traditionally not made for cable television subscribers. These comic acts soon gained astonishingly wild popularity. The current era can aptly be described as the golden age of stand-up comedy in India.

The YouTube generation of new comedians challenged the dynamics, structure and aperture of traditional cinematic comedy. They brought with them a vibrant new energy. The YouTube channels of comedy collectives like AIB, East India Comedy, The Viral Indian, TWTW, Being Indian and Bollywood Gandu alongside scores of other streams run by budding comedians were professionally crafted and viewed by millions. The comedy clubs that claimed blasphemy on the cultural norms started taking up abusive words or vocabularies censured as 'uncultured' and turned them into puns. In their skits, one could easily find palpable influences of Saturday Night Live, Comedy Central and the concept of the 'roast' that are popular on American cable networks. Popular YouTube comedy channels took up issues of social concern like censorship, bans, racism, arranged vs love marriage, politics and Bollywood by offering saleable critiques.

However, what they singularly overlooked was the political streamlining of racism that had been taken up by their American counterparts. American comedy became popular thanks to the African-American artists who injected fresh voices, themes and content into the existing scene. Giants like Bernie Mac, Martin Lawrence, Eddie Murphy, Whoopi Goldberg, Dave Chappelle, Chris Rock, Kevin Hart, Jordan Peele, Keegan-Michael Key, Leslie Jones, etc., provided an unforgiving sociocultural critique to the American public about its culpability for blind racism. This successfully tackled the issues of stereotyping of the black body, gender and sexuality issues, crime, politics, Hollywood, judiciary, music and almost every space available to public scrutiny.

However, the young comedy scene in India has not matured enough to offer a humorous critique to the social system that Dalit humour easily lives off. It is a far distance away from taking up sociopolitical issues the way their American contemporaries have done. From among the issues Indian comics take up, the historical ramifications of caste and untouchability are starkly missing. They seldom deal with the privileges of caste supremacy and rarely offer a wider perspective on the ills of Indian society. They're usually satisfied with issues of the middle class, which is a dominant caste concern, but in the enlightenment of the comedy era there is barely anyone—with a few exceptions—willing to take the cudgels of caste alongside class, religion and authoritarianism.[15] Therefore, we need to explore the internal spheres of the world of Dalit humour. These spaces are as much a revolt against as a relief for suppressed thoughts. They also carry a powerful counterculture of art that remains unknown to the rest of Indian society.

Dalit Universalism

Brahminism comes in various forms and formulas. The overarching tendency is to render the Brahmin influence invisible. Thus, everything a Brahmin does is presented as a Hindu project, including various anti-social activities executed by Brahmin-led organizations. However, Brahmin caste rituals, cultures and worship patterns differ from that of non-Brahmin Hindus. The Ganpati festival is a good example. Initiated by Bal Gangadhar Tilak, an orthodox Chitpavan Brahmin, this festival is widely celebrated for ten dedicated days. Initiated as a nationalist project, the ritual of *visarjan*—immersion of the idol into the river or the sea—was masterminded by Tilak. However, in a Brahmin household the Ganpati festival is wrapped up in three days. Even the extravagant public display of visarjan is absent in the Brahmin Ganpati puja. The idol is comparatively smaller in size and the function is meant only for the family, so no one belonging to another caste is invited into the sanctum sanctorum. A glass full of water is poured on the idol of Ganpati, which suffices for the ritual, as opposed to the hefty expenditure done by non-Brahmins. Even though the non-Brahmin Ganpati festival is celebrated under the strict religious guidance of Brahmins, Brahmin visibility is minimal when it comes to contributing to the large expenditures.

Universalism is appreciated for the commonality it commands and for the fact that it speaks to everyone. The Dalit, on the other hand, is considered a marginal, secondary category, infused with narrowness. The idea of Dalit universalism has never appeared in mainstream thought or social and political action. The commonly available discourse is based on fantasized abstractions of the Dalit experience. Therefore, Dalit universalism is not even considered, while stereotypical and misplaced ideas about Dalits are circulated in the privileged-caste public sphere. The theorization on Dalits corresponds with pulpit-oriented Sanskritic analysis that deliberately obfuscates the *material* experiences of Dalits—which are rooted in the universal experiences of human oppression.

The Dalit is represented as a fixed, unmoving category. He or she is the genteel server who is passive in reclaiming his or her share of justice, one who helps maintain the caste system. The theory of Dalit life is described through the lens of Brahminical actors, and therefore the ideal Dalit is shown as someone who does not threaten the established order. The experiences of Dalits are tied to the privileges of the dominant castes, and by excluding their material deprivation from the discourse, Dalits appear to be without aspiration. The experience of Dalits is comparable to that of other oppressed groups who fight for equal access to opportunity and financial security. However, Brahminical theory represents them as *ritually confined* beings, instead of as worldly beings. Dalit universalism locates the self beyond and outside the peripheral universality, beyond the peripheral identities that seek to prioritize their identities over other hegemonic orders. The emergence of the Third World, Global South or other modernist centred logos of humanity is premised on the uniqueness and exclusivity of identities. These appeal for a self-imposed isolation, whereas Dalit universalism appeals for a common humanism—a collective of everyone as human beings and access to a universal vision of humanity. A compassionate form of *maitri*, or fellowship, informs the humanist tradition that underscores Dalitness.

The idea of contemporary India is a Brahminical project designed by Brahmins. They dominate important positions in all sectors and are over-represented everywhere in India. Corruption, scandals and a rapidly failing state—these are the inevitable effects of the Brahminical project. Dalit universalism, on the other hand, is a moment of refusal to compromise with the ever-growing disasters. It offers a nuanced view of the mayhem caused by orthodox religious and capitalist forces.

Many progressive struggles that promised to subvert the existing unequal order reproduced another set of hierarchies. For instance, the communist revolution had promised a vertical order run by the lower classes. But the dictatorship of the proletariat merely became a new way of maintaining the unequal order. The Dalit movement, however, promises a horizontal order where no one is downgraded to sub-humanity. As Dalits lead honourable lives, their quest is to give the same to everyone.

Dalit universalism demands a complete annihilation of caste hierarchy, thereby inventing a new society for the oppressed to thrive—the Begumpura envisioned by Ravidas. An outright rejection of the tyrannical Hindu order is advocated, but the hatred is not directed towards any particular individual or group. The Dalit Panthers had succinctly observed, 'We are not looking at persons but at a system.'[16]

Dalit humanity calls for an equal position; it demands the *right* to be considered on par with other human beings. The Dalit

Panthers' Cultural Wing in Gujarat urged for treatment 'at par with rest of the human race'—a quintessential call of the Dalit struggle.[17]

Dalitness, Gangadhar Pantawane argues, is 'essentially a means towards achieving a sense of cultural identity' which weeds out the inferiorities imposed upon the Beingness of Dalits.[18] For D.R. Nagaraj it is a state of 'radical consciousness' that seeks to 'interrogate and challenge the previous stereotypes of the Hindu society . . . which smacked of patronizing pity'. The expression of Dalitness is harnessed in the 'politico-cultural expression of newly self-organized community' that rejects any forms of condescension and patronization. It challenges the state which is both an emancipator and a representative of dominant-caste control.[19] The struggle for freedom lies in the condition of truth which is to allow 'the suffering to speak', argues Cornel West. Therefore, Omprakash Valmiki's understanding comes closest to the Beingness of a Dalit: 'It is an expression of rage of millions of untouchables.'[20]

Although the 'tendency to be Brahmin' exists among all groups infiltrated with casteist interests, Dalit universalism is an antithetical instrument to the Brahminical project. It aims to participate in the global forces of humanism and liberate the oppressed from the clutches of casteism, capitalism, patriarchy and provincialism to upend structural inequalities.

Being a Dalit in today's world is to constantly fight, negotiate and ameliorate the abhorrent conditions imposed by society. The oppressors' influence on the psychic and material inputs entangles with the Dalit experience. Thus, an internal and external acknowledgement of Dalit culture in the public sphere needs to be taken seriously. Dalit art, music and literature need urgent patronage by supportive institutions and individuals as a project for the nation's self-reflection and self-realization. To see the world and experience it through the soulful touch and emotional metamorphosis of Dalits would enable one's humanness to speak for itself.

Being a Dalit is to desire to eradicate social discrimination and economic inequalities, and espouse a love ethic. Dalit Love, Dalit humour and Dalit universalism echo the articulations of Dalit freedoms. Now that we've estimated the Beingness of Dalit, let us cover the territoriality of the Dalit world.

~

Palestinian scholar Edward Said described the aspects of 'uniqueness' accorded to the colonized, the ruled population, in his path-breaking book, *Orientalism*.[21] Before I could make sense of my 'uniqueness' as a 'sub-oriental', I was out on the task of blowing up anything that came between me and my desires. Burning down the face of oppression and tearing it into pieces was a catalyst to bringing forth a certain affirmation to my sense of being. I had to inadvertently prove when no one asked me to do so. Why was I living under the orders of this *invisible* system? I was not part of it, and no deferential arrangement made sense! The Beingness of my Daliting came to me in a viscerally invisible form—not there yet so palpable under my skin, like a thorny vein pricking me from inside. I was living the pain of the furious blood in my body. My inability to retort at the time of humiliation and mockery keeps haunting me as a nightmare. Its sudden reminder brought rage. This time the rage was armed, and it was ready to blow up the oppressor who was perpetuating my oppression.

We measure ourselves through someone else's perception. This self is charted through a constructed vision—even we have not imagined ourselves in the form imposed upon us by the Others' thought, or visited our selves the way the seer does. Thus, it brings with it a two-ness of our identification. This means more demeaning harm to our unrecognized—and marginalized—self, the oppressed self that is freshly wounded by the derisive gaze of the outsider who is watching us. This watching transcends the mere act of subject objectivity. It is placed in historical junctures where watching someone is not to observe but to pass unqualified judgements on them. The gaze becomes even more painful when the seer and the subject have an unequal power relation that is built on the dossiers of oppression.

Jean-Paul Sartre describes what it means to look for self in the eyes of others.[22] It is the other's perfection that we choose to prioritize while presenting ourselves. Therefore, we constantly rehearse identity performances. Such repeated rehearsals add to the improvisation of how one finally comes to declare oneself. This becomes '*my* being without being-for-me',[23] meaning I am someone but I am not the owner of myself in this particular moment of interaction between the oppressor seers and the oppressed seen, the subject. This happens because, Sartre argues, we give up the agency of our self and willingly become an object for others. The audacity to giving up oneself comes from the historical experiences of punctuated fears that are inserted in our minds and bodies.

Not going into the details of Heidegger's conception of Time-Being, it is sufficient to note that according to him one lives in a tightly formed time space, and thus every action is codified according to one's action in a particular time. The question that then arises is what about those humans who have no accurate registers noting their presence in the time? My mother, for example, does not have a record of her birth. She does not know when she was born. The ownership of time is a privileged discretion of privileged beings.

It is in this light that the Brahmin lives in his or her own narcissist being without realizing the Other as a sacrificial human. Thus, in the decline of Brahminical acknowledgement, the Dalit acts for itself and for 'being-for-others' in a Sartrean sense.

We will delve into the lives of those that remain unprivileged in and with time, agency and the ethos of statism. This is the reason

Dalitism has to be reorganized because the question of agency and its quality is abated. Dalitism is a stark reminder that Dalits still own history and have their *being* existing in it. Socrates reminds us about the ownership of the commoner in bringing about universal peace. If the privileged take command of describing the spirits and powers of society, society will see no end to the saga of oppression. A Socrates dialogue with Glaucon, elder brother of Plato about a hypothetical city where the society measures and differentiates between justice and injustice can be only possible:

> Until philosophers rule as kings in their cities, or those who are nowadays called kings and leading men become genuine and adequate philosophers so that political power and philosophy become thoroughly blended together, while the numerous natures that now pursue either one exclusively are forcibly prevented from doing so, cities will have no rest from evils . . .[24]

2

Neo-Dalit Rising

'I don't know when I was born
but, for sure, I was killed
on this very soil
thousands of years ago.'

—Kalekuri Prasad

'Ambedkar taught us that character is the foundation of this edifice called the human society. When compassion and morality follow character, society achieves its real strength.'

—Baby Kamble, *The Prisons We Broke*

'Love is what
justice looks like in public
tenderness looks like in private.'

—Cornel West

'As she tore her ragged hair
in the darkness of frustration,
I, poison-drunk and restless,
would dig my fingers into the gooseflesh-navel,
profusely pouring black blood into
her psychic wounds.
'Hey, Ma, tell me my religion. Who am I?

What am I?
'You are not a Hindu or a Muslim!
You are an abandoned spark of the
world's lusty fires.
Religion? This is where I stuff religion!
Whores have only one religion, my son.
If you want a hole to fuck in, keep
Your cock in your pocket!'
—Prakash Jadhav, 'Under Dadar Bridge'

I was not brought up with fixed conceptions of race and gender. My community was alive with the humour that was peppered with healthy dialogues and equally shared amongst the members of my (extended) family—male and female alike. The concept of caste on the other hand was very banal to me, until the Other made me feel the inferiority of my caste position in a high-caste society—what appeared to me then as the norm; the *mothe lok* as my grandma often referred to them.

My school was cosmo-caste—a modern confluence of varied caste networks represented in a classroom, reviving the democratic sanctity of the space. Students came from different castes, although a disproportionate number were from the 'higher' castes as opposed to the lower end. There were three Dalit males and two Dalit females in a class of over sixty students. The three of us boys always comforted and naturally connected with each other. Nobody had to tell us about our shared affinity. The words 'Jai Bhim' would come to us naturally. Of the five Dalit students, I was the only one who came from a poverty-stricken background; the rest were second-generation upper/middle-class Dalits. That meant I was still the marginal among the marginalized. This would become apparent during lunchtime, when our tiffins would ooze with different kinds of spicy foods. My tiffin had a chapatti and cooked *methi bhaji* (fenugreek leaves) and not butter sandwiches or cutlets. I had probably not eaten butter more than six to ten times till high school. Butter was alien and did not form an important component of our food. Ghee too was highly valued. My mother would buy 100 grams of it, which was to be shared by five family members over the winter. Thus, ghee was an elite food enjoyed mostly by our dominant-caste classmates.

Ghee was equivalent to the positions of 'higher' castes, more so affixed to Brahmins. *'Bamanache lekra toop khaaun buddhine chapal va sudhrudh astaat'* (The children of Brahmins are sharp in the brain and healthy due to the dosage of ghee), my mother and grandmother would often say out loud. The dominant-caste students' lifestyle, food and study patterns were starkly different from mine. Their parents were educated and could communicate with them in English, in the language of the literates, to have a conversation about their coursework. The students had their own rooms in which they could hole themselves away to study without disturbance. On the other hand, I had to live and sleep in one room that offered no privacy to study, neither any alone time to think about exams. Television viewing, discussions, eating food—all had to be done in a single room divided by a thin wall. Although my parents tried to create a comfortable environment, the neighbourhood was a big distraction. I'd try to spend some time with my dominant-caste friends, and I would barely ever get access to their private spaces. I recall an incident in the eighth grade when I went to the house of a Marwari friend whose parents were physicians. This was the first time I was in the house of a Marwari family. They spoke in the Marwari language occasionally, but English dominated the conversation among the children, cousins and parents, who ensured that the kids ate together and traded information about the food they were eating and the various vitamins it had. I left the place empowered with new knowledge of vitamin C in the twenty-five minutes of my luncheon hangout. The kids were trained in accordance with the ease of their upbringing, and it was an easy segue for them to choose their career paths. It was the same with my other dominant-caste friends, who could look to their relatives or elders and draw inspiration to take up study options of their choice. These children had career paths set up for them with caste networks at their disposal. They did not have any difficulty in accessing the market and knowledge. With a smooth transition, they would be able to occupy important positions of power, reproducing the attitudes and norms of the hierarchical caste system (more in Chapter 6).

Thus, the Indian state–society is an entity of Brahmin supremacy. Every major enterprise in India functions under the strict dictums of Brahmins and other dominant castes. To emphasize his power position gained through inherited caste privileges, the president of a leading national party and a mascot for liberals audaciously declared his Brahmin lineage as a *janeu-dhari*, wearer of the sacred thread.[1] A person apparently in the race to represent over 1.35 billion people preferred to flaunt his Brahmin varna as aggressively as he could. This move to assert his Brahmin identity was also in line with his fears to not mess with the approximately 3 per cent Brahmin population of India, and reassuring dominant-caste Hindu voters that he had their interests in mind. This is how much Brahmin supremacy wields power. Every ritual in India is commandeered under the orders of this priestly caste.

The Indian Space Research Organization (ISRO), which is responsible for space-related projects, has launched missions to the moon and Mars. However, the take-off is always officiated by a Brahmin performing prayers. Even the directors working at the institution ensure that the Brahminic religion becomes part of its operations.[2] Astrology-inspired numbers and specific days of the week are considered when launching satellites. Such superstitious norms have ascended into space research projects. As far as ISRO remains under control of Brahmins, they will transport caste to the extraterrestrial world.

In the armed forces too, the pattern continues. The appointed priest in the barracks is by default Brahmin. Soldiers are disciplined to worship by having roll calls (attendance) at every Sunday Mandir parade. Citing the example of religious dominance, retired commissioned officer Lt Col. G.S. Guha writes that the Garhwal Rifles unit religiously observes the ten-day ritual of Durga Puja, and Lord Vishnu is its presiding deity established by Adi Shankaracharya.[3] This continues to transcend to the higher levels of defence. Very recently, Nirmala Sitharaman was anointed as the defence minister by a Brahmin priest.[4]

Jotirao Phule had commented on this way of Brahmin business in his famous 1881 book *Shetkaryache Asud* (The Cultivator's Whipcord). Phule chronicles how pot-bellied 'Bhat-Brahmins' exploit the commoner's fears. He cites the example of farmers toiling in the field round the clock organizing ceremonies to be officiated by a Brahmin who demands 'ghee and chapatti' and other expensive food items. The farmer is unable to afford these foods for his own children but readily makes them available for the Brahmin due to the fear indoctrinated through 'their selfish religion'. The Brahmin in India has deployed every strategy to be the supreme lord. And thus, from menstruating women to anyone's death, the Brahmin wants to be the primary point of contact so that he can further exploit the tears and pains of people. From the rituals before birth (*garbhadhan*), after birth (*janma kundali*, horoscope) to marriage up until death and even after death (*shradh*), the Brahmin has designed strategies to loot people. Phule observes Brahmins as freeloaders who seek to extort commoners. To explicate the beggarly attitude of Brahmins, Phule asks: 'Can such unsociable boisterous bloated beggars be found in any other country or community?' Phule also takes those Brahmin employees in the British government to task who doubly exploit the Shudra and Ati-Shudra peasantry. The British bureaucracy dominated by Brahmins worked in alliance to further harass the oppressed-caste people of India. The irrationality and superstition spread by Brahmins are primarily responsible for the descent of India's progress, which is very well seen in the fact that prayers are carried out before ISRO launches.[5]

As much as the constitutionality of the state emphasizes the spreading of social and economic equality and scientific temper, it does not, however, explicitly talk about the unequal stakes inherited by the traditional power brokers. The reconciliation of the horrid past that manifests into the present remains unacknowledged. As a result, the question of reparation and inherited privilege does not feature in the discussions of dominant-caste people. This lack of historical accountability creates a group of self-declared nationalists, religionists, supremacists and merit holders that parade around as pundits proffering distorted versions of Indian society.

No Controlling the Control Machinery

The government as a state institution is overwhelmingly run by legislators and ministers belonging to the Brahmin caste. The bureaucracy and top echelons of decision-making are manned by male Brahmins. The judiciary, which has the ultimate responsibility to decide the fate of a common person's life, is again dominated by Brahmins. A recent example is of the Dalit judge Justice C.S. Karnan of the Calcutta High Court. Justice Karnan was faced with a contempt of court charge when he mentioned that 'the upper caste judges are taking law into their hands and misusing their judicial power by operating the same against a SC/ST judge with [the] mala fide intention of getting rid of him'.[6]

No Dalit has yet occupied a seat in the Supreme Court, with the exception of Chief Justice K.G. Balakrishnan. Justice Karnan had earlier complained of discrimination against him by his dominant-caste peers, and he later sought to bring legal proceedings against them in three separate instances. He was eventually transferred from the Madras High Court to the Calcutta High Court. His fellow justices, the Bar Association and the Bar Council condemned and maligned the personality of Justice Karnan. The Calcutta High Court Bar Association reportedly denounced his misbehaviour and issued a statement boycotting Karnan's court. The statement read, 'We held a general body meeting wherein a majority decision was taken not to participate in any judicial proceedings before the court of Justice Karnan.' A sitting Dalit judge of a high court, Justice Karnan was eventually incarcerated for six months, an event that had never occurred in the history of the Indian judiciary.

What is worth noting is that not only were no remedial measures under the Prevention of Atrocities (SC/ST) Act sought on his complaint, but a twelve-judge bench heard the contempt case against him, which is rare. How is one to read such actions against a Dalit whose constitutional post is by default an outcome of his effective service and acumen in the judiciary? If this is any indication of what the Dalit workforce undergoes, we can positively contend that such anti-Dalit practices must exist in all public and private sectors in India.

Seven months down the line, in January 2018, a group of four sitting Supreme Court judges—Justice J. Chelameswar, Justice Ranjan Gogoi, Justice Madan B. Lokur and Justice Kurian Joseph—went live on Indian television screens one fine morning, sending alarming waves across the country. In their press conference, the judges alleged that democracy was in danger in India. They accused the chief justice of India, Justice Deepak Misra, for executing favourable attitudes in the assignment of important cases to judges who were junior to them to aid 'an orderly transaction of business'. In addition, they raised a concern regarding the untimely death of their colleague Justice B.S. Loya who was due to deliver a verdict on the allegedly fake encounter case of Sohrabuddin. Due to the interference of the chief justice, the disgruntled judges lamented that it 'adversely affected the overall functioning of the court'.

What happened next? Did they receive any flak from a majority of the judiciary, as was seen in the case of Justice Karnan? Did the state dismiss their claim and order a probe? Were they forced to take a mental health test? Were they rounded up and put behind bars?

The prime minister of India immediately summoned the law minister and took stock of the situation. It became a media carnival for a few days. The nation—on the right and the left—heavily discussed this issue and gave a fair hearing to the dissenting judges. During the Karnan episodes, although social media groups were abuzz with the unjust treatment meted out to Justice Karnan, some Dalits in the bureaucracy saw this as a warning.

An effect of such oft-repeated incidents is that many Dalit personnel share their experiences of humiliation and degradation only after retirement, and that too only in Dalit circles. Almost 50 per cent of retirees who shared their stories with me talked of the suicidal pressures they were put under. 'They have their caste networks in all the blocks [government departments]. The superiors are theirs, the police, CBI, politicians and even the judiciary belongs to them,' claimed a retired police officer. This police officer mentioned an incident wherein his children were admitted to a school where every bureaucrat's child was admitted. Being an Ambedkarite, the police officer had trained his daughter to be proud of her identity. Little did he realize that her dark skin and lunch box that did not carry vegetarian food would become a source of casteist contempt. Her isolation was marked by bureaucrat parents who discouraged their children from making friends with the Dalit classmate.

Liberal Constitutionalism and Ambedkar's Vision

The Dalit movement in India is yet to be fully formed with a sizeable consensus. It lives in various forms, sizes and shapes. It has not yet formulated a cogent programme to take in politically conservative Dalits by bringing them into the wider Indian democratic experience. Dalit scholars and politicians alike can be seen struggling to formulate a workable theory of Ambedkarism or Dalitism that would be a manifesto for common liberation.

By exclusively relying on the constitutionalism as a means of emancipation, this class of intellectuals argues for a utopian dream. The methods of attaining Dalit emancipation, however, remain unknown. The sooner India's oppressed realize this, the better. One cannot depend on the limited conceptions of constitutionalism for deliverance. Owing to the limited control of this institution, the Constitution has become synonymous to a grievance cell offering no immediate solutions.

The linguistic accessibility of the Constitution and its reach to the oppressed is extremely limited. Few peasants would consider the Constitution as a written word that would guarantee them protection from the landlord's real and financial whipcord. Similarly, beggars who are living on the mercy of donors' charity would think that this dossier guarantees them equality and access to freedom. The idea of the Constitution is romantic. No one really knows its limitations but lauds its profundity without testing it out. Many Dalits are repeating the state's narrative of constitutionalism as being the ultimate virtue—a god-sent panacea. It doesn't go further than merely applying a lotion to massage one's shattered ego. But when it comes to exercising the enshrined codes in the Constitution, Dalits seem to be harming their self-worth. This is because not everybody feels this document is close to their hearts as much as Dalits.[7] Not everyone has similar expectations from the Constitution. Thus, it creates genuine gaps while considering constitutional morality as a common virtue. Hence, in such a situation of one-sided applicability, mutual cohabitation is a long shot. One has to pierce through the devious agenda of casteist rogues by injecting a radical antidote to set a tone of mutuality and respectability. Unless this is settled, no further conversation can be foreseen that will yield real results.

As much as Dalits feel empowered in a constitutionally mandated democratic republic, any hope of their issues being redressed withers away when reality comes knocking. After every gruesome atrocity or everyday humiliation they undergo at the workplace or in their shared housing, the promise of constitutionalism shatters into pieces. Dalits are often accorded second-class citizenship. At the workplace, they do not get the requisite respect and attention from their co-workers. A senior bureaucrat friend, Tushar (pseudonym), who has an advanced degree from an Ivy League school, told me about his unpleasant experience. Prior to his departure to America, he was given a heavy workload with additional responsibilities by his immediate dominant-caste supervisors. Tushar narrated the story of how he was tasked to work on projects that demanded his extra involvement which in turn consumed more time than required. His selection to an Ivy League institution made everyone at his workplace insecure. He was regularly taunted with disparaging comments. 'What will you do after studying economics, which is not your field and different from the work you currently do?' Next, an inquiry was instituted against him in a corruption case that could delay his transition to America. Since his records were clean, he got the required clearance earlier and made it to the US just in time. He underwent a traumatic experience at the hands of jealous and insecure dominant-caste colleagues who couldn't tolerate a fellow bureaucrat scaling the heights. The friend could not do much about it. The promise of constitutionalism—that of equality—failed him bitterly even after he achieved a certain professional status.

One of the limitations of the Indian Constitution often echoed within Dalit circles is the absolute visionary absence of Dalit pride and the eruptive definition of liberation. Constitutionalism has proved to be an unreliable doctrine to influence perpetrators of casteism. The landmark case of *Surya Narayan Chaudhary v. State of Rajasthan* in 1988 exposes one among its many limitations. This case prohibited temples from discriminating against Dalits' right to worship and enter the sacrosanct spaces as a rule of law.

The verdict delivered by the chief justice of India, Justice J.S. Verma, pointed out the fact that 'mere enactment of such a law or guaranteeing a right in the Constitution of India is not enough and the change needed is really in our hearts and not elsewhere. It is the willing acceptance of the society which alone is the sure guarantee of eradication of any social evil.' He continued, 'The problem facing us is not the result of legal non-acceptance of equality of Harijans [Dalits] but of hesitation and refusal to accept honestly even that which we cannot openly deny or defy.'[8] The Justice J.S. Verma verdict expressed the inadequacies of legal provisions in the absence of society's willingness to acknowledge its prejudices. This goes in line with Ambedkar's comments on the uselessness of legislation in the face of social sanction.

Guarding the elitism of the Constitution and selling it under Ambedkar's name has come at the cost of Dalit radicalism. Ambedkar is now centralized as a sanctimonious figurehead. And in a country like India, to worship someone is to kill any critical thoughts about the person. Various ideological and semi-social and political circles play football with Ambedkar and enjoy the show put on by Dalits around his portraits. Ambedkar's image is used to silence Dalit rage around any issue, to the benefit of the oppressor, who is more than happy to co-opt Ambedkar into their vicious programme of hatred and violence. At the time of writing, every Dalit leader in the 2019 election campaign has spoken of protecting the Constitution. They found it a more appealing idea to attract the common mass towards 'Samvidhaan', as opposed to other traditional issues at hand, such as social justice, welfare programmes, education, health, taxation and the protection of the working class. The affection of Dalits towards constitutionalism is a curious subject of inquiry. No mainstream Dalit leader has dared to critically engage with the debate around Constitution and its encouragement of Dalit passivism.

Dalit rationality and radical conformity, on the other hand, retains a quality of elegance. This elegance is a result of its capacity to marshal adherent criticisms against vile Brahminical forces. By attributing the authorship of the Constitution to Ambedkar alone, the state as well as the casteist society plays into the banality of identity politics. Ambedkar is a father figure of the nation because he has authored the Constitution and therefore it is upon every Dalit to uphold it without understanding it adequately— this is a clever propaganda spread by the ruling caste in society. On the authorship of the Constitution, Ambedkar had once said exasperatedly in the Rajya Sabha: 'I was a hack. What I was asked to do, I did much against my will.'[9] This statement threw the House into unease. Members taunted Ambedkar by heating up the debate to solicit Ambedkar's response. To which he rose and added a blasting rejoinder:

> You want to accuse me of your blemishes . . . Sir, my friends tell me that I made the Constitution. But whatever that may be, if our people want to carry on, they must remember that there are majorities and there are minorities; and they simply cannot ignore the minorities by saying: 'Oh, no, to recognize you is to harm democracy.'[10]

Ambedkar's formula of minority and majority went beyond the statistical accounting of designating someone as part of the minority. The minority constituted an essential element in the life of India as every marginalized community with its vast history was a minority. Hence, the majority was an insufficient category in a liberal secular context wherein casteist ideology dominated in the making of a common Hindu identity. The majority possessed *chaturvarna* as the official doctrine which used 'caste discrimination as a sword' for political and administrative discrimination".[11] Every community according to Ambedkar practised inequality in its own forms.[12]

The same document that Ambedkar had so laboriously authored, he was now willing to burn to ashes.[13] He explained his position two years later, on 19 March 1955, when a colleague of the Upper House, Dr Anup Singh, reminded him of his earlier Rajya Sabha statement of 1953. Ambedkar clarified the rationale behind his forthright sentiment. In order to maintain the ideal of political liberalism, it was necessary that republican rights were provided to common and ordinary people. But he could see that this was no longer possible because Indian society was largely unequal, and the economic foundations were feudal and capitalist in nature. Thus, without abolishing social disparities, there was no point in talking about legal codes that were to suffer defeat at the hands of powerful landlords and priests who controlled the spiritual realm. Drawing an analogy with devas and asuras, Ambedkar had stated:

> We built a temple for god to come in and reside, but before the god could be installed, if the devil had taken possession of it, what else could we do except destroy the temple? We did not intend that it should be occupied by the Asuras. We intended it to be occupied by the Devas. That's the reason why I said I would rather like to burn it.[14]

The burning of a juridical text was not a foreign act for Ambedkar. It emerged from the tradition of radical love centred around the claim of equal rights for all. Ambedkar's episodic interventions with rigid Hindu society had already been made clear when he burned the *Manusmriti*, the oldest legal doctrine of Hindus.

His courage to denounce the repressive form of legality—as
represented by the *Manusmriti*, which propagated inequality
and oppression—connects to his commitment to the radical
pragmatism which believes in contemporary actions as opposed to
the settled doctrines of the past. It is a constant process of wrestling
with the past—its hazards and wrongs—as opposed to its vitality
to the present. Such codes of injunction deserve annihilation, that
is why he burned the *Manusmriti*; in the same way, he expressed
his frustration towards the handling of the Constitution of India.

~

The Constitution as a bearer of the state narrative suits the
governing castes well. Dominant-caste circles—liberal and
progressive included—view Ambedkar as someone who gave
them the Constitution, a nationalist, at best a revolutionary
constitutionalist who deserves recognition. However, by only
upholding his constitutional acumen, Ambedkar's rather more
important contributions to India's intellectual legacy are erased.
His harsh critiques of caste Hindu society, and the civic and
human rights movements he led, almost single-handedly, are
barely referred to. His intellectual and political struggles are
obfuscated from textbooks. Ambedkar's rights-based initiatives,
radical reforming movements and critiques of culture and
religions are the watershed movements in India's Brahmin-
controlled oppressive history. Ambedkar has given India many
reasons to stand in the world with pride, as someone who has
produced civil rights and liberties for its oppressed from day one
of its establishment as a republic.[15] By offering the Buddha's
philosophy to the modern world, he has put India back on the
global map as a nation with morale and sanctity. In spite of this
multidimensional work, Ambedkar is incessantly referred to as
an architect of the Constitution alone.

The authorship of the Constitution has also eclipsed Ambedkar's perspicacious scholarly command on topics like economics, law, philosophy, social sciences, religion, anthropology, linguistics, finance and jurisprudence. The person who undertook intellectualism as a method to organize and agitate is nowhere to be seen or credited for his scholarly achievements. Even scholars who have spent entire careers studying India's problems do not have an iota of knowledge about Ambedkar's colossal scholarship. Their cheap endeavours are visible when they rush to compare him with academically underqualified contemporaries. Major political leaders of the era are dwarves in stature compared to Ambedkar's persona. His laborious efforts to produce an alternative scholarship, to evoke critical dialogues in mainstream politics and to transform society from the bottom up are not to be found in his contemporaries. Academically underqualified leaders have become subjects of political and philosophical inquiries. These partisan scholars suffering from an inferiority complex and harbouring prejudice have espoused the magnanimity of India's founding nationalist leaders and other political mystics by making them subjects of study in every social science and related academic course one can find. However, they are not intellectually courageous enough to study Ambedkar. All of Ambedkar's works have been produced or translated into the English language. So there is no excuse of hiding behind the mask of vernacular inaccessibility.

Ambedkar's interventions in political philosophy have not got the attention they deserve, nor has his primary discipline: economics. I once inquired of a distinguished professor of economics at Harvard, who is an expert and writes on India's economic problems, about his thoughts on Ambedkar. He expressed to me his reverence of the man as a constitutionalist. On another occasion I asked a very senior Indian economist (who was also my professor at Harvard) about his comments on Ambedkar's economics. He lauded Ambedkar's move towards Buddhism, which he too found as the 'sensible option' one could choose. The economist Ambedkar is not a subject of inquiry, at least on the methodological plane, for economists or economic historians.

Ambedkar needs to be a subject of intellectual inquiry and there needs to be an engagement with his scholarship so that his erudite criticisms come to light. Ambedkar, then, will be available for larger public scrutiny beyond the circumscribed and idle interpretations of Ambedkar only as the author of the Indian Constitution and *The Buddha and His Dhamma* (1956). So-called experts have declared Ambedkar an eminent economist without adequately presenting his thoughts on economics as a socialist project available to ordinary people. The syllogism of 'Ambedkar's Constitution' is put on the face of every tormented Dalit who is still expecting a change.

Ambedkar's vision was a class-based solution for all castes. The society that was divided on social and economic terms still held on to social norms as a prerogative to everything they did. For land distribution, if it was merely a class issue, it would not have attracted the wrath of landlords. The land issue was primarily a caste issue and therefore an issue of social prestige. That was why Ambedkar concentrated on nationalizing land along with industries, insurance and education. This would give the state a rightful authority of being the welfare state looking after its subjects void of caste and class sentiments. Everyone in the village would be given land equally depending upon the standard sizes in the families. Ambedkar was a proponent of collective or cooperative farming in which intensive cultivation took precedence over the size of the farm. This gave more control to the farmer to focus on production and also helped the state regulate the revenue being generated from concentrated cultivation. This radical vision of Ambedkar surpassed every other binary of ideologies that were on the national scene in India. The Congress party disowned the agenda of land redistribution and did not seriously care for the nationalization of land as it was busy catering to the new landowning class which was extremely sensitive to its dominant position in society. However, overlooking the fact that Ambedkar talked of social divide and economic injustice in the same breath has limited the moments of Dalit pride in the broader sentiment of Dalit Nationalism.

Dalit Nationalism

The Dalit Nationalism project remains absent from radical and conservative Dalit political spectrums. Dalit Nationalism has the rightful potential to demand equality on its own terms and without frugal negotiations. This would set an uncompromising and non-co-opting tone of liberation. There are no national-level political calls for reclaiming Dalit land—land exclusively set aside for Dalits in rural and urban areas for the uprooted Dalit community—which is in tune with Ambedkar's thesis of separate settlement.[16] The agricultural census of 2015–16 states that 92 per cent of landholdings operated by Dalits comprised of small and marginal holdings, not exceeding 2 hectares. The poorest of farmers belong to the Dalit community whose operational holding is depressingly 78.06 per cent.[17] In a casteist economic order, Dalits are the most viable, accessible, loyal and determined labour. Hence, the logic behind putting Dalits closer to the chain of production is to extract undeniable labour. Yet, at the same time, the same system is seen to obliterate every liberatory move of Dalits.

Dalit Nationalism is also a space of congeniality and mutual respect. It is not a space that espouses ethno-centric nationalism. It is also not a geographically constricted spatiality. It is a consciousness of the highest standard based on the solid foundation of respect to everyone. Dignity and justice form the crux of Dalit Nationalism, which is a radical reimagination of selves in the topography of human virtues. Dalit Nationalism centres its attention on the lives of Dalits, the most vulnerable section of society, who need care and attention as the society mirrors the failure of collective humanity. By redrawing the lines of human-created boundaries, it breaks the axis of separation and encircles everyone who is willing to let go of their inhuman virtues. In it there is absence of hatred but a firm conviction to retort to the privilege-blind, entitled oppressor castes. It is not an *appeal* to the consciousness of the oppressor; it is a direct action of the oppressed.

Dalit Liberation as Opposed to Dalit Emancipation

The essentiality of 'liberation' and 'emancipation' presents to us the quandary of the current Dalit condition. Dalits want liberation as opposed to emancipation. Emancipation seeks to patronize the autonomous movement of self-liberation which is radical and uncompromising. Emancipation offers a suggestive liberal approach that is to work within structures that are often maintained by continuing oppression through different, albeit disguised means. Working in a system that operates on confining the marginalized to the ascribed position, emancipation suggests that rulers and owners should be gentle in their murderous treatment towards their subjects. It appeals to the consciousness of the governing class. It does not prioritize the urgency of the oppressed class; neither is it willing to work with the oppressed on their terms. It instead offers a prescription, a ready-made solution, to the oppressed masses on how to free themselves without holding oppressors absolutely accountable for the horrors they commit. And therefore, emancipation is a giving, a charitable act on account of the dominant who benefit out of the oppressive system.

The constitutional method as a route to Dalit emancipation precludes the call for the total liberation of Dalits. This over-

reliance on the Constitution—which did not make provisions for
the abolition of caste-based identities—has in effect kept caste alive
and intact by giving permission to uphold caste-derived virtues
which ought to be, but are not, unconstitutional. Thus, the thin
line between Dalit emancipation and Dalit liberation remains
blurred. Liberation equals radicalism, whereas emancipation
surrenders to the conformity of the status quo. Liberation is a fight
towards consciousness. However, emancipation takes away from
consciousness, thereby enslaving the totality of Dalit pride and
Dalit agency. The Dalit liberation doctrine brings with it the self-
sufficiency and confidence of Dalits becoming a governing class that
is equipped to self-rule without anyone else's deriding patronage.

Liberation has an agenda set by Dalits which is self-directed.
It has its own motives and goals that are predetermined and
not a negotiated compromise. Emancipation on the other hand
is a co-opted space. It is an ideology that suggests uplifting the
community not from the agencies or canons of Dalit experience
but from the experiences of the oppressor's side. Emancipation is
also a strategy to fit the Dalit into the narrative of the oppressor
circles. This liberation is not confined to Dalits alone. It transcends
the boundaries of gender, religion, race and sexuality, meaning
Dalits can echo other oppressed voices which are suffering under
similar dogmatic oppressions. Dalits can look around and say they
have the capacity and urge to liberate other oppressed people as
their history has been of challenging oppressive power structures.
They can channel their energy to liberate Brahmins and other
dominant castes who are trapped in the artificial make-up of the
caste hierarchy. Dalit liberation is the body politic of levelling
power relations. Dalit liberation is to take command of the self
and stand guard against potential attacks. It is not a subjugation
that relies on the patronage of the exploiting class. It is not a
petition to the oppressive ruling class. It is an action that relies on
blowing away the structures of oppression.

The likes of Abraham Lincoln and Gandhi are the archetypes of emancipators. Emancipation puts all the onus on the oppressor whereas the Dalit as an oppressed subject is asked to stand before the doorsteps of emancipators pleading for emancipation. The emancipator, as we all know, is not interested in bringing about liberation. The emancipator is only interested in freeing subjugated bodies up to a level that can ensure the continuation of his or her domination. It does not allow the shattering of oppressive structures. Instead, it performs the role of facilitating a dialogue within a hegemonic liberal framework that provides 'opportunities' for the upliftment of the historically exploited community. Schemes such as reservation are one such avenue where the entire oppressed group is given limited opportunities and has to fight over a small number of vacancies. It is inherently made to create rivalries amongst members of the oppressed group themselves and affect their solidarity. The emancipation project does not totalize freedom; it is an extension of dependence. Emancipation is the assimilation and accommodation of the few oppressed citizens into the framework set up by the privileged quarter of society. It considers charity a mode of associated living. It does not believe in giving up one's power and privilege, which are responsible for creating unequal structures.

The proponents of emancipation are mostly found clothed as 'moderates'. This group comes from the oppressive side of town but is willing to offer help. However, it turns out to be the 'great stumbling block'[18] in the move towards freedom of the oppressed group. Martin Luther King Jr viewed the member of such a group as one who paternalistically believes that they 'can set the timetable for another man's freedom', one who is adjusted to the 'myth of time' and one who is constantly asking the oppressed group to 'wait'. King observed this to be a 'tragic misconception of time' where people of 'ill will' are increasingly using this notion to delay the progress of the human race. King concluded with discordance that such '[L]ukewarm acceptance is much more bewildering than outright rejection'.[19] Ambedkar somewhat boldly understood secular Brahmins to be in the same bracket along with orthodox priestly Brahmins, dissolving the distinction between the 'moderate' and the 'extremist'. In his assessment, 'it is useless to make a distinction between the secular Brahmins and priestly Brahmins. Both are kith and kin. They are two arms of the same body, and one is bound to fight for the existence of the other.'[20]

Dalit Power

The answer to Dalit liberation lies in the resolve of Dalit Power. Dalit Power puts a premium on the conditions of the oppressed who are subjected to the vilified formations of life under the tyranny of a powerful minority. It is a programme designed to evince self-help as a method for execution. It is a secular space undivided by caste, religion, gender, sexuality, colour, race and nationality. It is the idea of universal liberation at the hands of those crushed under Brahminical conspiracies. Dalit Power has every possibility to bring voices and echoes on equal terms. Dalit Power prioritizes the oppressed Dalit. Dalit Nationalism holds history closer to the eye to learn from the sabotaged experiences of their movement. It is a non-co-opting and non-compromising agenda affirming its faith in radical, socialist, democratic politics.

To counter the flammable potential of Dalit Power's liberation project, the Brahminical apparatus graduates marginal Dalit political leaders into the mainstream. Recently, two Dalits were eagerly nominated for the post of president of the country; however, none of them has so far been considered for the post of prime minister. The mainstream Brahminical discourse about Dalit movement is limited to the struggle for civil rights. There is no understanding of the revolutionary character of Dalit Power.

The insincere dialogue on caste so far has kept the war on it covered, thereby securing the profanity of the Brahminical caste system.

Dalit Power of a strict order, where the system of radical democratic governance operated by Dalits and non-Dalits of a liberal-radical bent, would set the tone for visible forms of justice. Oppressive minority control is never the order of the day for liberatory politics. In the Indian context, dominant-caste minorities continue to exercise unquestionable control. Hence, the bandwagon of liberation mechanics idealized through the Constitution, whereby only one group adheres to its sanctity while another continues to disregard it, produces imbalance of a violent nature. This creates disharmony at the cost of Dalit lives.

Until we have the courage to criticize the criticisms, as John Dewey firmly stated, there can be no honest dialogue. The conditions in which this dialogue of criticizing the criticisms is initiated is under the false rubric of equality. The equality of unequals is what is on the table. We need to engage with the unequals before meditating on the abstract concept of equality.

Back to the bureaucrat, Tushar. Tushar finished his education with distinction. He taught a few courses during his time at the Ivy League school. He got good recommendations and was ready to come back and serve his country, albeit with some apprehensions. 'Frankly, I was nervous. I was not sure to whom I should report. I was not given a release order. And so, I did not have government-allocated housing. I was not sure where to go. My wife and child could also sense my anxiety. We landed in Delhi. I was hoping that a few of my colleagues would help me out.' Tushar hoped to receive at least some appreciation if not a grand welcome. He got neither.

He was given charge of a department far removed from his newly acquired expertise. He has now become a nine-to-five employee pushing files, and hopes to retire as a regular bureaucrat without his economic management degree ever being used for the advancement of his working environment. His educational achievement is not a source of pride for his workplace. To add salt to the wound, when his colleague's son got accepted into a US college, the department threw a big party facilitating the parents and the student. Tushar, sitting in the audience, stared at his lost future as everyone went on stage offering bouquets and showering praise.

Tushar represents an entire generation of educated Dalits who enrolled in prestigious government services with the aim of alleviating their society. Once they entered the service, they saw themselves getting intimidated by their dominant-caste English-speaking colleagues who casually flaunted their caste status through savarna mannerisms. With the caste limitations imposed on them, these Dalits were faced with intractable futures. Thus, they decided, as did Tushar, to help out the social justice movements in ways that were formidable and yet unseen. They organized closed-door meetings and shared their experiences. They looked out for each other and also financed some movements. However, this came with conditions. Many bureaucrats, unlike Tushar, expect silver-spoon treatment when they enter social movement spaces. Upon not receiving it, they turn to deception and self-loathing. In contrast, there are those who believe in subverting the order. They believe in themselves and are willing to be leaders and exemplars. It is people like this, and mostly students, working class and ordinary women, men, third-gender people, the old and the young who form the core of the neo-Dalit rising.

A Critique of Reason by the Dalit, for the Dalit

Dalits are in a rush to demonstrate their unity as a group, in spite of the inherent caste divisions, by forming new organizations without adequately addressing the issues of unity themselves. The idea of having an organizational platform to counter the hegemony of caste is appealing and equally profound. However, without addressing the pitfalls of democratic populism, these groups reproduce populism in new forms. Therefore, almost sixty versions of republican parties—the brainchild of Ambedkar—currently exist in India, each led by a flamboyant leader but riddled with self-interest at the core, euphemistically sealing the deal under the idea of Dalitism. The Dalit card is often played very well for self-proclamation in the situation of the caste identity crisis. The Dalit identity is auctioned at every circus of democratic representation, right from local government elections to membership of significant national bodies.

The erstwhile supposedly radical Dalit leaders can be seen in the pockets of Brahminical quarters performing all kinds of acrobatics to the command of their masters without sparing a moment of complaint. In this process, they dehumanize their own self and the totalized Dalit agency. By doing this, they get fractured in two ways. One, by virtue of losing the self-essence, and two, by losing Dalit recognition. There is, at the end, a plethora of loss for Dalit humanity, a catastrophe of its kind. The generosity that governs the deed of Dalit humanism is eclipsed in the self-hating dogma of Dalits.

Dalit Patriotism

Dalits are time and again dragged into the banal penance of proving their legitimate existence in India. This is done by questioning their patriotism and ardent nationalism. A Dalit, while subscribing to the views of Ambedkar and demanding his or her legal rights, always finds a need to footnote their nationalistic sentiments. Dalits are forced by caste colonizers to be patriotic in their own homeland.[21] The question of caste and Ambedkar's role during the independence movement is narrated from Brahmin diaries.

In these accounts, Ambedkar is portrayed as the handler of the British and an absolute colonial subject swayed by the seduction of Victorianism.

Instead of spreading Ambedkar's thoughts on the illegitimate exploits of caste colonizers, an educated Dalit in the office, school, college, sports stadium, cinema and every other common space spends time singing the greatness of Ambedkar's nationalism. The idea of patriotism built around the casteist nation is a treacherous concept. It is a crooked plot of traditional oppressors to question one's patriotism and resort to punishment if one has the temerity to even declare one's Dalitness. A Dalit youth was hacked to death in broad daylight in Ahmednagar, Maharashtra in May 2015. The reason: his mobile ringtone was set to Dalit music in praise of Ambedkar.[22] The mere act of embracing one's culture and being proud of it sends shivers of insecurity among oppressor castes. Thus, asking the Dalit to confirm his or her patriotism is to mock the mutilated and slayed Dalits in a country that breathes on freshly burnt Dalit bodies. Weekly, thirteen Dalits are murdered, five Dalit homes are burnt, six Dalit people are kidnapped or abducted, twenty-one Dalit women are raped.[23]

In spite of this, one can easily notice the demonstrative patriotism among Dalits. Every 15 August and 26 January, Dalits can be zealously seen posting messages of their affinity to the motherland, more than any other community I have come across. They reproduce quotes by Ambedkar, who had claimed his affinity to India: 'We are Indian firstly and lastly.' Middle-class Dalits still find the need to claim their legitimacy in the country of their ancestral birth. The immense sense of insecurity is the result of Dalits' outward rejection of the oppressive forces emanating from the state. Selective quotes from Ambedkar are used to sell their authenticity among their coterie of friends. Ambedkar's criticism of the state as an embodiment of elite masters' wishes is not given serious thought. The nation here is collaged according to the imagination of the oppressor, who is single-mindedly focused on stripping all the hard work of Dalits and the marginalized. The Dalit is asked to be disciplined if s/he pronounces her/his willingness to exercise the sacred writ of equal rights. In offices and in social spaces, a Dalit is disciplined to act and function within the codes of chaturvarna. Dalits are not allowed to have their festivals or marriage processions travel through areas populated by dominant castes.[24] For Ambedkar, effective patriotism meant collectively working towards annihilating caste.

Patriotism in an unequal society is a scheme conspired against Dalits to continue their subjugation. By questioning the Dalit right to belong, the nation handicaps them from performing tasks of their free will; for instance, Dalits cannot freely participate in protests against the state for legitimate demands. If they do, they are immediately branded as anti-nationals or India haters. No one is found discussing patriotism when farmer suicide rates grow at an alarming rate at the hands of village moneylenders—the Bania sahukar or the privileged-caste landlord. In the midst of an economic crisis, no one is seen campaigning for the nationalization of Indian temples that are the safe havens of priestly wealth as a patriotic sensibility. Even the secular/anti-religion Left Front has kept mum on this important issue. For various reasons, the Brahmin left continues to retain its hegemony.

A nation, as Ambedkar once observed, is not an entity built on the bricks of laws, but is an act of democratic morality. He goes on explain the pitfalls of nationalism and its ills in *Pakistan, or the Partition of India* and *Revolution and Counter Revolution*. Ambedkar thinks that nationalism is a psychological unity, a sensorial experience. He says:

> It is a feeling of a corporate sentiment of oneness which makes those who are charged with it feel that they are kith and kin. This national feeling is a double edged feeling. It is at once a

feeling of fellowship for one's own kith and an anti-fellowship feeling for those who are not one's own kith. It is a feeling of 'consciousness of kind' which binds together those who are within the limits of the kindred and severs them from those who are outside the limits of the kindred. It is a longing to belong to one's own group and a longing not to belong to any other group. This is the essence of what is called a nationality and national feeling. This longing to belong to one's own kindred as I said is a subjective psychological feeling and what is important to bear in mind is that the longing to belong to one's own kindred is quite independent of geography, culture or economic or social conflict.[25]

I see the position taken by Ambedkar with a deep appreciation for his full-time involvement in the internal cleansing of India before it was established as a constitutional republic. A nation with all its advances would fall prey at the hands of caste exploiters that hide under the guise of nationalists. Ambedkar referred to Indian power structures as a Hindu process, thus emphasizing the internal renaissance: 'Without such internal strength, swaraj for Hindus may turn out to be only a step towards slavery.' The incremental suggestions of Ambedkar to the wider Hindu community and to his own community have prohibited a series of bloodbaths and civil wars in India.

~

The suggestions of Ambedkar and the political future of Dalits remain with me as I stare at the scratched memories of my introduction to the caste system. This was the moment when the spark of the neo-Dalit rising was awakened. Rohith Vemula rekindled the suppressed voices of Dalits to be echoed in the horror chambers of Dalit atrocities. His suicide galvanized youth dissent into organic eruptions of movements. Many student- and youth-based organizations were floated in multiple university and college spaces. This injected the energy of youth into mainstream Indian sociopolitical movements.

Many Dalits armed with sophisticated English skills and savvy technical knowledge brought a newer version of Dalit radiance into the alternative world of rectangular screens. The rise of social media aided by cheap smartphones and affordable Internet data came as a boon for Dalits. Many young Dalits who were insecure and lonely in their identity struggle found a new space that helped them maintain anonymity and yet develop a community of fraternities and sororities. Online groups were formed and movements began to take shape. Many organizations took inspiration from the technology and media involvement of movements like Arab Spring and Black Lives Matter.

Rohith Vemula was representative of the movement that embraces Dalit beauty, Dalit pride and Dalit love. It is the commandership of Dalit agency that sits right at the centre of the neo-Dalit rising. Students and professionals, labourers and highbrow intellectuals, all joined the call for 'justice for Rohith Vemula'. In the feast of protests, Dalits once again demonstrated that they stand guard to the defence of freedom, equality and fraternity. Dalits remain defiant to the project of Brahminism and are willing to lay down their lives in the quest for freedom for all. Rohith Vemula gave us a moment of poetic reflection that at times remains missing amidst political revolution and social catastrophe. However, his sacrifice cannot be taken as the success of the Dalit movement. It demonstrates the pinnacle of the Dalit movement's failures. It is in Dalit radicalism and Dalit dissent that we taste the nectar of the neo-Dalit rising. It has begun and will become a life-changer for generations to come.

3

The Many Shades of Dalits

'We were animals and we continue to be. But dangerous ones. If people want to mess with us we know how to deal with it. We can even eat them raw. We are angry and the angst in us is incomparable. Our messiah Babasaheb is one such man who sought the right path for us – it is of human liberation – the path of Buddha. Those Nizams (a Muslim ruler in Deccan India admittedly known as the richest king on earth during his times) offered millions as a gift to conversion to Islam. The Sikhs came with their own demand. Catholics were in queue. But for my Babasaheb, Buddha was the only who could humanize us. To humanize us and to identify human as a human and a person of equality we have no other better option than my, our, Buddha.'

—Sahebrao Yerekar, a Marathwada Ambedkarite
folk singer (author's translation)

'The harvest of manslaughter is ceaselessly obtained here.
Seasons change only in accordance with the wind's direction
From east to west, north to south
harvesting never ends, round the year,
for vultures.'

—Ashok Chakravarti, *Harvest*

'When the diabolic thirst called Dalit conscience laid siege to my mind, I was spitting venom at the very word brahmin.'
—Aravind Malagatti, *Government Brahmana*

'Kapada na latta va khaya bhatta fajitee maay hoti lay mothi
Kakhet lekaru, haatat jhadna, doi war shenaachi paati,
Mahya Bhimana maiy sonyane bharali oti.'

[No clothes to wear, neither food to eat, it was a huge fuzzy, Child in arms, broom in hands, pot full of shit on head, my Bhim (Ambedkar) has filled my sack with gold.]
—Kadubai Kharat, an Ambedkarite Bhimwani singer and poetess who sings Ambedkar's song while visiting people in their homes and bastis (author's translation)

Dalits armed with revolutionary thought are departing from the fixed position assigned to them in the caste ecology. They are now emerging with a 'devil-may-care' attitude and ceasing to mimic their oppressors. Rather than adoring the lifestyle of upwardly mobile groups and aspiring to the status of the dominant castes, they are now changing the needle of their compass and looking inward, to seek inspiration. They are also looking globally to find cultural icons.

A Dalit child is sent to school 'to become Babasaheb Ambedkar' and not to occupy the position of a Class IV employee in the government sector. The replacement of other demigods of Hinduism with Ambedkar has offered another dimension of critique to the cultural politics of Dalits. Dalits now no longer desire to genuflect to these Brahmin and Hindu oppressor gods. They have discovered new temperaments that challenge their relation with the oppressor. They are taking their music to a high culture, their songs are echoed in the mainstream rap genre, popular songs in vernacular languages are big hits, and theatre, film and fine arts are reflecting the inner core of Dalit humanity. In the midst of such a cultural revolution, one may ask what the new identities are going to offer to Dalits.

Before addressing this question, we'll take a tour of existing Dalit categories. Dalit discourse is modelled to develop a morally strong character de-objectified from the narratives of market culture. Dalit discourse has an immense potential to suggest a virtuous rationality that incorporates scientific temper as its fundamental outlook centred on humanist values. These values engage not only with the Athenian principles of humanism that centred on human experiences, emotions and values, but also offer a deeply entrenched style resulting from an upbringing of a certain order.

In the present times, one cannot easily draw a clear line and declare one a Dalit or tribal leader without qualifying reservation or hesitation. The people who present themselves as representatives without moral consensus can be minimally described as salaried employees of Brahminical political parties. These appointed Dalits are forced to work under the tutelage of their Brahmin bosses who thrive in the Brahminical ecosystem. The best way to describe these groups is to categorize them according to the ways they operate.

Casteist behaviour is often from top to bottom, from upper to lower. Following this logic, privileged Dalits effectively execute caste codes upon the lower social, economic and political sub-caste Dalit groups. This hinders the formation of a united Dalit identity and further creates ripples in the battle against anti-Dalit forces. Chandraiah Gopani makes a claim for left-out Dalits in the process of democratic transformation.[1] The lowest of the low remain out of the purview of development. He finds the result of ignoring these communities a definite problem of the Dalit movement. Cross-caste solidarities among Scheduled Castes do not take place owing to the caste dominance of numerically strong sub-castes. Due to this, the left-out Dalits are co-opted by Hindutva forces into their projects of violence. Such groups act vehemently against upwardly mobile Dalit castes because there is a lack of social endosmosis amongst 1200 Dalit castes. Barriers are created through intra-caste marriage prohibitions, together with affixed caste occupations that force oppressed Dalit sub-castes much lower down the socio-economic ladder. The under-represented always feel oppressed and left out. Therefore, to gain legitimacy, they volunteer to not only confront the hegemonic Dalit discourse but also effectively puncture the dominance of the governing classes among Dalits. The various attitudes among Dalits could be effectively typified into four 'castegories' that aim to inscribe a contemporary lexicon of Dalitism. These are also overwhelmingly visible in the touchable–oppressive caste structures as they operate on a higher pedestal of immoral hierarchical oppression. The various castegories are an outcome of the strict management of the caste system, partially drawn from the law of imitation as explained by Gabriel Tarde and elaborated upon by Ambedkar with regard to Hindu caste society.[2]

Castegories of Dalits

The castegories of Dalits are an outcome of the autonomous yet co-habituated lifestyle of the Dalit castes. The 1200 Dalit sub-castes and approximately 4000 sub-sub-castes have retained their history and memories of independent tribes that were forced into Hindu untouchability.[3] Some of these independent sub-caste groups have formed their own universalism. And such variant practices do become visible in the various castegories below. Although the castegories that I have drafted below are visible across various castes, the twice-born savarnas included, the class loyalty across various Dalit castes remains particular. The existence of castegories is due to the independent sub-caste histories and their aspirations tied to their collectives futures. In addition to this, it is partly due to the fringe Dalit movements that has kept the sub-caste divisions intact by focusing entirely on the caste-based dynamics of Indian Hindu society.

Castegories of Dalits

Token Dalits
Conservative Dalits
Reactive Dalits

Elite Dalits
Salaried Hypocrites
Third-Generation Dalits

Self-obsessed Dalits
Harmful Dalits

Radical Dalits

Token Dalits

Ambedkar experienced this class of Dalits first-hand in his political and social career. In politics, the Dalits who emphasized their allegiance to the Congress's Hindu agenda presented themselves as an integrated part of Hindu culture. They contested against Ambedkar in the elections and were even successful in negotiations with the British. Ambedkar's All India Scheduled Caste Federation had opposing organizations such as the M.C. Rajah–led All India Depressed Classes Association, the Jagjivan Ram–led All India Depressed Classes League and Gandhi's Harijan Sevak Sangh, who claimed their authenticity over Scheduled Castes. On the social front, Ambedkar had argued for higher education benefits for Dalits from the British government. However, this class was to 'betray' Ambedkar's goals. They went on to represent the best of tokenism of the community they claimed as their own.

Kanshiram picked a term which was appealing to the masses. He named them 'chamchas' or stooges, who had given rise to 'an era of stooges': the 'Chamcha Age'. The chamchas wielded no direct power and were 'unable to operate on [their] own'. Therefore, it was through the chamchas that their operators attacked Dalits. Kanshiram was adroit in pointing out that the chamchas transcended the political spectrum, thus they could be found in legislature as well as the executive. Kanshiram identified chamchas in all Dalit communities, and they were 'the Dalits who hoped to gain from sabotaging the Dalit political discourse by enslaving their needs over the community'.[4]

Token Dalits possess a purchasing and selling power. They successfully present themselves in caste-politics auctions. They possess diverse skill sets and educational backgrounds and come from different sub-castes. Another common thing that connects Token Dalits is that they attest to their sub-caste category as a primary identity over anything else as it accrues more benefits in the political gamut. This produces an inferiority complex, and thus the only way they express themselves is by presenting a docile, subservient self. The dominant castes have spared Dalits a confined and narrow avenue of expression. This pertains to reiterating their lowly position in society. Trapped in this feudal ecology, Token Dalits see themselves as second-class citizens.

In this articulation, many Token Dalits assert a superior position over their fellow less well-off and less educated Dalit peers. They produce impermeable myths of their second-class identity. They are immensely insecure about their existence in the two worlds they inhabit: the Dalit world and the dominant-caste world. In the latter, their agency is no better than that of a loyal subject. The bi-located Token Dalits tackle their insecurities by repeating their stories of charisma and of their acceptance into the village Patil's *wada* or into the cars of MLAs, MPs or ministers. In one meeting of Dalit intellectuals, a former member of Parliament and a public intellectual of repute from Maharashtra boastfully claimed that he had had an opportunity to ride in the car of the chief minister of Karnataka. He felt that this was the only way through which he could emphasize his superior position in the company of fellow Dalit intellectuals.

Token Dalits can be observed primarily in subordinate positions at work, in politics and in social circles; they are clinging on in the garb of dutiful citizens. But they are nowhere to be found in places of worship or in the exogamous forms of intimate relationships with dominant castes. Many Dalit politicians make peace with the fact that they are unwelcome in the religious affairs of non-Dalit circles. Having accepted that they won't be allowed in, they endure a humiliating position in non-Dalit habitats—that of second-class citizens. However, some Dalits with class privileges becomes acceptable in caste society with a certain ritual distance.

To enforce their opinion upon the 'lesser' others, Token Dalits even hire a few affluent and muscular Dalits as their henchmen. For instance, a local councillor from Nanded, S. Gaekwar had no commitment towards his constituency. All he cared about was advancing his own needs using his Scheduled Caste identity. He was not favoured by the Dalit constituents. However, to retain his presence and maintain the pressure, he hired a few unemployed youths from the community. These economically disadvantaged youngsters were given motorbikes, salary, food to eat and liquor to drink. The councillor had to prove his importance to his political masters by keeping the constituents in a firm grip. He deployed the same strategy as dominant-caste politicians: hiring struggling Dalits as mercenaries.

Another style of influence involves recruiting influential speakers and intellectuals to propagandize for Token Dalits. For instance, a lawyer and a college professor who were eloquent in their speech were employed to influence people. Because they spoke in high-brow Marathi, semi-literate or uneducated working-class Dalits would flank to their events. These intellectuals would use rhetorical expressions and emotional appeal to garner support. Slowly and firmly they would invite the audience to appreciate the work of a Token Dalit. As the speech would proceed, the tenor would direct the attention of the public towards the Token Dalit leader by showering heaps of praises. Because people trust intellectuals more than opportunistic Token Dalits, public support would turn in favour of the latter.

Token Dalits, when encumbered with airs of pride and limited power, try to overshadow their position by demonstrating their control over destitute and helpless Dalits. Instead of becoming a positive vehicle of change, they represent the educated class that Ambedkar had decried in his 1956 Agra speech for having bitterly betrayed him. Thus, as the fable of casteism goes, the oppressed is interested in oppressing the one who is lower in the caste hierarchy. Rather than criticizing such a bigoted system, many Token Dalits flank to the lines of the oppressors. One thing to note, however, is that the Token Dalit is not part of a fixated category but a constantly evolving phenomenon. Because it is changing its appearance and form, one finds it difficult to pin down the Token Dalit category upon any one individual.

Fate of Token Dalits

Token Dalits are known to brag about their intimacy with their masters. The audience to this braggadocio are the dispossessed, crushed and oppressed Dalits. Token Dalits constantly feel the need to renew their value in the master's enslaving market. They sabotage their community's interests by auctioning socially acquired qualities of leadership, courage, speech and sound business acumen. Treachery, deceit, betrayal and disavowing their own groups' interest make their position stronger than that of other candidates. Some go even further to denounce other Dalit leaders in public by using abhorrent casteist slurs. By deriding their own caste folk, they deride themselves. An oppressed community is a stagnant mirror. It never changes. The good and the bad all reflect inner semantics to the outer world. Whatever one does and does not do is ingrained in the behaviour dynamics of a person. Therefore, if a person is degrading the other without spending rational thought, it is the result of the immense insecurities of the other.

Token Dalits pay and invest exponentially in order to be in the closer affinity of their masters. Spatial segregation does not deter them. They take a mortgage on their house just to be closer to the level of their masters. The master looks down upon Token Dalits. In private, he even mocks this buffoon for being his obedient, non-complaining subordinate.

Token Dalits also carry no responsible delicate reaction to the stigma attached to their lowly position. This can be understood through what Malcolm X defines when referring to the differences between a House Negro and a Field Negro.[5] A House Negro is a good-for-nothing-to-the-Black-community figure. He has blossomed with the idea of being close to his master and never thinks beyond the alternatives than the cosmology of his master's shadow. He is dismissive of every other possibility of survival. He challenges the Field Negro who demands liberation. He creates constant trouble and barriers in the execution of the project of freedom. The House Negro professes to be the best among the best of slaves.

One can consider how many Token Dalits resonate with oppressed groups on the other side of the Atlantic. In his monumental work, *Black Bourgeoisie*, Howard University sociologist E. Franklin Frazier examines the conditions of such a political class among the African-Americans that emerged in the post-slavery era.[6] This class of African-Americans benefited from the political opportunities offered by the liberal American north. Due to political power, they could vote and participate in civic life as office holders or citizens. Owing to this, they could resist the racial discrimination that was hurled on them in public and private spheres. However, in the Indian context, access to the political power won by Ambedkar after successful negotiation with the British colonial government unfortunately reproduced many Token Dalits. This was due to the callous Poona Pact that deprived Dalits of the autonomous political position they had gained at the Round Table Conference in 1931.[7] The opening up of opportunities for representation was taken as an affront by dominant-caste Hindus. Thus, they did not choose a candidate who would stand for the rights of Untouchables. Instead, they favoured someone who was a loyal and mute yes-man. As a result, this coercive act of Gandhi's saw the emergence of loyal Token Dalits who were encouraged in the political space.

Indian electoral politics clearly reflects the caste-based system, wherein subjugated castes have to be at the service of dominant castes who rule the political spectrum by default. Therefore, in contrast to the African-American experiences of resisting racial discrimination through political power, the Indian system, through the joint electorate, produced a power structure that was powerless for Dalits. A political Dalit in the quarters of dominant castes participated in reproducing casteist stereotypes and prejudice by fashioning an image of a corruptible, saleable and spineless character. Far from resisting caste discrimination, they denigrated the revolutionary liberation ethic. Token Dalits bid Dalit suffering as something to be sold in the caste market. This electoral system created a class of 'House-Negro Untouchables'.

To correct this, the Indian Constitution in 1950 reserved a percentage of seats for Scheduled Castes and Scheduled Tribes. But reservation politics has produced more Token Dalits than anything else among the Dalit classes. As long as they can produce more Token Dalits, the ruling castes will prefer having an intact reservation policy. Token Dalits excessively rely on the reservation policy and state social welfarism. They see this as the only avenue available for emancipation. Because they have benefited from this policy, they push for more state dependability for Dalits. These Dalits are self-centred and ready to profit from the common Dalit's struggle. Another reason that warrants the reliance of Token Dalits on the reservation policy is due to the purchasing power it offers. They are ready to auction their caste certificates at their master's doorsteps and divide organized Dalit unity. Because they can sell their credibility under the reservation regime, they are kept as sidekicks by the ruling classes who use them as per their needs. These Dalits do not possess a credible autonomous individual agency among the Dalit constituency or in their masters' quarters. They are seen hovering around the Brahminical political arena, flaunting their Scheduled Caste certificates to get a reserved constituency seat.

The tokenized Dalits render their Dalitness as a factor of negotiation to emphasize their importance as a political tool. In doing this, they conveniently and unethically vindicate the caste structure. Such people are committed to self-promotion. In order to retain their status, they embrace a stereotypical image of the Dalit community. These status-oriented Dalits devote their energy and attention towards immediate results by pawning off their dignity. Many end up becoming the butt of jokes and at best celebrity entertainers in Parliament. These leaders lack both oratorical skills and rhetorical timing. Simply by appealing to emotional outbursts and responding to Dalit anger, they feed into the narratives of a whiny but incompetent Dalit leadership, drawing spite from politically aware Dalits. Many refuse to own such a Dalit leader and often display contempt at this denigration of Dalit pride.

Most of the existing Dalit political leadership contributes to the anti-Dalit, Dalit-self-loathing paradigm. The Dalit community needs leaders who will exhibit courage as a bare minimum quality and remain committed to their roles in the movement. They need to emulate the prophetic gestures of truth, love and courage and adopt truthful and honest qualities to direct their actions. This would also mean looking at oneself beyond the confines of sub-caste and caste categorizations. Visionary leadership extends beyond anything that human narcissism has created: boundaries, me-ness and self-gratification over the larger cause of welfare to all. It embraces altruism as a working ethic and not an incentive. The leaders need to align such qualities with a strong moral force and offer democratic hope to the oppressed in times of hatred, anger and civic nihilism.

Conservative Dalits

Conservative Dalits prefer to stay in a confined space and operate within a regressive world view. Like all conservatives, Dalit conservatives are found in every religion. They use religion to dominate and suppress the dissenting voices amongst Dalit radicals. Conservative Dalits are fantastically myopic in their approach to the caste problem. They steadfastly rely on the traditional individualistic methods of looking out for oneself wherein protest or other radical measures by the more oppressed castes is discouraged.

Conservative Dalits despise fellow Dalits and are notoriously against any challengers from the Dalit community. Their enduring faith in the karmic theory pushes them to be regular visitors to the Hindu congregations of babas and sadhvis to seek guidance for the next life. Some continue to practise Hindu dogma even after conversion to other religions. They are not aversive to the Hindu identity. Their belief in the religious life is granted with a faith in the supernatural to warrant acceptance in caste Hindu society. Although, treated differently, Conservative Dalits still hold on to their position as their approach lies in not completely disturbing the order but following certain set rules. They believe that the latter might prove beneficial in the larger context.

Many among Conservative Dalits have graduated into the ranks of top leaders in various fields, from politics to arts, literature, sports and religion. Due to their education and upwardly mobile background, they have flanked a new class of educated Dalits who are neither radical nor totally submissive. They credit their success to hard work or faith. Their changing lifestyle and presentation of the self immediately set them apart as outliers. Conservative Dalits prefer to run the world based on their principles, which are not pluralistic. They are convinced that their methods are the only genuine ways for Dalit liberation.

However, the ideals of Dalit liberation are not practised in the private sphere. Their daughters do not have the desired independence; they treat women as secondary to men and expect them to submit to patriarchy. Father, mother and the extended family compel the female child to pursue a life of subordination. Their way of salvation for the female person is confined to her husband. Unsurprisingly, Conservative Dalits prefer intra-caste marriage and oppose inter-caste marriages. They detest the lower-caste/class Dalits, and ostracize inter-caste and inter-subcaste couples.

Conservative Dalits parade around as liberal and open-minded; however, when it comes to personal relations and the private sphere, they discriminate against Dalits from lower sub-castes. While they do not mind getting their toilets cleaned by manual scavenger Dalits, they do not allow them to enter their house. They carry an arrogant air, which is the outcome of their economic and social status. These conservatives try to imitate and present a moderate image of their Brahmin masters who have effectively maintained their supremacy by downplaying the role of women. These Dalits aspire to become idealized Brahmins without realizing the inability of the caste system to grant them Brahminhood.

In a Conservative Dalit household, women are strictly made to live under Manu's dictum—under the control of the men of their family. They do not have equal rights and are treated shabbily. The men exercise undisputed authority and thus reproduce patriarchal violence upon women's bodies. The women also control the lives of other women, deriving legitimacy through conservatism. They discourage other women from loving freely, making independent choices or choosing career over marriage, and so on.

The premise of any social institution built over centuries, whether caste, race or patriarchy, is fertilized by human subjugation. Ambedkar deals with this phenomenon in detail when he anchors a sharp anthropological understanding of the caste system. It is the endogamous practices among Brahmins that get imitated across the caste hierarchies that are peculiar to the mystery of the caste system.

The caste system is fundamentally premised on the oppression of women. Ambedkar had distinguished the persistence of caste discrimination functioning as being primarily an anti-women system. He charted out this proposition in a 1916 essay[8] where he identified the genesis of caste Hindu society. He observed that it was the practice of endogamy that was used to control the sexuality of women across caste groups. He characterized three prevailing customs that depicted the barbaric nature of caste Hindu society: 'Sati or the burning of the widow on the funeral pyre of her deceased husband; (ii) Enforced widowhood by which a widow is not allowed to remarry; (iii) Girl marriage.'

Considering the above, it can be said that the Conservative Dalits' indefatigable commitment to Brahminical values is overwhelmingly seen in the marriage system. These Dalits align their faith with a strict class-based consciousness. Thus, they indulge in the regressive practice of demanding dowry. The women do not hesitate to inflict domestic violence on their daughters-in-law just as they had suffered it at the hands of their mothers-in-law. An abiding faith in superstition influences the habits and norms of the family—for instance, cooking only at certain hours, cutting nails in a specific corner of the room, using certain rags during menstruation and performing religious rituals on a specific day and time, and so on.

Conservative Dalits love fellow Dalits who attend their congregation and regular sermons of their favourite priests, pastors or godmen/women. Anything else is received with suspicion. Conservative Dalits are in a dominating position in various circles. They get heard whenever oppressive forces want to put down Dalit radicalism. The conservatives are used as tools by the oppressor castes, and become examples of Dalit buffoonery. They enjoy this position as long as it brings them some benefits. Their struggle is confined to personal gains and thus it remains limited. They are uninterested in going beyond and crossing the inner borders of Dalit, that is, sub-caste-centric issues.

Conservative Dalits believe in the free market and are supporters of capitalism as a mode of social and cultural production. They rally with free marketeers to enhance the capacity of Dalits in the capitalist mode of production. They want to create concessions and facilities for Dalits in the free-market regime.[9] Compared to other submissive caste groups, Conservative Dalits undergo another layer of graded humiliation due to their disadvantaged position in the graded caste ladder.

Reactive Dalits

Reactive Dalits have no ideology or programme to offer. They ride on the principles of negating the other. In doing this, their approach is entirely dependent on others. They have no genesis of originating organic constructive criticism. They rely more on reproduction of ills than resolvability. Their victory is laden with the destruction of the other. They do not have a concrete programme to take over state resources. Instead, they partake in momentary masculine pleasure offered to male bodies to vent out their frustration in public. The venting out of frustrations is aptly seen in the reaction of Dalits to episodic anti-Dalit state actions or court orders against the provisions granted for the welfare of Scheduled Castes and Scheduled Tribes. Along with other groups of Dalits, Reactive Dalits can easily be spotted holding their placard in all directions.

The Reactives profoundly invested in gaining legitimacy from the Dalit community in order to attract their dominant-caste masters' attention. They are the reserved foot soldiers who are ready to sacrifice their community's priorities for a slice of the leftovers. They wag tails as per their masters' wishes. They eulogize them by repeating the masters' generosity time and again. They click pictures with local leaders and superior party wo/men, and proudly display themselves as loyal servants. They are not concerned about their autonomy and their role as equal partners in the democratic game. They are relegated to the position of a first-class servant, a second-class citizen, and a third-class individual.

Reactive Dalits have indoctrinated a similar line of thinking among their followers. They live with a single goal: to get a ticket to contest the assembly elections or elections to the local bodies. I know of a strong national party foot soldier who is a mature, lucid and courageous Dalit. He had served his Maratha master so loyally that he even took the charge of his master's crimes upon his head. He was incarcerated for over a decade. During our conversation in his three-storey house, the only one of its kind in the Dalit area, he whisked out a cigarette and spoke in despair about the lack of respect from his colleagues in the party. 'It is akin to *peshwai* [feudal rule]. Their gaze has declared us inferior,' sobbed the strong Dalit politico. He was a suspicious mushroom among the dominant-caste party members. Therefore, he had to double his efforts to demonstrate his loyalty to his Maratha master. He was frustrated and embarrassed. He did not have anyone whom he could speak to. The Dalit constituency liked him but limited themselves to a transactional relationship. Whenever the master needed a strong public presence for a public function, this Reactive Dalit was called upon to get Dalits out of their *bastis* for a wage of 100 rupees per day.

The politico once told me, 'They will never treat us fairly. We should be aware of who we are and not expect more than what is served by the boss. If we rebel now, I am sure he will eliminate me and my family members. They know the grips to keep one in control. They do this by making you a shareholder in some underhand business.' The government contracts and other sources of income come from the political master's patronage and often this kind of business is done through illicit means. Invariably, the Dalit is made a collaborator. This Dalit leader has been in the government contract business for the past decade and is aware of his master's exploits. He has been debarred from having big political aspirations, with a stern warning to not dream big. Contrary to this, his dominant-caste colleagues who are well known for their corruption scandals walk freely, aiming for higher positions.

This Dalit leader was told by the party office that once his master became a minister in the government, he would be in the pipeline for a position in government-run organizations that focus on SC/ST development projects. When I asked him why he did not ask for more, he said that the *relatives* of the master—read, dominant-caste men and women—were in the queue and the master would prefer them over us. 'Us' meant the Dalit community.

Another friend, a mainstream Dalit political party's state unit office-bearer, considers having 'pragmatic' alliances. Thus, he supports his party joining hands with Hindu right-wing conservatives 'for as long as they value us, we will work with them'. It could also be read as 'for as long as they value us, we will continue to enslave our human personality on account of community dividend'. It so happened that the alliance with the right wing never worked. They had to go back and forth repeatedly getting things approved as none of them were reaching a fair compromise.

With all the benefits that Reactive Dalits grant to the Dalit movement, their energy is misdirected into a hollowed vacuum. This confines their actions to multiple repetitions and thus its temporal nature is limited to reaction-oriented action. Due to the absence of long-term time spans, their position remains unsettled. This fragility in regard to ideological belonging results in no concrete action. Their performance as Reactive Dalits only gets acknowledged in the momentous rush. Owing to this, they find it difficult to win support among the masses and thus develop a flimsy public image which is neither trusted nor counted upon in the midst of reactive battles that are evoked after every other pogrom or atrocity upon Dalits.

Reactive Dalits have a good standing among the poorer Dalits. They come with an established background and can be also found working in bureaucracy and education. Because of their status and background, they carry weight. Their suggestions are fused to create further tension in the community. After the Bhima Koregaon violence[10] in 2018, I heard a top Dalit bureaucrat suggesting to a Dalit student leader to not align with other non-Dalit progressive forces when a united struggle was fermenting the country.

Such Reactive Dalits are loud in private and prefer to pass on their message to the community via their handlers who are working amongst poor Dalits. At the time of backlash and repercussions they are nowhere to be found. A student leader once acted at the behest of an influential Reactive Dalit against an organization in public. The Reactive Dalit fed the fearless charismatic leader with misleading information. When the backlash happened, the student leader was arrested. The Reactive Dalit bureaucrat merely stared into his eyes. Later he confessed that he was helpless and was only 'suggesting' calling out people's names in the public. Thus, Reactive Dalits befool fellow helpless Dalits day in and day out. At the time of their direst need, they prefer to save their own backsides. Many hint that they work in the background because they are afraid of the government machinery. The fear is passed down to the community and the suffering Dalits are also told to be afraid of the state machine. They are discouraged from breaking the back of the system of dirty caste politics which is responsible for their exploitation. The Reactive Dalits who puncture revolutionary zeal by suggesting liberal methods of working with oppressors do not have radical consciousness. They are a product of extended caste-based biases existing in various circles in India.

Elite Dalits

This is the most ungrateful class of Dalits and it benefits the most from the Dalit caste identity struggle. Such Dalits profit enormously from their surreptitiously kept Dalit identity. They can be found in politics, public and private sector jobs, and in the field of arts and culture. The term Elite Dalit might sound misplaced, but in the quest to attain elitism among Dalits, there is a desire to claim upper-class status. It is a desperate attempt to replicate upper-caste class-ness in Dalit social circles. The number of Elite Dalits are nowhere close to the relative size of dominant castes. However, they validate their status from the majority of the poor, oppressed Dalits. It is in relation to lower-class Dalits that Elite Dalits draw their powers in order to execute their wishes upon poor Dalits.

Elite Dalits have a different vision of reality. They prefer to work within a system that continues to oppress Dalits instead of working towards challenging and eventually dismantling the apparatus that adversely affects their work. This loyalty offers them individual security and stability. But this class is seldom found by the side of struggling Dalits who are fighting for accessing equal rights for all Dalits irrespective of their status.

Some Dalits in this category have rarely been as vulnerable as the majority of Dalits. They have seldom suffered the torments of the caste system as rigorously or openly. Even if they did, they had a different language for their oppression. These Dalits have an 'a-Dalit' understanding of the caste system. Their epistemic reality is premised on distant Dalitness and thereby they cannot relate to the expressions of Dalit Beingness.

Elite Dalits suffer from restlessness until they get into the corridors of power. Many prominent Dalit intellectuals, even the ones who participated in shaping the Dalit Panthers movement, with a few exceptions, have rendered their salutations to the masters of political power. Although they did a great service to their community in their heyday, their rush to acquire elitism pushed them to the subservience of political powers. This is the case with almost every publicly visible desirous Elite Dalit, who either assimilates with the governing state's offer or settles down with a government-approved position. Many are seen heading some important committees of the government or pursuing the state to provide transparency with regard to the Dalit, tribal and minority question. While the Dalit agenda is indeed fruitfully handled by a handful of influential intellectuals, others without clear vision end up dancing to the command of their political masters. Even with a strong will at hand, these slaves of political ambition are unable to provide motivational leadership to their destitute community.

Such Dalits have changing wall patterns. Their walls change colour and design depending on the type of guests they are hosting. If it is colleagues from office who most likely do not belong to the

Dalit community, various tactics are employed to please them and to not make them feel awkward. Their walls are painted in neutral colours. The photos of idols belonging to their caste hanging on the walls are not permanently fixed, and so when colleagues visit, these caste gods and icons go into the basement. I had once noticed this at a Dalit friend's house; he had put life-size portraits of caste icons behind an almirah amidst cobwebs.

Every aesthetic which could give an indication of Dalit belonging in the rooms of wall-changing Dalits are double-checked. They even change book racks, kitchen spices (removing masalas for non-vegetarian dishes, for instance) and CDs on shelves. A most 'neutral' environment is presented so as to make their guests feel 'welcome'. Food for their guests is also made in the style of a different cuisine, and not the regular hot and spicy kind that is consumed by them. They are subservient and humble so as to please their colleagues. They drop their specific style of speaking and pick up an elite accent. If sensitive issues like caste enter the conversation, these wall-changing Dalits are the first to condemn Dalits for their inability to protest and their inaction. They excitedly join the ranks of dominant-caste colleagues criticizing Dalits in order to ensure that the friendship is not jeopardized. Few make the effort to explain the position of fellow Dalits.

The walls of the house change again when they encounter Dalits—they go back to Ambedkar's portrait and books, and loud discussions on caste issues and Dalit revolt animate their conversation. This time, they are assertive about their identity. They even discuss Dalit issues they have recently read and cry foul about their casteist colleagues.

This experience alludes to the earlier works done in a similar field wherein the Dalit middle class aspiring to be elite suddenly found itself in a new social environment different from the origin of their parents. This new environment is heavily controlled and disciplined by the dominant castes. This doesn't benefit their own status. Although economic mobility has granted them limited access, the social codes overarchingly dominate their behaviours and attitudes as is seen in the case of wall-changing Dalits.

In the two scenarios, one theme remains common, and that is to put the blame on fellow Dalits for the failure of the Dalit movement, and conveniently changing the narrative as and when required. They are constant in their decrying the victimization their community undergoes. To avoid this, some smart ones do not bother to flaunt their culture; they hide their opinions in their hearts, thus, giving the flavour of a 'neutral' household. The neutrality is presented through the Buddha's artistic portraits and statues on display in their common rooms. The neutral Buddha sans Ambedkar is their version of trying to be both Dalit and non-Dalit.

Once, I was invited for a luncheon at a top Dalit bureaucrat's government quarters in Gujarat. He had a lavish property, a two-layer security detail and close to twenty-five house staff members. He identified himself as a strong Ambedkarite, meaning a Dalit with an Ambedkarite consciousness who is aware of his enslavement in the caste system and is willing to take the mantle to liberate himself and his people. His house was a British-era chateau whose stylistic influences were obvious. In addition, there were nails at a number of places on the walls throughout the house. The earlier occupant had been a Brahmin bureaucrat who had taken special permission to put up images of gods. Some of these gods continued to adorn the kitchen. Despite having nails already available on walls, this Dalit bureaucrat decided to keep his right to religion a private matter. He kept the portraits of Ambedkar and the Buddha only in his bedroom.

During my visit, our discussion ranged over many things, from social conditions to the cultural and political scenarios of the country. This Dalit bureaucrat also had a portrait of Ambedkar in his office, which was adjacent to his residence. He had two Ambedkars—one private Ambedkar, and the second, a public Ambedkar. The private Ambedkar was someone who empowered him individually and also his community. It stood for his rights and was there to inspire him whenever he was put down. The public Ambedkar, on the other hand, was due to the government orders he had to adhere to. He had clearly marked two phases and faces of his affiliation to the icon he talked so vociferously about in private. The demarcation of his private self and his public self was a tightrope walk of convenience. While his predecessor could leave behind permanent marks of his religious and cultural belonging, this bureaucrat, seemingly embarrassed by his affiliations, dodged every opportunity to talk about caste and proclaim his identity. His defence: 'I am a public servant; therefore, I belong to everybody, I need not show that I am biased towards Dalits. To avoid that suspicion, I present myself as neutral.' Can the same logic be applied to his predecessor who flaunted his religious beliefs? Does his Hindu affiliation get to be seen with suspicion while performing his duties? If the answer is negative, we live in a society where a top Dalit bureaucrat feels insecure about exercising his constitutional right to religion, culture and private life. The casteist bureaucracy has still not created any safe space for highly educated Dalits to just be themselves. And nor has the capitalist economy, where many Dalits employed in managerial positions and above cannot decorate their thirty-first-floor condos the way they please. They remain hidden for fear of the potential gossip about their caste in their friendships with colleagues.

However, Elite Dalits can exhibit more courage and be more vocal about it rather than give in to the prejudiced discourse. They have the power. A cobbler on the street or a porter on railway and bus stations or a lower-class employee does not have the same leveraging power.

Salaried Hypocrites

Thanks to the reservation policy, many Dalits are acquiring higher education, which has opened vistas of opportunities for better jobs and lives. At the workplace, due to reservation policies, some of them get to climb the ladders of job hierarchies and ascend to responsible positions. However, very few manage to reach the top due to the institutionalized caste barriers imposed en route. The few who manage to do so immediately shun their caste identity. They live in a fictitious world, anonymizing themselves. The quality of hypocrisy changes as we navigate through the hierarchies and seniorities of professional employment. A junior staffer has a different approach towards society than the Dalit who is at a relatively higher position. Their approaches are conditioned by their caste vision and class belonging.

To this class, a sense of belonging to the community brings unspeakable shame, so they prefer to drop their names for fear of being identified as Dalit. This educated lot has become a privileged layer which continues to dissociate from community interests. Due to the fluidity of their economic position, they make every attempt to bring up their children in a manner similar to their dominant-caste colleagues, and in the same family culture. They keep their children away from the realities of caste. They do not discuss it and most of the times do away with their last names.

Their children are sent to private schools where they purportedly grow up 'neutral' without a sense of their identity. They live in an insular bubble. They shun contact with fellow Dalits who talk about their identity and declare them as 'radicals' or 'extremes'. By living as non-Dalits, these Dalits benefit from their anonymity at the cost of poor, working-class Dalits. In the midst of Dalit oppression, they do not speak out. They also make sure that they do not utter a word of support in favour of Dalits lest they be exposed for being too sympathetic. They are quick to put the entire blame on working-class Dalits who face the harshest forms of economic, caste, gender and other exploitation. Almost entirely, they successfully manage to live as an anonymous corpse with a falsified identity. And they pass this on to their children.

Their line of defence is preposterous: We want to 'protect' our children from the casteist slurs and inferiority complex they might have to suffer. Their children assume the Dalit identity only at the time of contesting elections on a Scheduled Caste ticket or finding a marriageable partner or getting jobs. Caste survives on the practices of endogamy, and so this lot eventually tries to hustle into other Dalit households, trying to find a suitable partner for their children. It is when they require social recognition that the community becomes inherent to their identity.

Sukhram, a Dalit working in the state services, had ascended to a higher position. His kids grew up in a family surrounded by portraits of Ambedkar and the Buddha and celebrated the festivals of Ambedkar and Buddha Jayanti. The children were warned to not hang out with the children of poor Dalits. However, Sukhram continued to maintain contacts with his Dalit ghetto, occasionally visiting the basti on his two-wheeler motorbike.

As his kids grew up, Sukhram started looking for a match for his daughter. He could not rely on his non-Dalit networks as none of them was interested in marrying their son to the educated daughter of a Dalit colleague. Employing his caste networks, he was able to find an equally educated and well-positioned groom. His community came to the rescue at the time of need. The same can easily be observed in people belonging to other aspiring castes who have broken their community ties and have never brought their children into that fold. Thus, the children need not be bothered about their parents' background and social life.

Consequently, when Salaried Hypocrites are found amidst a crisis at the workplace or elsewhere, their Dalitness comes to the fore, and they parade themselves as victims of the caste system. However true it might be, such Dalits only summon their community for help in the time of *their* need. They only come to realize this when their desire to cling to the buttocks of the dominant-caste leadership results in an expensive demand on their honour. Salaried Hypocrites, by virtue of being in a dominant position among their social groups, direct their contempt towards poor, destitute Dalits. It is due to their lack of moral vision that they derive wretched pleasure from corrupting the conscience of society.

Salaried Hypocrites in the bureaucracy, for example, are one of the finest examples of helpless, pitiable creatures. These highly talented people with amazing abilities and hard work now see themselves trapped in the alienating caste system. It is not that they never knew caste or did not bear the brunt of it, but hitherto they had never imagined they would not escape its shackles. They get called names deriding their caste and are put under pressure by their superiors, who will in most cases be non-Dalits. They remain silent because they do not have strong political or collegial backing. They suffer and lament about these experiences in private. They cannot summon the courage to challenge their superiors because they find themselves trapped in a system that has little or no solidarity with them. Lack of a support system and transparency is one of the important reasons for their suffering at the hands of dominant-caste colleagues. It is the caste habit that gives enormous power to the privileged-caste colleagues who go about doing the things they want to without being held accountable for their actions—which are overwhelmingly unconstitutional. During my conversations with Salaried Hypocrites, I often notice them following a ritual. They look around, adjust their seat, and whisper in a low tone before discussing their experiences of caste oppression at the workplace for fear of being caught airing the violation of their constitutional rights. The same fear was demonstrated by a few at Harvard. One Salaried Hypocrite would whisper when it came to talking about caste issues. He would immediately look around for fear of anyone spotting him discussing the issues affecting him and his community.

The caste system has enormously denigrated the Salaried Hypocrites' intellectual labour and achievement; in spite of their attaining rightful positions in their jobs—which is an outcome of hard work—they fear to utter a word against casteism within dominant-caste coteries. There is an unwritten rule that prohibits them from declaring their religious and social beliefs in public. Due to this, many of them end up with a misplaced sense of identity. They are neither recognized as equals by their dominant-caste colleagues nor by their own community. Thus, post-retirement, they try to help their community by setting up NGOs or private-aided institutions.

For instance, in 2017 in Bangalore, I found myself sitting in a room surrounded by a group of Dalit retirees who had worked in the government. They considered their personal goals to have been met, and they now wanted to turn towards the community. The retirees, mostly in their sixties, demonstrated the zeal of someone in their thirties. They had established an NGO and also an employee welfare fund. They wanted to use this platform to help Dalit students and asked me for some insight. The retirees had immense potential, but sadly their current positions did not draw the same power as while they were in service. Although they had the urge to do something, their timing was misplaced. While in service, they could have fronted progressive policies for Dalit students or sanitized departments which otherwise frustrate Dalit students by not granting complete scholarships and disbursing these in time. Moreover, they could have issued government orders to make strict rules to protect Dalit students on university campuses or to form an alliance against every attack of the government on the welfare of Dalit students.

Unlike them, many new scholarship schemes, including the foreign scholarships, were designed by other Dalit bureaucrats at the cost of their careers. It was due to the integrity in their work ethic that they could be successful.

Third-Generation Dalits[11]

The third-generation educated Dalits mostly inherit their parents' lifestyle, approach, practices and attitudes towards society. Very often, educated parents with salaried jobs and balanced lifestyles expose their children to the issues of caste as an economic problem—that of poverty alone. Therefore, they reason that begging has not been eradicated due to a failure of economic policies. The social disabilities that lead to economic disadvantages for lower-caste communities are seldom discussed. Thus, third-generation educated Dalits are class-sensitive and caste-blind. Due to this, they submit to the class structures in society as being the model of development for Dalits. They have very little to do with Dalits who do not fit into their class category. They are well off and have good lives, many of them joining the private sector and not asserting their existence in society.

While on a trip in Australia in 2018, I met a third-generation educated Dalit, Saaket, who had done well for himself. He had received a doctorate degree in engineering from a reputed institution in Australia. He was frank enough to acknowledge that he grew up in a relatively privileged Dalit family where both parents were educated and had managerial positions in the banking sector. He was keen to know about life in the US and at Harvard. As we talked, I inquired about his family and their commitment to the society. He replied with a hesitant nod that his parents do go to slums and offer school-going students clothes and shoes. 'They do it every year on Ambedkar Jayanti,' Saaket asserted with enthusiasm. Then he told me in detail about his life and the problems he faced as a student. Till now he hadn't referenced his identity as Dalit. He would use euphemisms such as oppressed people, non-privileged people, at times struggling to find a vocabulary to describe Dalits. His problems of discrimination in Delhi were a result of his skin colour. He also listed out the kind of food he ate and the girlfriends he had dated. The problems Saaket noted fit the bill of urban middle-class problems. He was fond of the AAP (Aam Aadmi Party) style of politics that promised service delivery on time and the eradication of corruption because he had once experienced hostility at the revenue office of his city while applying for an income certificate. Thus, he concluded that the government was corrupt and needed fixing. Middle-class politics inspired Saaket's interest. He watched debates on TV supporting the liberal candidate's views, but seldom did he take the opportunity to hear a Dalit viewpoint.

Similarly, I met another person in New York City, Ketan, the son of a senior government official, a third-generation Dalit. Ketan grew up in Pune and attended an Ivy League school in the US. He was groomed to be a cosmopolitan kid. His interests were heavy metal music and magic realism literature. His parents were sensitive about caste issues. Ketan, however, had a hard time connecting with the problems in India. He lamented about the unworthiness of India's politics. Upon being asked to give solutions, he talked about the many differences that existed in politics along caste, religion and regional lines. This was the first time Ketan mentioned caste, albeit in passing. He did not dwell upon the caste question. When I pushed him on the topic, Ketan declared that it was Indian politics that was primarily responsible for retaining the caste structure. I had heard this line of argument multiple times in dominant-caste student circles.

There is another subcategory—third-generation educated Dalit millennials, which includes those who are relatively well-off compared to the previous lot of third-generation Dalits. These millennial Dalits are born into spaces of technological accessibility, comfort and viable social space. Almost all the Dalits in this category are educated in English-medium schools. They are based in urban areas and have a family that enjoys high salaries. They are shielded by their families and class networks, and because they grow up in colonies or apartment societies that had a strong Hindu influence they end up emulating Hindu practices in their households—vegetarianism, worship of certain gods, fasting and visiting certain religious sites among them.

The social life and cultural avenue of third-generation Dalit millennials are strictly limited to their dominant-caste networks. They envision their future along with their dominant-caste friends. Thus, many manage to go to good colleges in India or abroad to pursue higher education. Sometimes they are marked up for reservation, often they are not. Their understanding of India's social relations is not empirically informed. They have a theoretical conception of it, with their knowledge of the world mostly mediated via popular cultural platforms and social media. Due to their elite lifestyle, the Dalits in this category live a life of a-caste cosmopolitanism, thinking about the world without knowing or acknowledging the very real presence of casteist sensibilities in society. Their references are often based in Western geographies. Influenced by the social activities in the Western hemisphere many feel 'woke' when it comes to their social problems. Thus, these woke citizens vehemently fight for the rights of the LGBTIQA community. They are also seen standing in solidarity with the Muslims and Christians of India, and some take up the cause of communities based outside India, either in North America, the Amazon basin, the Middle East or Africa.

When these third-generation Dalit millennials look at caste issues in society that are pertinent to them they feel a disconnect. Their a-caste cosmopolitanism removes them from their historical memories and social conditions. For them the caste reference only comes up when they talk about their grandparents, but not because they feel they identify with it. Due to this, their attitude towards caste-based problems becomes that of charity or the saviour-social-worker complex. These Dalits, although having emerged out of their caste identity, have no agenda or vision to work for the annihilation of caste. Due to their inability to connect with the large Dalit populace they do not bother about the Dalit movement. They remain mute and passive participants in observing casteist abuses hurled at their fellow caste men and women. This generation of Dalits awaits the possibilities of a certain freedom which is not necessarily tied to the poor Dalit's project.

Self-obsessed Dalits

Certain Dalits have a dual stand on reservation policies in India. They believe their measure of success comes from individual-centred achievements. Many educated Dalits who start off as liberal by standing guard to protect their rights turn to conservative values as soon as they get accepted in the mainstream Brahminical market, which advocates for the reduction of state intervention in public policies. They emphasize 'merit' instead of other structural inequalities. This space offers a profit-oriented future. By suggesting that Dalits need to overcome their lazy attitudes and start working hard, the market puts the onus on suffering Dalits. Upon learning the new metaphors of hard work, lazy incompetence and freebies, the Dalits who have recently joined the Brahminical market club seek to find these qualities among fellow Dalits. Thus, they start identifying the above-mentioned stereotypical epithets in other Dalits, instead of encouraging a struggling Dalit or extending a helping hand. The Dalits who achieve limited success in the Brahminical market are sent back into their community as role models by the managers of the market. These 'role models' fail to mention the sacrifices of the community done on their behalf. The many 'success stories' in fields such as business and public and private office are some glaring examples wherein Dalits, by upgrading to the lifestyle of the Brahminical market, goes about peddling its agenda.

Any Dalit who goes up to the Self-obsessed Dalit for advice or help is schooled on how to distance oneself from the lowly Dalit status and shouted at for claiming the Dalit identity. A Dalit PhD student in an elite university in the US benefited from his elite Dalit networks. His statement of purpose and letter of recommendations benefitted from counselling by a fellow Dalit who had completed his PhD from an Ivy League school. This student never invested in nurturing the next generation of Dalits who solicited his advice. He once told me that the Dalit students who asked for guidance were lazy and untrustworthy. 'They keep asking me for advice and they would not follow. So I gave up on guiding anybody. They want everything on a platter.' After this assertion, he narrated his story. He said he was not a motivated student in his college days in India. Although he went to a posh school, his training and support system were not supportive. His school environment did not encourage him to pursue foreign education. One of his Dalit friends, on the other hand, had acted as a guiding light for him.

This Dalit PhD student could not understand from his own experience the lack of cultural capital that many poor, rural and urban Dalit students face. The nomenclatures of confidence, laziness and hard-working are alleged by the same Dalits who should ideally be sitting by the side of poor and struggling Dalits and investing in their future. This Dalit student had effectively bought into the logic of the Brahminical market.

Another incident that comes to mind is of a Dalit postdoctoral scholar in Germany who had studied at the best schools in India and completed his PhD in Norway. He had an extended network of high-school friends who supported his endeavours. In the final year of his PhD he reached out to me for advice for a postdoctoral position in America, more specifically at Harvard. He opened up about his experiences of being a Dalit student in a private school in India and how isolating it was for him to assert his identity irrespective of the fact that his family was staunch Ambedkarite Buddhist. As things progressed and mutualities were shared, I requested him to guide a few students from his disciplinary background for doctoral studies. He immediately demonstrated his contempt. He began by declaring that he did

not distinguish between a Dalit and a non-Dalit. 'The Dalits need
to be serious in their life if they want to pursue foreign education.
It is not a simple thing. It is a gargantuan task.' By saying this, he
conveniently absolved himself of all responsibility and distanced
himself from anything to do with his fellow Dalits. Although
we still kept in touch and I did help him, he did not see that as
community solidarity but a result of his individual achievements.
This despite the fact that his individual performance was notable
but that was not the only aspect considered by the people who
offered job recommendations to him.

People like this can be seen benefiting from the Dalit identity
but later in their career-oriented lives they discourage and despise
the same community. This acculturation in the Brahminical
market has exposed their vulnerabilities to such an extent that the
only way they can preserve their credibility is to denounce their
fellow Dalits. Hence, they lend their voice against the reservation
system as well. They feel that the reservation system is putting
Dalits down in the eyes of the competition-centric dominant
castes. They are convinced that merit favours hard work and hard
work is rewarded in competitive spaces. Little do they realize that
all the epithets of merit are used against Dalit emancipation. In
the capitalist Brahminical market, caste and capital are rewarded
rather than the mythicized hard work. In their research, Sukhadeo
Thorat and Paul Attewell[12] found that there was favouritism in
hiring processes. Irrespective of the fact that applicants 'were all
highly-educated and appropriate qualified', their 'sector, caste and
religion proved influential [in] determining one's job' even at the
first stage of the recruitment process. Comparatively, Dalit and
Muslim applicants had a lower chance to receive a call for interviews.
The distressing part of this process is that when a qualified Dalit
application was sent as opposed to an underqualified dominant-
caste Hindu, the latter had higher chances of being called for
an interview.

In another study, S. Madheswaran and Paul Attewell[13] report that there is rampant discrimination against Dalit and tribal workers in the public and private sectors. This proves that the reservation policy is poorly implemented and that candidates from Dalit, tribal, Muslim and Other Backward Castes (OBC) background face enormous obstacles in accessing equal opportunities in the labour market.

Self-obsessed conservative Dalits believe that Dalits should own up to failure that is not necessarily an outcome of their own failure but rather a systemic one that has institutionalized casteism and patriarchy. These Dalits worship the dreams of capitalist advantages. Success is the ultimate step that is propagated. The rich tradition and ethical values that hold community as a marker of success is rejected over individual greed. Whatever a Dalit achieves, it is an outcome of the collective struggle that worked for him or her to reach success. The values of sacrifice, dedication, love and hard work alongside fair competition, respect and dignity inform their connection to their ancestral aptitudes.

Self-obsessed Dalits talk about the 'nation' first without explaining the locus of nation or what constitutes nationhood. They parade their identity with the singular monolithic Indian sentiment—which is a caste-centric framework masquerading in the 'secular' outlook without taking into account the caste differences that result in inequalities or diversity of cultures. Due to this easy identification with the dominant majority, Self-obsessed conservative Dalits severely lack an internationalist vision. They cannot relate to the activities of other oppressed groups in the world. This can also be seen in their responses to issues where they are hand in glove with the Hindu majoritarian view, opposing credible dialogues on topics of global concern like the international human rights issues of Islamophobia and political battles around the world over contested territories. This is due to the dilemma Dalits find themselves trapped in. One peculiar and recurring sentiment that

has emerged towards Dalits is that they are 'anti-national' because
of their constant run-ins with the state that repeatedly attacks their
welfare and frustrates them from accessing state resources, and the
second is their dire need to claim a populist position rather than
having to defend their opinion which might sound unfavourable to
the ruling elite. One of the prominent reasons for such a situation
having arisen is due to the failure of Dalit liberal and Dalit radical
space. Dalit radicals spoke of economic emancipation without
accounting for the subtleties of caste-based grievances that stood
like a stiff wall in each direction of revolution. And Dalit liberals
put every responsibility on the state and asked Dalits to rely on the
state entirely without challenging its structures that operate against
Dalit progress. Hence, this fissure of overlooking important social,
economic and cultural factors and at times overemphasizing any
one of them has given those in favour of the status quo an occasion
to recruit more Self-obsessed conservative Dalits to their side. These
multifarious situations among Dalits suggest that they're a diverse
community acting under the pressure of the aggressive casteism
imposed on them.

Harmful Dalits

Many educated Elite Dalits who fail to acknowledge the experience
of caste are harmful and most often a burden on the community.
Instead of paving a path for subaltern Dalits to speak, these Dalits
themselves become the spokespersons of the community. Because
they could afford to go to good schools and make connections
with the dominant-caste tribe, their imagination is constricted in
the techno-modern caste cosmopolitanism, an apparently caste-
neutral and welcoming space for all which does not exist in reality
but has a say in their imagination.

   In the wake of the Rohith Vemula movement, for example,
Dalits started connecting across regions and developing

harmonious ties. New acronyms started being formed that addressed the concerns of Dalit Bahujans and Ambedkarites. In this fiesta, many developed confident social media contacts, and trust was built over likes, retweets and private messages without meeting the owner of a social media profile in person. As was the case in the past, when people believed everything that appeared on their TV screens—from commercials, to films and TV series—today this habit has extended to social media. Whatever appears on discussions of social media groups is taken as authentic. Its credibility often remains unchecked. Anyone writing provocative comments or creative posts becomes the leader of the Dalit social media world. However, the risk of not knowing a new supporter's profile exposes the Dalit private space to manifold vulnerabilities.

In the aftermath of Rohith Vemula's suicide in January 2016, English-educated Dalit youth started commenting on it furiously and without fear.[14] This caught the attention of the English media, dominated by non-Dalits, who solicited their views and opinions to feed on the Dalit murder market that thrives on the murder of young Dalits, working people and those who are most vulnerable. Many Dalits who could amplify their tone in the language of courage got recognized primarily due to the cultural capital they had accumulated. The Dalit youth who had studied in English-medium schools and brought up in the safety net of a-caste Dalit households where silence on caste reigned, were now being asked to speak for the Dalit community. Many of these Dalits had experienced caste through class and colour complexes, not as it is actually lived. Caste has the unique factor of being embedded in one's birth—and not necessarily through any distinguishable outward characteristic like skin colour, race, etc.—which leads to a sense of non-belonging if there is any exclusion. Many of these youth in their testimonies had clearly admitted to not having had any pressures to learn anything about their Dalit identity, nor did they express any interest in knowing it now; these were the same people who were now being asked to theorize the Dalit experience.

Thus, many went to libraries and purchased books on Dalit literature. First-timers started making sense of Dalit jargon. However, this confused state of being and non-being multiplied their complexities of 'Being-in-itself', which is to perform and simultaneously be under the same experience permanently. As many individuals started finding the sense of their worth, they started coming out as Dalits. Many did so to hint at their suppressed suffering that had remained undiscussed. While the movement was hot, Rohith Vemula became a default profile picture, but as the heat cooled down, his image and quotations got buried under the commentaries of newly discovered Dalit experiences inscribed on Facebook posts and Twitter feeds. Soon, these Dalit youths started calling out everyone who had discriminated against them so far. Their rage demanded apology and invited solidarity from other Dalits. A sudden proclamation of their being Dalit brought benefits to these people who wanted to make a career out of this newly discovered identity. On the other side, it encouraged many to break the shell and think about their humanity on equal and self-defined terms, which were the result of their ancestral struggles. Without subduing the dominant-caste narrative, many owning up to their Dalit selves was a positive shift. This led to many in dominant-caste circles to acknowledge and report about the events.

Many people who participated in the Rohith Vemula movement profited from it; however, they rarely paid attention to the ongoing struggle of Rohith's comrades. One of them, Prashanth Dontha, continues to face eight charges. His regular visit to courts and frequent meetings with lawyers eats into his time for writing his PhD. The students who witnessed the fallout of Rohith Vemula's suicide from afar travelled to foreign countries to discuss the importance of the Dalit movement, while Prashanth is still struggling to get a passport owing to his pending court matters. Like him, other students affected by this incident still have to face such realities, which are far removed from the glamour of media bites and Facebook likes. The Brahminical media religiously reported the updates of other non-Dalit student leaders who enjoyed caste comforts in a casteist society. And student leaders like Prashanth and many others were left to suffer without any update on their struggle for justice and student activism.

The ones who lost the most from the Rohith movement are the Vemulas, Radhika and Raja, who continue to live in dire poverty. The money that Rohith would send them out of his stipend has now stopped. Raja managed to buy an autorickshaw on loan and struggled to maintain his business. His auto had Ambedkar's image, but because casteist people have a strong dislike for Ambedkar, Raja's assertion of his identity brought huge socio-economic losses. When I last spoke to him in Guntur in 2017, Raja was struggling to meet his monthly EMI for the auto and was about to give up on that sole business, which threatened to push the family further into debt. A year later, he had given up on the auto business as well as a promising career in geology. Radhika Vemula continues to be summoned by Dalit and non-Dalit progressive communities to offer guidance and light. She is a crowd-puller at events, but once they end, the leaders who invited her are nowhere to be seen. She is kept at the beck and call of the leaders' party cadres.

The Rohith Vemula movement is also a bitter reminder of how self-oriented Dalit energy has become. Many promises were made by Dalit and non-Dalit groups to support the Vemula family in order to continue Rohith's legacy. Barring a few, almost all of the promises turned out to be fake.

The suicide and its aftermath also brought with it an entourage of untrained youth cadres from urban privileged backgrounds who believed in their experiences but could not articulate their sense of freedom in the language of sustainable movements. Other Dalits who had remained oblivious for a good twenty years or more had now suddenly become aware and were getting attention for their assertive views. With this sudden recognition, they did not get enough time to process the multiple meanings of Dalit, and not just the class term but its caste, gender and spatial location. However, the show went on and performance was rewarded; the struggle on the ground, however, was forgotten. Elite Dalits went back into their gated communities to be reassured about their future by their friends and families. Two years on, the Dalits who wrote unending columns and gave lengthy sound bites in the media frenzy are difficult to spot. Dalit genocide continue to take place. After Rohith, it was Muthu Krishnan,[15] but at that time the short-term activists who had emerged during the Rohith Vemula movement were nowhere to be seen. The young activists, having done their share of extracurricular activities, are now desperately seeking a career where Dalit murders are appreciated and Dalit lives don't matter.

As I write this, another Dalit PhD student at IIT Kanpur, Bhim Singh, hanged himself.[16] Such suicides are a form of social lynching that put the premium on Dalit insecurities without addressing its concerns. Dalits in India have a long history of being murdered by the social orders of dominant-caste society.

Relatively privileged Dalits who are armed with access use their voices and get the attention of the media because they operate in the same ecology as dominant-caste media personnel. The arrogance of the media was challenged by well-versed and articulate young Dalits who narrated the experiences of their community.

The strong distaste and apathy towards Dalits by Brahminical society is one of the causes of Dalits disowning themselves. They don't have a free and cosmopolitan space where they can own themselves without being judged or intimidated.

Radical Dalits

This category can be found in any class or sub-caste of Dalits. These Dalits could be poor, middle-class or rich. Their reactive sense is out of an urgency to place themselves in defence against any attack on their caste folk. They are very proud of their caste and Dalitness. They are different from the token category discussed earlier. Radical Dalits are committed to their struggle and are radicalized in process of realizing their sense of being. They love their people and hate the oppressor. They have experienced caste hatred first-hand and are hateful of such a system. They know the tactics of dominant castes. Thus, they stand guard against the oppression that they practise. Radical Dalits keep their identity close to their hearts and want to engage with it actively. They do not shy away from caste; in fact they hold it up as a primary locus of understanding the world.

Whenever any assault or offence is committed on Dalits, an army of Radical Dalits work overtime to ensure their case is heard. They are on the streets and on virtual platforms. They appease the Dalit constituency by offering criticisms of the Brahminical discourses of oppression. They work with polemics and use the language of the subaltern to direct their criticisms. Explosive reactions are valued in their social circles. Therefore, they believe in reacting uprightly without considering the totality of the condition. In doing this they mimic irrational caste offenders who tend to use the language of abuse and derogation. Radical Dalits believe the best way to respond to an offence is to produce a counter-offence. Violence for violence and humiliation for humiliation is the theory they have complete faith in. The extent to which they believe in their counter-activity is phenomenally an understudied segment in the domain of behavioural sciences.

Radical Dalits tend to demonstrate overzealous energy and enthusiasm. Due to this, they get recognized by political elites.

Sometimes, this group is also found wandering in various political circles of diverse ideologies. They are able to amass supporters. Thus, they designate the responsibilities of their actions on to their admirers. The Radical Dalit belief in counter-strategy makes them counter-revolutionaries. They put their oppressor on the defensive. For instance, the Aryan invasion theory declares Brahmins as outsiders.[17] Therefore, in the same thrust, Muslims and the British are considered outsiders who colonized the country. Radical Dalits blame Brahmins for the country's loss of glory and suffering. Going back to the history of the formation of the Hindu caste system, Radical Dalits prove that the current oppression is due to the outcome of the historical injustices carried out in the form of Brahminical dominance and oppression. They mistrust their oppressors and are unwilling to work with Brahmins. They believe in strengthening all oppressed persons sans the dominant castes who are responsible for their suffering.

Radical Dalits have a sound process of creating cadres and have a reach in almost all major districts in India. They hold annual conventions and regional meetings regularly to share their strategies and work on countering oppression. Their demands include a complete upending of the system. They want to be in charge of the state and other important avenues from where they can extract benefits for their community. They do not want to work under the patronage of anyone but rather run the country on the premise of being the ruling class. They believe in creating a force of all the oppressed people and giving agency to all in the complex system of caste. They look at their problems not through the lens of the Brahminical media but rather through the experiences of humiliation and depreciation given by dominant castes throughout history. History is a strong guiding point for their actions. Thus, learning from the mistakes of their ancestors, they are firm about not repeating them. In the vein of finding the enemy in others they are also aware of the enemy within, so they loath Token Dalits as the children of the Poona Pact.

Dalit Intellectuals

This brings us to the Dalit intelligentsia who are placed in institutions of knowledge and who are witnessing the synergies of the neo-Dalit uprising closely. Many Dalit faculties in India command a stature of producing original knowledge which is then disseminated to the general public for consumption. Dalit scholars are often summoned by the community to educate the public on various issues of societal concern. In the majority of Dalit-centred movements, the role of intellectual thought is prominent. During an informal chat, a national-level BAMCEF organizer once invoked Immanuel Kant to offer a criticism of the banality of Brahminical society. He located his thinking in the tradition of Bhakti revolt that articulated the multiple meanings of freedoms through the devotion of one's self to the larger cause. The 'larger' here implied the social structure. The Dalit movement owes immensely to the Dalit intellectual tradition that has kept the community intellectually agile.

Many Dalit scholars with oratorical skills and command over vernacular languages get recognized by the community for their contribution to the world of knowledge. Thus, each public event of the Dalit community has at least one Dalit scholar on the podium. Dalit knowledge informs the ethical dimension of the community's thought process. Prominent Dalit scholars are divided over multiple streams of thought. Some identify with orthodox Marxism; some with Marxist-Leninist revolutionary methods of liberation; some with the Bahujan-centred Phule–Ambedkar tradition; some ascribe to the OBC unification theory; some with Ambedkarism (be it radical, progressive or

orthodox); some with Buddhism; some with the Black liberation
theology; and some with the global movements of feminism,
environmentalism and other issues of concern. In broader
strokes, they could be classified into four categories: caste radicals,
pragmatic Dalits, Ambedkarites and Marxists.

Attached to these are different philosophical traditions, and
Dalit scholars demonstrate a commanding role in advancing the
knowledge of these particular traditions. They bring with them tools
of sharp analysis and life experience. By adding their experience, they
graduate the historical tradition to a tradition of serious analytical
thought relevant to contemporary times. Dalit scholars dedicate
their lives to uplifting the values they cherish. Their honesty and
determination in themselves through the community ethic—which
is a careful responsibility for all—is one of the added values that
non-Dalit scholars do not bring to these traditions. The grassroots-
based understanding of the community informs the development of
new theories. It is a bottom-up practice of drawing theories from the
organic experiences of the community.

For sociologist Vivek Kumar, the Dalit intellectual tradition
can be traced to the emergence of the Dalit literary movement of
the 1960s. Kumar observes that by invoking the experiences of
self and refuting the hegemonic settled order of the 'mainstream'
dominant-caste Hindus, Dalit intellectual space has carved a path
for itself. In small periodical magazines, newspapers and journals
in multiple languages, one can find emerging Dalit intellectuals.[18]
However, in contemporary times, there could be persons in some
Dalit intellectual circles who draft Dalit emotions to rally behind a
cause that suits their personal interests en route to Dalit liberation.

The Dalit experience remains core to the founding of various
contemporary debates happening in both radical and moderate
traditions. Dalit scholars have occupied positions of prominence
in their own social circles and they disagree with each other most
of the time. They bitterly criticize their colleagues in these circles
and in private conversations vilify each other. Although they could

all be towering giants in their own right, their contradictions stem from the ideological punctuations they misplace. For instance, Marxist Dalit scholars have a different style of operating, and thus their radical stand is often attuned to the emancipation of the toiling classes from caste discrimination. Their belief in the class struggle comes from their experiences as a subjugated class. There is a hope in this Dalit intellectual circle that when the class struggle culminates, caste identities would wither away. These are in tune with Marx's naive reading that the railways and industrialization in India would undermine caste-based discrimination.

Some Dalits are obsessed with the class question, while some prefer to single out caste as the only problem responsible for their suffering. In these debates, the important factors of gender, sexuality and intra-caste hegemony often remain untouched. The debate over superstructure of caste or class sucks away the juice from the threadbare debate of caste over class or vice versa. Moderate Ambedkarites interpret every derivate of their suffering under the cudgels of Brahminical supremacy. Traditional Ambedkarites try to bring in the religion perspective as the interpreter of the situation.

Dalit scholars in various schools of thought have managed to create an impact in and beyond the academic circles. Their ideological orientations offered them space in various quarters and they benefitted from that privilege. However, they have overwhelmingly failed to consolidate and institutionalize their efforts and line of thinking by not establishing independent Dalit-led research initiatives. Simultaneously, they failed to create critical solidarity initiatives with other oppressed groups around the world. They produced knowledge for the general public and their immediate colleagues. The original thought did not create any solid foundation for subsequent Dalit scholars to relate to. It is in this sphere that we see a handful of institutions and journals produced by the Dalit intelligentsia. In the vernacular stream, there is a rich tradition of scholarship accessible to the public. However, in the English language, there is deafening silence on the academic and non-academic dialogue that singularly focuses on the lives of Dalits and other oppressed-caste citizens. Many Dalits who offer public policy interventions do it in their individual capacity as opposed to being a representative of a Dalit research organization or institution, with a few notable exceptions. Thus, ideological and scholarly disagreements take precedence instead of the formulation of a Dalit public conscience.

In their disagreements with each other, Dalit intellectuals marshal a sophisticated epitome of prolific knowledge. While some become the assigned member of the 'Dalit Brahmin' clan that Limbale adhered to—those who theorize the struggle but never join it—others walk the talk.[19]

Dalit Women

The privileging of certain Dalit voices—Token Dalits, for example—is carefully planted in dominant-caste circles. The Dalit female identity is put down, pushing it further into the darker corners of non-existence. Dominant-caste males, progressive and regressive dominant-caste female movements, Dalit males and some Dalit females are responsible for this regrettable situation.

The Dalit female belongs to the most oppressed group in the world. She is a victim of the cultures, structures and institutions of oppression, both externally and internally. This manifests in perpetual violence against Dalit women. The experiences of Baby Kamble, a working-class Dalit woman, are testimony to this:

> I suffered every kind of sorrow. When in the field we had to fear for our modesty and at home we fear our husbands . . . Not a single day of my youth was spent happily. Beating, quarrels, crying and starvation—these were routine.[20]

Her experiences come from a husband who was a participant in the Ambedkarite movement and primarily responsible for encouraging her to participate in it. 'We would both take parts in meetings and demonstrations. When we came home there would be quarrels and arguments, and I got beatings too.'[21] The imperious control over the civic and private life of women has given rise to the reports of Dalit women in the movement. In the movement too, Kamble reports:

> We always get different treatment as women. Whenever an institution is established in our community, only men are chosen to be in it. The women have done more effective work than them . . . but they are forgotten when the time comes to contribute to the executive committee.[22]

Caste, religion, patriarchy, class and spatiality function as the five-fold structures of fixed hierarchy in the Dalit woman's life. The Dalit woman is placed on the edges of sources of power. Because she offers the most powerful resistance to the structures of the caste system, she is most devoutly oppressed.

To counter this attitude, many firebrand Dalit women lead solidarity campaigns and organizations that guard women's expressions of sexuality and sensibility from patriarchal oppression. In addition to external forces of oppression, Dalit women have been subjected to patriarchal tendencies within the Dalit movement.

The Dalit woman's narrative rarely gets discussed in the mainstream. She is not considered an agent of change or one who has participated in the revolutions in history books.

Consider this story. We all know Laxmi Bai as the brave queen of Jhansi who fought against the British army under General Hugh Rose. At the age of twenty-two, she tied her infant to her back and went into the war zone. The portrait of the sword-carrying, horse-mounted ferocious fighter is presented as a measurement of women empowerment. Guess what? Laxmi Bai was not the one who actually fought that battle—that was her adviser and soldier, a supreme fighter trained in sword-fighting, Jhalkari Bai, who looked almost exactly like her. When the British were certain of entering the fort, Laxmi Bai wanted to escape. Jhalkari Bai offered to fight the British troops by disguising herself as Laxmi Bai to allow her time to escape successfully. Laxmi Bai was successful in getting out of there and going into hiding in the dense forest of Nepal Tarai.[23]

Many are surprised to know of Jhalkari Bai in the story of Laxmi Bai. Brahminical historians preserved the memory of Laxmi Bai as a martyr and eliminated Jhalkari Bai. However, references to her couldn't be prevented from entering literature, to the credit of Dalits who kept her memory alive through oral traditions and rituals. Jhalkari Bai finds a reference as early as 1907 in vernacular writing. Although some books talk of her contemptibly by showing her as a menial servant or simply referring to her by her caste, Kori, the acknowledgement of Jhalkari Bai couldn't be entirely eliminated from the grand narratives of the Battle of Jhansi.[24]

Laxmi Bai was a Brahmin born in the household of Peshwa Baji Rao II. Her original name was Manikarnika Tambe. And Jhalkari Bai? She was a Dalit born into a Kori caste family. Jhalkari Bai offers us many reasons to celebrate her as a brave Dalit woman who took it on herself to enter the battlefield and fight the colonizers. She epitomizes the chivalry of a women warrior who violated all the regressive religious codes that confined women to kitchen and family. But a modern feminist icon with her name remains missing. The acknowledgment of Dalit contribution to the freedom struggle and its stories of valour are buried to withdraw any occasion of pride and empowerment. This is out of fear that such stories will inspire Dalits to fight against oppression and cause a Dalit rebellion.

Therefore, Dalit women are either presented as menial figures, caricatured in certain stereotypes or in the position of someone unqualified to make contributions to humanity. Roja Singh, in her ethnographic study of rural Dalit women in Tamil

Nadu, presents the universalist values that Dalit women in rural parts incorporate in their humanist Beingness.[25] In their poetry and their expressions of 'singing bodies and dancing minds', universalist humanist values shine through the dark chambers of societal caste pressures.

Influential writings by subaltern Dalit women have not yet become part of the rectitude in progressive circles. In spite of Dalit women's scholarly inputs in the writings of Indian women, there are no definite efforts to acknowledge these important moments in the creation of new knowledge. Neither are there any urgent projects to supplement their work in the struggle.

Some noted Dalit organizations in the anti-caste struggle are led by Dalit women: the National Campaign on Dalit Human Rights (NCDHR), All India Dalit Mahila Adhikar Manch, National Dalit Women's Federation, Navsarjan Trust and the Ambedkar International Mission(s). Dalit feminist groups are asserting their rightful position as leaders in the movement, which have been apparent since the year 2000.

Dalit women from rural, semi-urban, urban and metro areas have started to organize and challenge the inbred casteism that operates in various forms across and within castes. The resultant expressions of such acts contribute to the movement of the neo-Dalit rising.

Regular interventions by Dalit women at international conferences are watershed moments in the history of the Dalit rights campaign. The Dalit women leadership which was previously invisible or marginalized is now coming out with powerful assertions to claim their equitable position not only in the domain of caste-confined activism but also for universal human rights. The powerful assertion of the Dalit women constituency has brought the most marginalized into the spaces of discussions. Like never before, a solid Dalit women leadership is articulating its own grievances and leading the struggle without anyone else's intervention. The glaring visibility of Dalit women at the World Conference against Racism, Asian Social Forum, World Social Forum and scores of other important interventions post-1990s is a watershed moment in the Dalit movement. To assert their right to speak for themselves, the Dalit Mahila Sangathan was formed to prepare for the Beijing World Conference on Women in 1995.[26] It was notable in the sense that it provided an autonomous axis to Dalit women's agency in an international space. Dalit women challenged Brahminical patriarchy. They went on the offensive against the resurgence of Hindutva alongside neo-liberalism led by the state. Noted women like Jyothi Raj, Ruth Manorama, Vimal Thorat and Pushpa Valmiki are some of the leading names that made an incomparable pitch at the World Conference against Racism in Durban in 2001.[27] Such firebrand assertions and universal claims led some to concede that 'Dalit women talk differently'.[28]

The Dalit women's movement is a stand-alone category that is illustriously located in the international global rights movement. Taking stock of global developments along with other feminist movements, Dalit women narratives appeal for their inclusion in global frameworks. Dalit men's support to the autonomous, self-reliant Dalit women's unit and its legitimacy in global struggles offers the Dalit rights movement a historic position, which is the acknowledgement of patriarchy mediated via Brahminical influences within the power structures of Dalit assertion.

In addition to this, the ignorance, silence and appropriation of caste issues by non-Dalit women has led to the problematics of the touché moment—the precise moment of realizing the missed part. In addition to the representation of middle-class educated Dalit women on various platforms, the question of class and gender places important emphasis on the mandate of Dalit liberation. Friedrich Engels had argued, in his famous thesis *The Origin of the Family, Private Property and the State*,[29] that the issue of gendered subjugation and subordination is primarily class-oriented. It was the ruling class that offered a male-centric industrial job domination, thereby putting the interests of women and family in a secondary disadvantaged position. Access to capital in return for labour made women dependent on their male counterparts and this created a massive gender inequality. Marx's basic premise of economic surplus being the reason for political and intellectual control of the ruling classes fits into the analysis of gender discrimination. The economic surplus at the hands of the male labourer invoked the condition of control that is enmeshed with the desire for oppression. Thus, we can see the clarity of gender discrimination in its origin. However, beyond economic capacities, there are cases where the female as productive labour is promoted. In matriarchal societies, the female being the head is the most productive form of labour. She not only controls the potential birth of productive labourers but also commands a distinction over inter-group relations. However, in the Brahminic realm, it is caste that overshadows and outweighs class subordination, thus making the caste system a free market of women's oppression.

Ambedkargodism

He [Ambedkar] is far greater to us than the maker of the universe. Was there anything that he did not [do] for us? First, he gave us life; then he made us human beings. The first need of a human being is education. He made it possible for us to receive education; he even spent his own money for that. He encouraged us to be graduates. He helped us obtain prestigious jobs. He made our households rich. He empowered us to obtain wealth and power. He demonstrated

to the whole world that we had the ability to reach the highest
position; that we could even be ministers. He strived hard and
brought comfort to our doorstep. Obviously, since he made
all this possible, he is our god. Nay, he is even better; he is the
god of gods for it is because of him that the age-old suffering
of millions of people could be wiped out within fifty years.
He is certainly superior to god. He achieved what even god
has not been able to do.[30]

Let us turn our attention to the spiritual sphere of Dalits where
multiple identities are contested over belief in the community
as one's primary identity. Ambedkar has become a fairy-tale
hero who has solutions to every problem. Perhaps due to the
amnesia of any heroic stories or inspiration of the recorded
ancestral past, Ambedkar and his work have become the subject
of legends. Grandmothers and parents have redrawn the sources
of inspiration from little-known aspects of Ambedkar—through
ballads, music and stories. Popular stories often invoke exaggerated
parables. Although Ambedkar was popularized in Dalit and other
backward-class communities, there were comparatively fewer
popular cultural affirmations on the initiatives of Ambedkar
during his lifetime than after his death.

The story of Ambedkar growing up in poverty and studying
under street lights is always recounted to students in Dalit
households. It is often used to direct the child's attention to
the 'lavish' life s/he has compared to what Ambedkar had as a
student. Ambedkar's overtly respected personage comes from his
singular achievements in the face of heavy oppression. He acted as
a spiritual and moral compass to me while growing up in a semi-
literate family that emphasized hard work and merit. This was
meant to show the world that put us down by clamouring about
the lack of so-called merit among Dalits.

The emphasis of the Ambedkar legend in Dalit lives comes from
a culture of respectability and worship. In the context of human

worship and faithfulness, Ambedkar becomes an alternative norm of embrace. Added to that are Ambedkar's soaring and unexpected academic achievements that become glaring features of veneration.

Alongside the Ambedkar legends, we also have Ramabai Ambedkar, his wife, and Savitri Phule, the first female teacher and spouse of Jotirao Phule, the founding father of the modern social revolution in India. The female icons have varying characteristics; some demand valour, while some epitomize strong motherhood, some ask to rebel against patriarchal culture while some ask to be loyal wives. In the make-up of such characteristics, the embrace of ancestors by Dalits remains an important foundation to Dalit efforts to recreate their history and establish the present. The future is an impoverished epoch which sanctions spiritual catastrophe by slapping psychological inferiority upon oppressed minds.

The Dalit spiritual sphere is extremely diverse and does not constitute a homogeneous entity. Private and public spiritual practice is a disputed space. Due to multiple interpretations of the Dalit spiritual sphere, various versions of religious dogma have been erupting in recent years. Since Ambedkar's conversion to Buddhism, many spiritually motivated people have tried to find refuge in the diverse practices of Buddhism. There are any number of differences of opinion and practice amongst religious Dalits. Some look at the Buddha as a person most often remembered in the meditation pose guiding people towards liberation of the self from the ultimate cause of suffering. While some take the Buddha to be a social reformer who appropriates the reason against Brahminic karmic faith of birth-based purity. This argument was put forward by Ambedkar in his magnum opus *The Buddha and His Dhamma* wherein he argues for a walking Buddha, a Buddha in action who works in the community and is not confined to asceticism or isolated from the world. For Ambedkar, the suffering of the world for the Buddha meant that he needs to go to people and teach them about the basic causes of suffering. That's why Ambedkar sees Buddha's sangha as a far superior motif than the communist parlance. Some are staunch in their belief in the rebirth and karma theory, while others rebuff this as another form of superstitious Buddhism. Whatever the differences may be, spiritually diverse Dalits are united in their resolve to abide by the trust they put in Ambedkar and his guidance of accepting Buddha's teachings.

Dalit Buddhists

Dalit Buddhist is a category that sutures the ritual- and rites-based practices of Hinduism with Buddhism. The work of Dalit Buddhists is identified with that of the 'silent revolution'.[31]

People in this category have replaced portraits of Ambedkar and the Buddha with that of Hindu gods and goddesses. Thus, because of this, similar forms of worship and devotional practices are exercised over Ambedkar and the Buddha as opposed to Hindu gods.

My grandmother would pray to the Buddha and Ambedkar, requesting them to bestow some guidance on me. Her sense of devotion to the Buddha and Ambedkar came from the indigenous religious practices that upheld the virtues of individual ancestors as deities worthy of worship. 'Bhagavanta' in this context is used to refer to the Buddha as opposed to the eternal god that was an earlier point of reference. Therefore, the requests that are made to the Buddha are similar to those made to any Hindu god or goddess. There's a sacred room in the households of Dalit Buddhists that enshrines the Buddha's images and idols with incense and candles being burnt in front of them throughout the day. Many Dalit Buddhists I know have a daily ritual of burning incense and offering prayers before and after work. Because the picture of Ambedkar is placed alongside one of the Buddha in various ceremonies, it has acquired the status of ritual with the Buddha as god and Ambedkar as a demigod. From marriages and birthday celebrations to death ceremonies to private home events, Ambedkar and the Buddha have become centrepieces.

Dalit Buddhists and Ambedkarite Buddhists pay their respects to the Buddha and Ambedkar alongside other social revolutionary figures like the Phules, Shahu, Birsa Munda and Shivaji by lighting candles and incense at their portraits. On some occasions, I observed that during festivals, plates of food, fruits and heaps of cash were also offered up. Each practice that Dalit Buddhists adhere to is inspired by the Hindu tradition that they still hold dear. They put vermilion on their foreheads and have wrist bands that display Buddhist artefacts. Their dress habits are also influenced by such standards of religious bearing. Most of the time these religious habits—in most religions—are not inspired by any form of commitment to a religious doctrine. They are forms of blind worship owing to one's insecurity and unhappiness. This group also believes in meditation-based Dhamma as a virtue of being Buddhist.

Dalit Buddhists prefer the Buddhist tradition sans its historical heritage of struggle. Thus, Buddhism's limited interpretation is used for spiritual guidance. These Dalits continue following Hindu rituals by adapting them into Buddhist forms. A friend who built a house invited about thirteen monks to perform rituals at the housewarming. The capacity to get a large number of monks meant he had power and influence. After the rites, the monks were fed and the event was wrapped up. There was no discourse on Buddhist philosophy. Offering some highbrow interpretations of Buddhism and prayers in Pali, the monks had fulfilled their part.

Certain sections of Dalit Buddhists who have embraced the Buddha still engage in discriminatory practices of sub-caste-based superiority. They have contempt for other Buddhists who do not follow rituals as closely as they do. They generate a sense of superiority over uninformed, illiterate Dalit Buddhists after acquiring a modest education on Buddhism.

In the sociocultural and political sphere, Dalit Buddhists, particularly those from the middle and rich classes, prefer to align with Buddhist organizations only. Their relation with the Buddhist sociocultural sphere is based purely on spiritual tenets. Anything to do with the sociocultural Dalit struggle is seen as a political problem that is beyond the interest of the Buddhist congregation.

Their Buddhism is psychosomatic and an opportunity to join non-Dalit Buddhists who otherwise would not allow them into their social circles. Unfortunately, non-Dalit Buddhists entertain contempt towards Dalit Buddhists. A caste Hindu friend practises Japanese Buddhism. His devotion led him to embrace Buddhism. He did not hesitate in expressing his spite towards Dalit Buddhists as those who did not know what Buddhism was and therefore did not know how to practise it.

In almost all major cities in India and abroad, Dalit Buddhists have embraced their Buddhism because it offers them a somewhat neutral identity over their Dalit identity. These groups have weekly closed-group meetings that are firmly class-based and where the lower classes are excluded.

Festivals are important segments of Dalit Buddhists' religious practice. They prefer celebrating Diwali, Holi and other Hindu festivals by legitimizing them with a mythical story that is different from the Hindu narrative. Dalit Buddhists are more like convenient Hindus who want to be part of both religious institutions.

The calamitous practice of dowry is still prevalent in this community. The idea of prestige and the supremacy of one's position is re-envisioned by promulgating Hindu feudal practices of flaunting of one's material strength.

Fasting too is prominent among this group. In this their aim is the same as the Hindus: they fast to secure favour from their traditional gods. And during the fast, vegetarian Hindu food is preferred.

Ambedkarite Buddhists

Ambedkarite Buddhists predominantly belong to dominant Dalit castes. Due to the radical awareness and proximity to dissent, they adopt an identity congenial to protest movements. Their approach to Buddhism stems from an aversion to Hinduism. Whatever practices are seen in the Hindu order are deliberately rejected by Ambedkarite Buddhists. As a consequence, ritual-seeking Dalit Buddhists become the butt of jokes and contempt. Ambedkarite Buddhists tend to find their legitimacy in Ambedkar's version of Buddhism. *The Buddha and His Dhamma* is a guiding doctrine for them. Superstitious practices are not welcomed in their circles.

Ambedkarite Buddhists have developed a form of radical Buddhism which questions the persistence of caste in every aspect of Indian society, Buddhism included. They make the issue of caste central to Buddhism, spiritualism and religion. The phenomenon of caste that predates Buddhism becomes the moment of departure for them. The Buddha's caste background is brought into focus while deliberating over the acceptance of Buddha and his doctrine in a feudal casteist set-up. These Ambedkarites claim that Buddha's Kshatriya (warrior) background played an important role in the acceptance of his dictum by the people. If one has to become the Buddha, must one have caste privilege? Why has there not yet been an Untouchable Buddha? If there is, why are his stories not part of the mainstream narrative? These questions are raised while dealing with the idea of spiritualism alongside Buddhism and Dalitism.

They have successfully formed a cult centred on the Buddha and Ambedkar, where the latter is prioritized as the liberator. Thus, Ambedkar's meditations of Buddhism are considered valid passage to revisit Buddhist ethics. The twenty-two vows ordained by Ambedkar on the day of conversion on 14 October 1956 are essential components of becoming a Buddhist. The Buddhist avatar is seen as a recuperation of rationalism that was lost in the denudations of Hinduism.

Ambedkarite Buddhists denounce the purity-based ritual aspects of the evangelical form of Buddhism. Their vision is to make 'Prabuddha Bharat' (Enlightened India) or 'Buddhaymay Bharat' (Buddhist India)—a nostalgic gesture to the era of King Ashoka who had reigned under the Buddhist values indoctrinated in his vast kingdom.

Ambedkarite Buddhists firmly believe in the philosophy of Ambedkar's Navayana version of Buddhism. The libertarian theology of Socially Engaged Buddhism is given precedence.

For Ambedkarite Buddhists, a radical antidote to casteism is the crux of being a Buddhist. Anything to do with a-caste experiences does not contribute to the making of Buddhist ethics. The Buddha is seen as a rebellious anti-caste revolutionary, someone who walked the talk and sublimated the oppressed culture of caste.

Ambedkarite Buddhists prefer to institutionalize their Ambedkar–Buddha approach. Thus, schools and cultural and educational centres are established upholding the legacy of the Buddha and Ambedkar alongside other pantheons of the Dalit history. The curriculum and daily activities of students are designed to keep them engaged in the Ambedkarite Buddhist tradition. Many Ambedkarite Buddhists have floated cultural and educational institutes across India. These help foster critical dialogue on the issues of caste, religion and communalism. In addition, they are socializing spaces for youth living in nearby areas. Buddhist retreats are frequently organized at such venues.

Ambedkar Dharma

I met a few individuals from Andhra Pradesh and Telangana who told me in detail about their plan to begin a new religion that centres around Ambedkar's philosophy.

'Our people are attached to the religious realm. They cannot escape and thus they are the most convenient agents for the Hindus to be recruited in outlandish episodes of violence. We want to be able to channel their belief into something that is not Hindu, Christian or Muslim version of belief,' proposed one gentlemen who has been working on a project to achieve this for a few years now. His plan is to get Dalit villagers from various Dalit sub-castes to subscribe to the 'Ambedkar deva' project for solidarity amongst spiritually and politically divided Dalits. The project is designed to offer alternative options that are radical and close to the political ideology of Dalit emancipation. The belief is that drawing away those Dalits who are already embedded in superstitious religious practices is going to be a very difficult task. Any opposing views to religion or a rationalist approach to organized religion does not have purchase among the toiling and oppressed masses. They need a spiritual realm to wake up and hope for the good. The invisible power has a superior influence on the lives of the dispossessed. Thus, they need to channel their spirituality into another domain that would seed the possibility of gradual change through Ambedkar Dharma.

The individuals behind the project have also set up the ritual process and recruitment of overseeing priests who would conduct ceremonials in the Ambedkar Dharma tradition. One civil servant who subscribes to this project told me that he plans to make it a mass movement so that people do not submit to oppressive Brahminical violence.

The attempt is to insert Ambedkar in all aspects of spiritual practice. One gentleman has created an *aarti* (prayer) for Ambedkar that replaces the word 'Brahma' with 'Ambedkar deva'.

The tune and tonality is of the same pitch with each verse ending with 'Ambedkar Devo Swahah!'

While discrediting the existing priestly order and other forms of organized religion, the Ambedkar religion team has completely missed out on considering forthcoming generations. Their focus is limited to the present generation that is trapped in religious dogma, their rational and radical focus still confined within the shackles of a religion with a monotheistic outlook. By glamorizing Ambedkar, he is presented as a prophet who has the qualities of god. While he could very well be the most important person in the history of Dalits, this group aims to deify him and institutionalize his personality and work around the tradition of mysticism.

Through these myriad celebrations of Ambedkar as an individual and a representative, Dalits have managed to live a life of continuous rebellion. In essence, they have internalized the universal values that come within the frameworks of spirituality, politics, community and humanism. This humanism is so essential to the project of Dalit universalism that without moral fraternity, ethical equality and pure liberty, it ceases to advance further.

Dalit humanism is to claim an equal position. It is argued as a *right* to be considered at par with other human beings. Dalit humanism does not claim for an unjust subversion of order; rather it professes an equal order. It is due to the belief in the other person's humanity that it gives a chance to the fallacies of human deficiency and aims to establish equality. The subversion of a hierarchical oppressive system would produce more inequality and not resolve it. Thus, Dalit humanity does not contend with having a divided hierarchical order. Rather, it advocates for dismantling the rigid structures that differentiate humanity by affixing its position in society. Dalit humanism is a modernist doctrine with ethical actions diffusing bitterness and hatred, and searching for love instead.

4

The Dalit Middle Class

'Whatever I have been able to achieve is being enjoyed by the educated few, who, with their deceitful performance, have proved to be the worthless lot, with no sympathies for their downtrodden brethren. They have surpassed my imagination, they live for themselves and their personal gains . . . I now wanted to divert my attention towards the vast illiterate masses in the villages who continue to suffer and remain almost unchanged economically.'

— Ambedkar, 31 July 1956, Delhi

'Educated people have betrayed me. I expected that they would do social service after getting higher education. But what I see is a crowd of small and big clerks who are busy in filling their own bellies.'

—Ambedkar, 18 March 1956, Agra

'I do not ask
for the sun and moon from your sky,
your farm, your land,
your high houses or your mansions.
I do not ask for gods or rituals,
castes or sects
Or even for your mother, sisters, daughters,

I ask for
My rights as a man.
. . .
I want my rights, give me my rights.
Will you deny this incendiary state of things?
I'll uproot the scriptures like railway tracks.
Burn like a city busy your lawless laws.'
                    —Sharankumar Limbale, *White Paper*

'Small minds big mouths,
spitting venom all around
Your ancestors were sick people, there is no turnaround . . .
All you know is five words, Dalit, Merit, Caste, Ambedkar,
Reservation.'
                    —Sumeet Samos, Dalit hip-hop artist

The existence of various organized movements in the Dalit rights struggle since the nineteenth century is a testimony to the organized struggle of Dalits. Various regional groups in the north, south, the Deccan, east and all over India could be seen working towards the cause of anti-untouchability. Some groups followed the tradition of the Bhakti movement, albeit clinging to the variants of Hindu religion, but also challenging the discriminatory practices within it. However, some came out with an anti-Hindu diagnosis, appealing for a separate Dalit identity independent of the Hindu identity.

In this chapter, I look at the formation of the Dalit middle class, which is arguably influential and a setter of trends. Following which I offer a set of introductory remarks on the taxonomies of caste and the caste system, then differentiate the caste system with the growing consciousness around Dalits. Towards the second segment, I engage with three important moments that have unsettled and destroyed our collective amnesia of vicious Brahmin supremacy. Caste and Dalit are not separate issues, neither are they issues of the Other—external, unrelated to someone in the caste ecology. They are not peripheral, they have to do with the quality of personhood—the humanness of a common collective existence. They affect the oppressed substantially but also the one who is doing the oppressing. They are oxymoronic positions to theoretically discuss the formation of caste as a system while at the same time being adjusted to the dialectics of Brahminism—benefiting out of it and reproducing it.

Therefore, we need a frontal Dalit attack on all forms of human bigotry. There can be no Dalit humanist tradition without offending, attacking and being honest with the oppressor. It cannot be a dialogue primarily to comfort Brahmins and other dominant castes and secondarily talk about caste. Therefore, participating in the Dalit struggle is the difficult exercise of speaking and hearing the truth.

The oppressor castes in India continue to thrive, committing more offences and accruing sympathy from their community. The proponent of Brahminism, a Brahminizer who is casteizing every other discourse and method, cannot be taken lightly. Brahminism has to be dissected and cut through with a sharp instrument of visionary critique. The Brahminical comfort of the dominant castes is antithetical to a discussion on caste, which is invariably distasteful. A 'feel-good' approach is not going to advance an adequate politics of liberation. Many mainstream Dalit movements are forced or called upon by the dominant castes to lessen their severity of language and limit their outwardly style. The mainstream Dalits who get quoted are generally middle-class Dalits with upwardly mobile sensibilities.

Defining the Middle Class

The middle class has been of much interest to scholars of economics and politics, especially in light of the postmodern capitalist society.

This class is seen as influential and dominating. A middle-class income group in India is significantly different from the ones found in Western economies. Hence, we come across various arbitrary numbers for the middle-class population in India. Sanjeev Sanyal quotes various sources that estimate the size of the Indian middle class. According to figures presented in *Times Asia*, it is about 250–300 million persons, while McKinsey's number is down to 50 million, while the Institute of Applied Manpower Research, New Delhi, shows that the Indian middle class in the past decade did not constitute more than 26.4 million.[1] This shows that there is no consensus in quantifying the middle class category. Moreover, the Dalit middle class is not yet established with epistemic clarity. Who qualifies to be part of the Dalit middle class? Is it the middle class among the Dalit socio-economic variable, or does it derive from the non-Dalit middle-class base?

Historian Gyanendra Pandey intervenes through his survey of the global culture of the middle class. He suggests the middle class is the productive unit that is under-employed or unemployed and which was formerly known as 'the masses'.[2] This middle class is the product of an innovative technological revolution. Particularly in the case of developing countries like India, jobs in the IT sector brought a sense of freedom, which along with economic independence influenced cultural norms.

Although India is still a poor country—according to Pew Research 2015 data—as of March 2019, we have the largest ever Dalit middle class in history. Though there are no clearly known numbers for the size of this category, there are ways to support the hypothesis by considering factors like Dalit access to education, employment and the struggle to gain access to public health. The Indian middle class constitutes close to 2 to 3 per cent of the total population.[3] Most Indians fall into the lower-income segment, which, if divided caste-wise, would reveal those working-class Indians who live in depressing economic circumstances. The working class largely comprises lower-caste OBCs and Dalits. In spite of this, there is a commonly held view, which is accurate, that the Indian middle class is an opinion-maker. Most reports and movements that float in the metros focus on the middle-class population. The Indian political class also caters to the middle class, for instance, giving it advantages under the garb of progressive taxation policies.

Gurram Srinivas and Nandu Ram do intervene at length on the question of the Dalit middle-class.[4] The formation of the Dalit middle class is a generational change brought by welfare measures like the reservation policy wherein the generation that benefited from the policy fits into the new middle-class category. In addition to work status and pay-scale hierarchy, the entrepreneurial aspiration to become independent professionals and business owners informs us about the making of the Dalit middle-class. Thus, an average of 5 to 10 per cent of Dalits scaled to the upper and middle classes.[5]

Other commentators put the middle-class population at the higher end. Pavan Verma suggests that the proportion of the Indian middle class could be well over 50 per cent in his book *The New Indian Middle Class*. Without offering any evidence to support his claim, Verma puts the guesstimate as 'anybody who has a home to live in and can afford three meals a day for the family, with access to basic health care, public transport and schooling, and some disposable income to buy such basics as a fan or watch or cycle'.[6] According to him, anyone making between 20,000 and 1,00,000 Indian rupees ($280–1400) per month is qualified to be identified as a middle-class Indian. He presents a polar opposite picture from the middle-class census. This would mean that larger sections of India could easily fall under these randomly drawn borders of the middle class. While describing the features of the middle class, Verma makes a passing comment that the 'stranglehold of caste on the middle class has verifiably loosened'. The reason: migration. Verma unconvincingly declares that the middle class is now the new liberal class that has a-caste aspirations and is willing to overlook caste distinctions because of the oft-repeated reason of migration from villages to cities being the ultimate dissolver of caste sensibilities—because caste is a rural, backward thing of the past, and now that Indians are mostly salaried they are without strict caste sensibilities like the rural population. There's no evidence to suggest that caste no longer matters, but this is a quite widely held assumption and is often used as propaganda.

Verma's opinion contradicts the research on the ground. National Sample Survey Organization (NSSO) data presents to us a grim picture of the Dalit condition in urban areas, where the reported incomes of the dominant castes are 65 per cent more than that of Dalits.[7] In addition, Dalits largely work in the lowest-paying jobs in urban areas. Verma goes on to argue that in light of the consumerist surge, the preservation of caste purities undergoes a change. This echoes the narrative of neoliberal capitalism, according to which the market is outside of and impervious to caste. 'People want to buy an apartment irrespective of who lives next door; they are willing to work to earn more whatever be the caste of the employer.'[8]

Verma gives a final call that the experiment of Indian middle class-ness has become a melting pot that is diluting caste distinctions. However, empirically, his statements do not hold true. People still inquire about the caste of their neighbours and choose apartments where people with 'safe', dominant-caste names reside.[9] Employees who work for Dalits harbour casteist sentiments of utter disgust. Many Dalit bosses and employers have narrated stories of how their juniors or employees ensure that the practice of separateness is maintained. A senior broadcast journalist once narrated the story of a Dalit entrepreneur from Mumbai whose staffer refused to drink water from the same jug. He brought his own bottles from home. Upon inquiring, the entrepreneur was told by his employee without hesitation that he had caste rules to follow and could not consume the same water as he drinks. The Dalit entrepreneur was stunned. He couldn't initiate any action. So he simply started carrying his own water bottle to avoid the inconvenience to his employees. Even though he is responsible for feeding his employees' families, he is forced to act and behave according to the caste rules his employees follow. Thus, in light of the NSSO data and empirical findings, it is difficult to accept Verma's claims.

However, there is one thing that is accepted across the board, which is the 'sensibility' of the middle class and its bent towards higher education. Surinder Jodhka and Aseem Prakash argue that there are historical and sociological factors that place the middle class as a 'bearer of new values and lifestyle' in addition to economic factors. 'Anyone who belongs to the middle-income category may not necessarily be a middle-class person, subjectively or on the basis of an objective sociological criterion.'[10] Premised on this indicator, Jodhka and Prakash survey the literature on middle classes in India. The figures in these studies vary anywhere from 28 million to 91 million. A possible explanation to these fluctuating numbers is the attitude and approach of a particular class. However, one thing that remains constant in their argument is that the sensibility of the middle class is devoid of caste.

According to Pandey, on the other hand, the democratization of the middle class in the form of its adaptability has increased the number of middle-class clubs. The growing Hispanic and Black middle-class population in the US, dovetailed with the immigrant middle class, has made countries like the US a middle-class centre. India, in contrast, adheres to the stringent and fixed caste-based hierarchical social order. This undemocratic nature of the middle class in India is testimony to the unattained 'middle class-ness' in the Indian field.

It is in light of this that I will look at the Dalit middle class. The aim in this chapter is not to exclude the non-middle class from my hopes for Dalit liberation. On the contrary, it is to remind this upwardly mobile Dalit segment of its responsibility towards subaltern Dalits. Earlier research on the Dalit middle class has found that the Dalit middle class sees itself an in-between category wherein they remain outcastes in both circles: the dominant-caste social sphere and the internal Dalit sphere. This is because they are never at par with Dalits economically, and nor are they on the same plane as the dominant-caste social hierarchy.[11] Thus, remaining in the middle provides no definite loyalty to a group, which makes it a solidified class of its own, which effectively happens with closed groups. However, a certain section of the Dalit middle class is enamoured of the Ambedkarite ideology that sees organizing and revolting against injustice as the way forward. Thus, they are involved in strategies rooted in the future that involve gradual success. Therefore, education becomes the salient selling point in their vision.

There is no straightforward definition of the Dalit middle class. Some argue that it is defined by the attitude and social values that one carries, which refers to those who place emphasis on higher education and English language.[12] Another methodology to define the middle class is within an income category. These definitions still do not create a workable model as the social and economic indicators are liable to change. The change could be inspired from various factors—changes in income, attitudes and approach towards a certain degree of stability. Stability could be ascribed to a decent job and the fulfilment of material requirements. For some, stability alone may not satisfy the hopes and expectations from the liberal market economy. And, as we have seen, income bracket is an unreliable factor in cataloguing the middle class as income is relative to other factors which are not as measured as desired. Those factors are historical and social in addition to political.

The term 'middle class' could be ascribed to the social position gained through education and 'convention behaviour', not by occupation and income alone.[13] Convention behaviours are the attitudinal dimensions of a particular group that are tied to the overall social values of the larger group than any specific one. Thus, the Dalit middle class can be better described as a salaried, wage-negotiating class which mostly works in the service industry or public sector and exercises its influence as a politically conscious entity over the politics of the state. This class represents a false image of Dalit improvement, which relies heavily on pretensions of economic security while little changes in the social sphere.

The middle class, according to Pandey, remains unrecognized due to the nature of changing formations.[14] As a 'political class', Pandey argues that those who are in steady employment are seen as middle class. Among the 'working class', bourgeois aspirations and attitudes bring about the sense of middle class-ness. However, this uncertain drawing of lines to define the middle class has put it on to the peripheral boundaries of the 'economic society', which is organized around economic structures in a social context.[15] This has largely inflicted a damaging impact on their performance as a civil and political society that is aspiring to become an economic society. Thus, protests against service delivery, Occupy Wall Street and anti-corruption movements are imagined merely as alternatives on offer within the ultra-models of neo-liberalism, which according to Pandey, speaks to different aspects of the middle-class dreams.

Sudha Pai has offered some introductory remarks on the emerging, new Dalit middle class, taking from the Bhopal Document, 2002. The Bhopal Document was an outcome of a conference hosted by the government of Madhya Pradesh in 2002. The conference, known as the Bhopal Dalit Conference, aimed to address the socio-economic challenges of Indian society pertaining to Dalits and Adivasis. It concluded that the state would intervene in the business of Dalits and Adivasis by promising 30 per cent procurement from these groups. This policy aimed to integrate Dalits and Adivasis into the mainstream by creating a path for them to share the possibilities of the liberal capital market through government loans and credit lines, otherwise exclusively accessible to the capital-owning class mostly comprised of dominant castes,

that is, Brahmins, Banias and Kshatriyas in addition to the newly
emerging Shudras. According to Pai, the Dalit middle class is an
outcome of the late 1990s political activism that benefited the
younger generation through better education. It now commands a
sizeable influence in society—public and counter-public—which
is produced in opposition to its exclusion by society. This class,
according to Sudha Pai, is the 'small elite section within the Dalit
community'.[16] The 'small' is unquantifiable.

This new Dalit middle class wields considerable power to
participate in and question the policy of reservation in the public
sector. Its consciousness pushes it to re-examine and redefine
the state-sponsored policies for Dalits. Although reservation has
benefited a huge mass of erstwhile disenfranchised Untouchables;
however, the upward mobility of the Dalit community with regard
to social and economic status has not improved comparatively. This
new Dalit middle class is largely urbane, aware, conscious and ready
to fight, and is committed to their conviction for the community. It
is well placed in the bureaucratic order, it is English-educated, can
articulate in global idiom, and can comfortably draw comparative
lines with other marginalized groups in the global rights struggle.
It is the product of globalization policies that shifts directions in
light of the changing international economic policies. Some look
up to globalization as a boon to break free of the shackles of the
vicious caste-based labour cycle. Such a class had also emerged in
the post-Ambedkar era that was banked upon by Kanshiram from
the 1970s forming a 'pay back to society initiative' via BAMCEF,
a non-Brahminical, largely Dalit, caste organization of employees.

~

The middle class is an outcome of exterior forces, with capital-
intensive industrial and techno-capital work being one of the
leading factors. The middle class is often, as evidently referred
to, in the 'middle' passage. It has the possibility of climbing a

step up or sliding one down. That the middle class becomes important is due to the sheer amount of energy it can attract. Due to the demographic weightage and more numbers in its box, the middle class in developing and developed societies wields significant attention. It is a dominant class by numbers. Thus, though it is economically nascent, it draws powerful political influence for the social and cultural movements.

Recent developments around the world like the Occupy Wall Street movement, the overwhelming protests against climate change, and other service- and capital-centred movements convey the middle-class angst, which, according to Pandey, speaks to different middle-class dreams. Therefore, to win over this group, there are related efforts initiated on the policy and social levels. However, the crucial question remains: Does the middle class of the underclasses have the prowess to yield recognizable strength? The middle class among Dalits is not a new phenomenon. It has been in existence since the colonial era. Although insignificant, the surge of this class was noted by all sections of Indian society.

Ambedkar, in his 1942 address to the All India Depressed Classes Conference, enumerates the positive developments of his movement for the rights of Untouchables.[17] Describing the enrolment of Untouchables into higher learning, Ambedkar was referring to the emerging professional careers that were being considered by the educated Dalit class. A tiny minority of educated Dalits by this time were trying to occupy positions in the government, political offices, police, army, etc. The way they dressed and presented themselves as part of mainstream society was a reference to the 'aspiring' emerging class. Referring to women, Ambedkar expressed his satisfaction about the social position of Untouchable women. The change in the attitude of Untouchable women marked a stride of 'progress' that was the most 'astonishing and encouraging feature of his movement'. The contemporary women who have far advanced socially and economically go into the making of the Dalit middle class.

If 'aspiration and attitudes' of the underclass is taken as a marker of the middle class, as suggested by Pandey, the Dalit movement had already started to show early signs of these. However, it must be noted that this number was nowhere comparable to other minority groups because of the added layers of everyday discrimination, stigma, exclusion and repression singularly carried out against the Untouchable communities.

Going back to the process of the patronage of the middle class by the state and capital, Ambedkar reminded his followers of

the record of progress of which we may all be legitimately proud. It is a progress for which we have not to thank anybody. It is not a result of Hindu charity. It is an achievement which is entirely the result of our own labor.[18]

Thus, we are left with the question of what leads to the emergence of middle-class attitudes vis-à-vis ideas, aspirations and sensibilities. Is it the support of dominant capitalist forces? Or is it the opportunity created to render an accessible working situation that defines the middle class of underclass?

Significant attempts have been made by Dalit intellectuals and activists to demand a fair share in the government's coffers. A cursory glance at the statistics of Dalits in the employment sector presents to us the huge backlog in this regard. Even after Dalits occupy all the resources available to them in the public and private sectors, there will still be a sizeable portion that will remain unemployed. Therefore, apart from drawing benefits from the state and the private sector, what are the other avenues Dalits should look for? We do not know yet.

Characteristic of the Dalit Middle Class[19]

The Dalit middle class is a powerful mediator between poor Dalits and regular society with caste–class privilege. Presently, most Dalit movements in India are run by Dalit middle-class people. The political and social organizations are an outcome of Dalit middle-class visions. They are responsible for floating an enumerable number of bodies, unions, organizations and political parties. Work-based SC/ST employees welfare unions are an outcome of the Dalit middle-class desire to fight oppression at their workplace. Many organizations that are active in the Indian cultural sphere give credit to Dalit middle-class articulations. By acquiring education and achieving a relative economic and social status in society, the Dalit middle class assumes the role of Dalit leadership due to the immense vacuum in the changing political and cultural scenarios in the country. In most avenues of society, the Dalit middle class is playing a consequential role in filling the gaps and offering a Dalit perspective and Dalit leadership. They wrestle with the non-Dalit sphere to gain recognition and add their voice on equal terms. Due to the presence of many organizations and the implicit inter- and intra-class wars, the Dalit middle class faces hostility for embracing its ideology as well as class status from amongst its own.

The one thing that the Dalit middle class has effectively managed to do—which we will see later in the chapter—is to offer ideological guidance. They have matured the critical theory of Dalit liberation and made it publicly accessible for the general mass. By bringing Ambedkar, the Buddha, Ravidas, Kabir, Iyothee Thass, Basava, Jotirao Phule, N. Sivaraj and Mangu Ram Mugowalia, among others, to the everyday dictum they have managed to create a positive consciousness amongst the masses. The Dalit middle class actively promotes progressive values that defy the regressive backwardism imposed by society and religion. Education and jobs are placed on a high premium. Thus, there are an uncountable number of coaching centres sponsored by salaried people and community activists who fit into the bracket of the Dalit middle class. They offer scholarships, mentorship, free training to students from slums and lower-working-class backgrounds to prepare for competitive exams from grade ten onwards till postgraduation. At school level, children are groomed with the ideology of community but also the ethos of striving for merit. In his research, Srinivas found that more than 54 per cent respondents comprising salaried people across job hierarchies and professions were involved in more than one social activity which included extending financial help, creating education and skill opportunities, political mobilization, showing solidarity and participating in an existing organization. An interesting observation of Srinivas's study is that his respondents believed even the 'smallest' work in the Dalit community amounted to contributing to the development and welfare of Dalits, of which political mobilization attracted most interest.[20]

A certain section of the Dalit middle class carries a responsibility towards the community. A self-conscious Ambedkarite or Dalit takes it upon him/herself to be at the service of the community. However, the majority of them who go with a self-centred objective end up preaching to the community their maxims of Dalit liberation. Many times, rather than listening to the community's problems they become preachers to the community. Thus, instead of grasping the condition of regular Dalits, they strive to provide a leadership based on their self-experiences which is often far removed from the experiences of their larger non-class community. The Dalit middle class is responsible for creating consciousness irrespective of the manifold factions it has. Although a fragmented yet solid unit, the Dalit middle class has the power to redefine structures. Whatever the positive outcomes that Indian society has seen since Independence, one can count the Dalit middle class in its success story. Therefore, whatever positive developments we may see will be relatively due to the Dalit middle class. However, due to the presence of a certain class consciousness this Dalit middle class is also responsible for the calamities that the Dalit public sphere has witnessed in the past five decades, and if it remains unchecked it would reproduce this in an exponential form.

The non-agreement on various issues amongst the Dalit middle class has proffered much space to the oppressive casteist structure to produce anti-Dalit attitudes. This is validated in the policies and politics of India that rampantly carried out exclusion of the same Dalit middle class from jobs, deprived them of important positions at the workplace, excluded them in budget allocations, imposed cuts in welfare schemes and marginalized them in holding and household expenditure capacities. Thus, this chapter is an attempt to critically examine the Dalit middle class that has assumed the character of Dalit leadership and the aspirations of the Dalit future.

State-Sponsored Liberals

The Dalit middle class is a flexible class that has a strong potential to speak with the players of the socio-economic gamut—like colleagues, to begin with, in government and non-government offices, universities, businesses, workplaces, etc. This Dalit middle class has elevated itself to the level of having a dialogue on an equal basis that was impossible until the enactment of the Constitution due to the imposed caste regulations. It is an established understanding that the middle class in the feudal era—dominant-caste people with access to learning and writing—and the advanced capitalist era was always focused on its goals and aspirations. It was most feared because it could form its own opinions, which was often different and contradictory to the established dogmas. Today, due to its strategic position that has a good standing in the market and electoral polity, the Dalit middle class is usually entrusted with the responsibility of the future of Dalit population.

The Bhopal Document intended to concretize Dalit 'emancipation' by asking for an equal share in the national distribution on account of being qualified for equal citizenship. However, the Dalit here moved away from the realm of the 'Untouchable'. As Kancha Ilaiah argued in his column in *The Hindu*, the Bhopal Document did not pay 'more attention to the institutional causes of untouchability. Untouchability in the spiritual realm led to social segregation of people who were not allowed to participate in agrarian capital in the feudal and pre-feudal economy of India'.[21]

This document focused more on pacificatory measures. It aimed to propose a 'non-conflicting' solution by taking into account the 'existing opinions in society—both Dalit and non-Dalit'.[22] Since it was a state-sponsored event, it discouraged any radical measures of liberation. It instead cajoled Dalits and Adivasis by distributing state patronage, by offering a slice of the pie while trying to distribute a larger bite for the dominant castes. These 'equal-share measures' were inspired by the African-American example of inclusivity into the American economy, both national and private, and the slower progression of capital ownership. This meant that capital ownership would happen more gradually as more people from the African-American group got included.

Rather than criticizing the bedrock of Dalit oppression—the caste system inspired by Brahminical dominance in varnashrama dharma—the solutions in the Bhopal Document were unstable in their approach and avoided denouncing the real cause of Dalit oppression.

Recently, a group of Dalit entrepreneurs and executives met with Congress Party officials and presented their demands, reiterating concerns similar to those in the Bhopal Document. They demanded regulatory flow of credit and financial capital to the Dalit community. They also requested educational loan guarantee schemes at an interest of 4 per cent per annum.[23] Their entire approach was to taste the slice of the smallest pie given to Dalits. These Dalits demanded their share according to their intellectual opacity. They couldn't stand their ground for the solid constitutional demands of distribution of land to the landless, universal health care and a common education programme beyond the ones based on the 'liberalism' of the Constitution overwhelmingly discussed in mainstream media.

However, the Dalit vote base—which is largely working class— is disenchanted with the flimsiness of the Dalit liberal space. Dalit liberals promote a state-centred, welfare-oriented society. This idea is dangerously inadequate; it does not offer a complete picture of economic progress. Both Dalit and non-Dalit voters are unhappy with the liberal politics in India. While liberal politics offers a critique to the right-wing majoritarian view and counters the hatred spewed by the casteist Rashtriya Swayamsevak Sangh (RSS) or Bharatiya Janata Party (BJP), it does not address the urgent needs of struggling people. The right wing benefits due to this blatant oversight and the scant attention paid to economic problems by liberals. Thus, most of the country's contemporary issues can be traced to the failure of liberal parties, and the liberal elite have become the primary target of anger, having invited the wrath of working people. Communal hatred is conveniently whipped up by the right wing, and those supporting liberal values are downplayed as those who support oppression. The downgraded and repressed populace gets easy traction with the right-wing promises that appeal to their immediate needs. The hatred towards the elite due to dynastic or nepotistic arrangements in politics or the workplace where the common man seldom has access is manipulated by the right wing to recruit the disgruntled masses. Liberals have failed to provide a model to the subaltern groups that will offer safety and security to their future. As these groups see no other option before them, the conservatives are able to feed off their reactionary mood.

The careers of Dalits with neoliberal sensibilities—whose presence is vital in the Congress Party's liberal policy— mushroomed under the canopy of the feudal landlordism promoted by the Nehru–Gandhi dynasty. The Dalits who found the leveraging of economic advantage a primary programme for their upliftment subscribed to the policies of the ruling Congress Party despite its casteist make-up. Each Dalit ghetto in India has a Dalit Congressperson. The Congress Party worker is enamoured of the promises of neo-liberalism and thus s/he acts on the orders of rich landlords who are by default Congress supporters and who have profited out of its successive regimes.

A senior Congress leader who is also a member of Parliament and operates in the inner circles of the party once told me, shaking his right hand in hopelessness, that asking the party to change its feudal policies and demanding to democratize its leadership from the local to the national level 'simply is not going to happen'. He accepted the feudal workings of the Congress as a given model upon which the party was firmly established. The primary money and muscle that sustains the party is feudal in nature. It is not by default but by design. It manufactured a political class among the rich landowning Shudra farming community in rural India.[24] Since the inception of the Congress Party, the caste elite in Indian society single-handedly ran the Congress project as a private enterprise. The movement towards Independence provided a golden opportunity to mobilize the masses, and its emotional appeal was effectively used to advance the caste elites' goal of establishing their rule. M.K. Gandhi was used to shepherd a 'cause' that was never meant to weaken the caste hegemony.

Many Dalits who took up the membership of the Congress Party were seduced by three aims: immediate personal gains, providing community support, and the Congress's liberal ideals. However, the liberal ideas that the Congress and later (more recent incarnation of) the Bahujan-oriented BSP also offered did not guarantee recourse to the suffering, working-class poor Dalits. When the BSP attempted to work with a *sarvjan* liberal model, it suffered a depressing defeat. Following the road map charted by the Congress Party, all post-colonial central governments adopted similar policies of liberalism. By doing this, they continually brushed aside the liberation agenda of Dalits. One should note that majority of the party leadership is drafted from the middle class.

Many of the BAMCEF activists were primarily salaried employees who filed behind Kanshiram's leadership. Thus, people with a job in the state or central government devoted their time and resources to strengthen the organization. The cadre camps were designed around creating a mass consciousness amongst the educated folks. Notwithstanding its poor and working-class agenda, the cadre camps were a democratic space that valued everyone equally irrespective of their status at the workplace. The comrades *saathi*s of the BAMCEF movement were committed to the dream of ruling India that will be established on the principles of equality, liberty and justice. Kanshiram reiterated Ambedkar's vision of the governing class sharing political power in terms of equality, or '*shaasan karti zamaat*' (ruling class community), or, as he put it, '*hukmaran* samaj' to refer to the Bahujan class rule.

This vision of becoming the ruling class appealed to the conscience of Dalits and non-Dalits. The Bahujan identity was effectively deployed as a model for political and social unity. Middle-class Dalits found this space appealing and refreshing and one that brought with it a sense of confidence and valour to think about oneself as a person with authority and command. It did not intimidate their status in society and at the workplace. In fact, it offered a space to utilize their 'time, talent and treasure' in the service of society. Due to its vast middle-class base, BAMCEF could take a risk to articulate its political visions via the BSP. During BAMCEF and now with the BSP, the committed cadre sacrificed itself to ensure that the dream project of the ruling class was implemented. Here, the Dalit middle class played an extremely positive role. It ushered confidence amongst the lower classes of Dalits. It could do this by participating in the everyday activities of lower-class people.

Many salaried employees of BAMCEF flanked Dalit bastis doing door-to-door campaigns. They also raised money and recruited more cadres. They spent time with the people oppressed by Brahminism and capitalism. They discussed their problems with them and found common solutions. A space of intellectual carnival was fermented. The cadre base was effective and strong because it united people across various class and castes through subliminal humility.

In this scenario, the Dalit middle class is a new group that certainly benefits from the state's assistance. It is the first group to adequately fit into the global category of the middle class. Thus, its debutant presence in the production scale and economic segments like ownership of capital is exposed to vulnerabilities. It is weak and not yet ready to fight the challenges imposed by traditionally powerful groups that harbour right-wing conservative sensibilities.

There is a pre-existing reliance on state resources, civil society and the capital-oriented market. The implicit faith in the state and the commitment to work within the structural parameters of the government or the market have not been fully examined by Dalit groups. Often, it is these structural spaces that act as a legitimate hindrance against the Dalit revolution, thereby convicting Dalit rebellion as unlawful. How far can one go in relying on the ostensible measures of justice-seeking that are enmeshed within the citadels of oppressive caste power? Power is central to understanding the issues of Dalits.

Every avenue of Dalit resistance is directed towards the state. The calls for change on the streets and in Parliament overwhelmingly rely on state resources. Hence, the issues of reservation in the public and private sectors and extending affirmative action to state-sponsored private enterprises are placed before the state. Beyond-state thinking does not exist in the larger liberal Dalit public sphere. This exclusive reliance on the state is a seriously stabilizing measure for the government and other actors invested in maintaining the regular flow of Dalit labour.

Among popular Dalit middle-class circles, there is no dialogue on rebellion against the state. Rather than questioning the legitimacy of the state led by the dominant-caste minority that is in charge of the interests of lower-caste groups, the Dalit middle class is instead focused on the gathering of state resources.

The liberal Dalit middle class with its bourgeois sensibility is a most disoriented and status-symbol-hungry class. It revolves around conveniences for the self, followed by family, and if time permits, concern for society comes towards the tail end. It has no definitive loyalties and is willing to change its colours and fashions according to the requirements of the moment. It works day and night to preserve its composition in the class–caste make-up.

This class often falls short of critiquing the hegemonic narrative. Therefore, by duplicating the demands of the Brahminical class it embraces the norm of self-hatred. It does not miss a chance to mock its own caste folks. Instead of adopting the originality and novelty of their own caste, the music, art and other mediums of Dalit existence are loathed and shunned out of embarrassment. It is the Brahmin-defined quality that the educated Dalit imposes on his community. This class attempts to emulate Brahminical methods and tries to be equal in Brahminical circles. However, despite attaining professional and political status, they are still considered Untouchables. And as their experience of equality is being not quite equal nor unequal, they are somewhere 'halfway to equality'.[25]

Discourse of Non-Dalits in an Un-Dalit World

Dalits remain absent from prominent views and images of our perceptible imaginations. They get represented in their absence. Thus, writing about Dalits in times of nihilistic conduits is similar to being on a deserted highway without any hope of coming across a generous person who can give a lift to a lonely traveller. There is no single prescription for casteism, and thus the experiences of caste and its forms of credence are drastically different for different caste groups. Therefore, to identify caste oppression only with influential individuals from the Dalit community is to downplay the rigour of caste oppression. Manual scavengers, kiln workers and landless farmers will have different experiences of caste than drivers, teachers, students, executive officers, government officials, those in the judiciary or a head of state. However, even in the diversity of their experiences, one common aspect remains, and that is the blatant execution of caste as a supreme method to denigrate fellow human beings.

However, Brahmins and other 'upper'-caste Indian academics and influential scholars attempt to divert attention by making a case in terms of class. They are ready to replicate, almost plagiarize, the theoretical analysis from Western concepts, without adequately and critically examining the theory as well as the empirical thresholds. This is evident in the indexes of their books where barely any Dalits are cited let alone acknowledged, suggesting their casteist logic of undermining Dalit knowledge production. However, if rigour is to test virtue, the proportion of Dalit citations reveals their limited grasp of the ontological depth of Dalit scholarship.

Then, there is a public sphere in India, which, according to Jurgen Habermas, can be loosely articulated as a marker and market of 'public opinion'. It is a closed inward look at the public sphere that offered the bourgeois-implicit determinant as a public opinion: 'The self-interpretation of the function of the bourgeois public sphere crystallized in the idea of "public opinion".'[26] Building upon this logic, the Indian public sphere articulates opinions of dual authority: state and society. The ruling elite who describe the public sphere are the ones who are in fact empirically bankrupt. Their knowledge is limited to the well-known and oft-repeated examples of Mayawati, former president K.R. Narayanan, President Ram Nath Kovind and the emerging Dalit capitalist enterprise Dalit Indian Chamber of Commerce and Industry (DICCI) as proof of their claims of Dalit emancipation. The public sphere's list is exhausted beyond this handful of examples. Consider this in light of the number of rapes, murder and torturous crimes along with the everyday physical and mental humiliation that an oppressed-caste, second-class citizen has to undergo. In the caste crime statistics and reported incidents of *everyday casteism*, the graph is harrowing. The crimes are so persistent and conviction-free that it calls for a serious intervention, a reframing of the globally holistic terminology of crimes against humanity. About half a million crimes were committed against Dalits alone in the decade from 2006–16.[27]

Anti-Dalit Indian Attitudes

The graphs of education, poverty, housing, incarceration rate, health, lifespan, access to housing and land, among other socio-economic issues, presented by NSSO data and the Socio-economic Caste Census (SECC), agricultural census, crime records and prison statistics demonstrated that Dalits and Adivasis are being pushed further to the bottom of the ladder towards near annihilation.[28] The official data available on the Ministry of Statistics and Programme Implementation website refers to SCs and STs as being the most deprived section of Indian society.

A compilation of national data findings shows that 21 per cent of Dalit families live in houses with thatched or bamboo roofs, 78 per cent stay in one- or two-roomed houses compared to 68 per cent of the whole population (meaning two-thirds of the Dalit population do not live in three-room houses which include a kitchen, a common room and a bedroom), 35 per cent have a drinking water source within their home compared to 47

per cent overall, 41 per cent do not have electricity compared to
33 per cent overall, and 66 per cent do not have toilets compared
to 53 per cent overall. In rural areas, the comparison gets bleaker.[29]
According to the SECC 2011 that was released in 2015, SCs
constitute 18.45 per cent of the total Indian households in rural
areas. House ownership among Dalits in rural India is as low as
17.69 per cent, of which 0.46 per cent rent the house and 0.28
per cent live on other means and not more than 3 per cent in total
have a kuchcha, pucca, semi-kuchcha or semi-pucca house.[30] For
STs, 10.50 per cent own a house, 0.26 per cent rent and 0.20 per
cent live on other means.[31]

The exclusion of Dalits and tribals in terms of material
ownership of wealth and income is glaring.[32] The data for
households owning 2.5 acres or more irrigated land with at least
one type of irrigation equipment is 0.24 per cent (Dalit) and
0.19 per cent (tribals); households owning 5 acres or more land
irrigated for two or more crop seasons is 0.16 per cent (Dalits) and
0.14 per cent (tribals); households owning 7.5 acres land or more
with at least one type of irrigation equipment is 0.09 per cent
(Dalits) and 0.14 per cent (Tribals).

The percentage of households that make less than 5000 rupees
per month for SCs is 15.41 per cent, between 5000–10,000 rupees
per month is 2.17 per cent and more than 10,000 rupees per month
is 0.86 per cent. These statistics refer to the total household income
and not the earnings of an individual member. SECC shows that
only about 4 per cent of rural Scheduled Tribe and Scheduled
Caste households have a family member in a government job.[33]
For SCs in rural areas, it was 0.73 per cent in the government
sector, 0.17 per cent in the public sector, and 0.45 per cent in
the private sector. For STs it is even more depressing with only
0.48 per cent employed in the government sector, 0.06 per cent in
the public sector, and 0.16 per cent in the private sector.

If we take the parameter of source of income for SC households, it boils down to the issue of land-related ownership: 3.39 per cent of Dalit households rely on cultivation, 12.41 per cent on manual casual labour, 0.40 per cent on part-time or full-time domestic service, 0.05 per cent on foraging or ragpicking, 0.19 per cent on non-agricultural own account enterprise, 0.07 per cent on begging/charity/alms and 1.92 per cent on other kinds of work.[34] For STs it is 4.41 per cent on cultivation, 5.63 per cent on manual casual labour, 0.22 per cent on part-time or full-time domestic service, 0.02 per cent on foraging or ragpicking, 0.07 per cent on non-agricultural own-account enterprise, 0.03 per cent on begging/charity/alms and 0.83 per cent on other kinds of work. If we compare these numbers with the non-SC and non-ST population we come face-to-face with the depressing reality. Dominant-caste groups feature heavily in cultivation and non-farm business activities.[35]

Educationally, one in every ten students is either an SC or ST. Of them, the percentage of students who complete their grade drops from 81 per cent in the 6–14 years' age group to 60 per cent in the 15–19 age group. It plummets further to just 11 per cent in the 20–24 age group in higher education. This fall is noticeable across communities and castes but it is the sharpest among SCs and STs. The dropout rate among the Dalits is depressingly the highest.[36]

Similar forms of exclusion are overwhelmingly found in other spheres of Indian public and private life. In the elite government services in 2015, for example, of the 393 positions at the secretary, joint secretary and deputy secretary levels in various central ministries and departments, only thirty-one (around 0.08 per cent) belong to the SC category and sixteen (around 0.04 per cent) to the ST category—much lower than the reservation officially granted to them.[37]

Representation of SC/ST/OBC Officers in the Government of India

Sl. No.	Post	SC	ST	OBC	Total
1.	Secretary	3	3	-*	70
2.	Joint Secretary	24	10	10*	278
3.	Deputy Secretary	4	3	10	45

Details of officers recruited under the general category prior to introduction of OBC quota are not available.

The judiciary adds to the unrepresentative character of Indian democracy and state machinery. In the twenty-four high courts in India, there is not a single Dalit or Adivasi chief justice. No Dalit judge has been elevated to the Supreme Court since K.G. Balakrishnan in 2010. According to an *Indian Express* report, the Supreme Court collegium responsible for the appointments of judges and promotion to the superior courts does not have clarity on the rules and criteria.[38] There are indications of nepotism and *parivaarwad* in judicial appointments. More than 70 per cent of the judges are connected in one way or another to 132 families.[39] One report by *Outlook* magazine stated that eleven out of twenty-eight sitting Supreme Court judges had relatives within the law fraternity.[40] In the Allahabad High Court, the appointment of nineteen judges in 1999 indicated nepotism. Of the nineteen, two were sons of former Supreme Court judges, another two were offspring of former advocate generals, one was the son-in-law of a former high court judge and one a junior advocate of the former chief justice.[41]

The Ministry of Law and Justice released information on the representation of gender diversity in the appointment of judges.[42]

Although the communiqué stated information on women/SC/ ST/minority judges, it did not explicate the representation of SC, ST and OBC judges, stating that 'no caste- or class-wise data of judges is maintained' owing to the nature of their appointments under Articles 124 and 217 of the Constitution of India that does not provide reservations based on caste and class differences.

It can be inferred that due to the non-representation of SCs and STs in the top judiciary, there must be glaring holes in the deliverance of justice. The judges who oversee the fate of SCs and STs do not belong to their community. Hence, social experience, chronic violence and routine oppression do not come under the purview of a judge who has lived a privileged life. Former chief justice of the Supreme Court P.N. Bhagwati had commented: 'Judges are drawn from the class of well-to-do lawyers . . . they unwittingly develop certain biases.'[43] This is reflected in the court's palpable bias with regard to the policy of reservation and affirmative action for socially marginalized communities. The Supreme Court has put a ceiling of 50 per cent reservation for 82 per cent of the population, thereby providing an open field of 50 per cent 'reservation' to the already dominant 18 per cent. A large percentage of this 18 per cent have a grip over resources, jobs and ownership and use their caste networks so that these continue to circulate among themselves generation after generation. This 'general' category hides under the disguise of unproven 'meritocracy', while actually ensuring casteist hegemony through nepotistic means. This applies to all realms of the public sector, including the judiciary.

On the question of equal representation in important portfolios, Dalits are barely seen in positions of decision-making. A similar pattern is seen in the list of national awards given by the government of India for their extraordinary achievement in

film, arts, social life and culture, where the representation of
SCs and STs is embarrassingly low. A quick caste tally would
uncover the casteist mess created by the colonizing tendency
of the oppressor castes. This also elucidates the supremacist
mentality of the privileged castes which do not give due
weight to Dalit intellectualism. This attitude can be clearly
seen in the European project of enlightenment and subsequent
colonization in which Africans and Asians were degraded as
black or yellow non-beings without agency or thought, and
their subjugation was thus justified. Similarly, the Dalit is a
wretched Other who is responsible for his own condition in the
depressing Brahminical era.

Anti-Dalit Attitudes in Budget Allocations

Similar instances of gross under-representation are seen in
budget allocations. The 2017 budget of the government of India
scrapped the Scheduled Caste Sub Plan (SCSP) and the Scheduled
Tribe Plan (STP) that were made a constitutional guarantee in
the 1970s.[44] These plans' premise was simple: funds would be
distributed according to the demographics of caste. However, each
successive government has sincerely failed to allocate the desired
funds. Dalit activists have been staging demonstrations in the
capital ever since, which have gone unnoticed by the dominant-
caste propaganda machine: the Indian media.

International Dalit rights activist N. Paul Divakar calculated
the government's deficit towards SC–ST welfare.[45] He observes
that the allocated budget according to the Jadhav guidelines
was 4.6 per cent of the total budget that was supposed to be
directed towards SC development and 2.3 per cent towards ST
development. However, the government only redirected half the
budget, meaning 44,246 crore rupees instead of 96,638 crore
rupees for the SCSP and 18,073 crore rupees of the total 44,246

crore rupees for the STP. It gets worse as we add the gender factor. For SC/ST women the budget allocated is a mere 0.99 per cent. In addition to this, the money directed for specific schemes do not even reach those at the bottom of the pile, and more than half the government schemes do not operate in their entirety. Various promises by the government for the social and economic development of the marginalized remain a shadowy matter when budgetary cuts are increasing for development schemes like the National Scheduled Caste Finance Development Corporation, credit guarantee fund for SCs, self-employment and rehabilitation of manual scavengers fund,[46] food and public distribution, environment, climate change, national overseas scholarships and pre-matric scholarships for Dalit students. This results in the present government spending a mere 1.3 per cent of the total budget towards an underprivileged population that comprises 16 per cent. The Twelfth Planning Commission admitted the government's failure in addressing this serious deficit (the remodelled NITI Aayog continued to mete out similar disgraceful treatment for SCs and STs in budget allocation).

Despite the fact that the TSP and SCSP strategies had been in operation for more than three decades, they could not be implemented as effectively as desired. The expenditure in many of the states and Union territories was not even 50 per cent of the allocated funds. No proper budget heads or subheads were created to prevent the diversion of funds. There was no controlling and monitoring mechanism, and the planning and supervision was not as effective as it should be.[47]

Crude strategies of not implementing the budget and thereby letting the amount lapse have become the norm for budgetary allotments meant for SC/STs. A social welfare secretary in Karnataka once requested me to help him spend the allocated money by suggesting some policies that could be used appropriately so that the budget would not lapse. The money was allocated under the sub-component plan; however, due to the delay in depositing it in the department's account it ran the risk of being taken away. Such tactics are used to derail the work of social welfare departments.

Another grosser outcome of the SCSP–TSP project is the misdirection of allotted funding. The money meant for the welfare of the Dalit and Adivasi communities is spent on non-Dalit, non-Adivasi schemes. For example, the construction of roads, flyovers and jails and other infrastructure that has no bearing on the life of the poor Dalit community. The government actively participates in this misdirection of funding. The Commonwealth Games scandal is one such well-known instance from the recent past. This scandal exposed the corruption of the Delhi government under the Congress. From 2006 to 2011, it consistently redirected its budget from the SCSP towards the Commonwealth Games; this amounted to 744 crore rupees.[48] However, this misdirection of funds remained an undiscussed, undebated and underrated topic. The money was meant to build healthcare facilities and schools and fund micro-credit projects for the development of poor, disenfranchised, under-represented Dalits. The same funds had been set aside for ending the practice of manual scavenging.[49]

In the 2019 finance budget of the central government, the mockery continued. An analysis of the National Campaign for Dalit Human Rights observed that of the estimated amount (Rs 5,05,015 crore) only Rs 2,75,772 crore was released. Of this, only Rs 81,155 crore was allocated through direct schemes and the remaining Rs 1,48,088 crore through indirect schemes.[50]

SCSP–TSP Schemes in Union Budgets FY 2014–18[51]

	2014–15 BE	2015–16 BE	2016–17 BE	2017–18 BE
Total Budget Expenditure (BE)	17,63,214*	17,77,477	19,78,060	20,91,735
Total allocations for SCs	50,548	30,851	38,833	52,393
Amount mandated by policy (SC)	81,460	82,119	91,386	96,847
BE on SC schemes as % of total BE	2.87%	1.74%	1.96%	2.50%
Total allocations for STs	32,387	20,000	24,005	31,920
Amount mandated by policy (ST)	42,141	42,482	47,276	49,992
BE on ST schemes as % of total BE	1.84	1.13	1.21	1.53

*Values in Rs crore

Myth of Dalit Political Unification

When a Dalit fails, it is the community which has to carry the mantle. When a Brahmin commits an offence, it is the individual sans his caste who is the culprit. Or, if a Brahmin fails, adjustments are made to accommodate him into the dignified labour market, whether through monetary corruption or the 'arrangement' of caste networks because a Brahmin simply cannot fail; if he does, the argument of meritocracy no longer stands. Brahminical society conveniently has different parameters for different sections. Dalits exist as an energetic political category and therefore Dalits are convinced about their political raison d'être. Thus, every discussion on Dalits, among Dalits and with Dalits concerns the political location of Dalithood.

As we have seen in the previous chapter, certain sections among middle-class and elite Dalits are not of much help to the Dalit struggle; rather, they are a burden on the subaltern community. They live amidst fears and insecurities and loathe themselves and their caste folk. Their hatred of the self mirrors their lapses and failures towards the community. Many of them are 'passing Dalits', meaning those who are constantly trying to escape their identity. They think it is possible to do so; little do they realize that they are walking blindfolded in an assumed non-Dalit self when non-Dalits view them only as Dalits.

In his autobiography, *Akkarmashi*, Sharankumar Limbale ponders over the extreme fears he lived under in the office space where he had to interact with his dominant-caste colleagues. To avoid any untoward incident, Limbale 'thought it safer to be secretive about my caste in such a terrible situation'.[52] In order to assimilate better he wrote to his friends instructing them 'not to write Jai Bhim in their letters since casteism was predominant'. He adds, 'I deliberately wrote letters to my friends whose names were Patil and Joshi, informing them of [my] new job. I hid the photographs and books of Dr Ambedkar in my trunk. Instead, I started reading novels by V.S. Khandekar, and detective stories.'[53] Limbale was constantly in fear that his 'caste would be revealed', so whenever he 'happened to see Dalit friends approaching [he] quickly altered [his] route'.

'If I happened to be going with a high-caste friend and someone greeted me with a "Jai Bhim", I felt like an outsider,' reminisces Limbale. In order to avoid the humiliation of mistreatment at the hands of dominant-caste colleagues he kept his 'caste a secret' and still his 'caste followed him like an enemy'. Limbale concedes, 'I was a Dalit who had become a Brahmin by attitude, but high-caste people didn't even allow me to stand at their doorsteps.'[54] Limbale's situation resonates with many Dalit middle-class persons in India.

Another way to escape this situation is to give up the caste name and adopt a classical Vedic name that has no totemic relationality to Dalit being. Names like Advait, Vedika and Brahma continue to animate Dalit identity cards. Dalits also change their names to the names of their villages and at times get Brahmin surnames just to be safe. The names partly escape the enormity of casteism. As a result, they continue to live in a relatively good position in society. They also partake in typical Hindu festivals and visit temples. However, back in their villages or intimate circles they are not given equal status in temples and private spheres.

Greedy Dalit Class

The greedy and aspirants among the middle-class Dalits—who are, as some scholars have argued, 'authors of Dalit ideology and identity who influence, inspire and motivate the Dalit masses'[55]— end up becoming the face of the community. Without having the everyday experience of living as a Dalit—in rural and urban centres—they tend to occupy the cultural and political avenues of Dalit expression. They consist of Harmful Dalits and Elite Dalits (see Chapter 3).

Many salaried-class Dalits in India and in the diaspora recognize their oppression. Almost all, irrespective of their religion, blame the caste system for their suffering. They have stories of horrors and pain. In their narratives, one can easily notice the immense caste burden they had to carry while growing up in

India. An IIT alumnus, a Dalit executive who now works in New York City, told me about the horrendous experiences of his life in IIT. 'This is the pinnacle of Brahmin fiefdom, our seniors [Brahmins] ensured that we were given bad treatment. From ragging to professorial treatment, all was marked out by caste epithets.' Although graduating from IIT boosted the confidence of the Dalit outlier, twenty-five years later he still carries the scars of his mistreatment. Many such heart-rending stories bear witness to the failure of Indian social reform movements.[56] Unfortunately, in their suffering, many Dalits from the middle class shy away from further engaging with this question. They do not use powerful narratives of pain to organize around these issues and build solidarity. Instead of showcasing their presence as an immediate retort, using their stories to challenge stereotypes and speaking up for their community, these marked Dalits keep the pain inside their hearts without channelling the rage to transform society.

This class in turn becomes a liability for the radical transformation process. By remaining mute, it passively participates in reproducing the ills of the caste system. These Dalit middle-class citizens prefer to remain within their safety nets. On the questions of reservations or Dalit atrocities, they proffer a liberal understanding of the problem by putting the blame on Dalits instead of the system. This liberal approach looks at the surface-level problems that are most apparent. If a Dalit student or employee is unable to perform well, they shift the blame on to struggling Dalits without inquiring into the background, history and structural societal inequalities that make Dalits vulnerable and the dominant caste an oppressor. They are unwilling to take on the establishment and the state for multifaceted violations.

Instead, they join the tirade and denounce Dalits and the Dalit leadership. But by using the same logic with which they criticized the Dalit leader, they end up getting no one—fellow Dalits and dominant castes—on their side, eventually putting the entire

blame on the struggling Dalit political class without accepting
personal responsibility for the failures of which they are part.
The Dalit political class is an outcome of societies' aspirations.
Ask any aspiring middle-class Dalit about his/her opinion of the
Dalit political situation. Without delay they will point to the lack
of unification among the Dalit leadership. Due to this lack of
unity, Dalit votes are split, which sustains the problem. By an
oversimplified logic, they brush aside the political complexities in
the make-up of casteized democracy.

By pushing for an agenda of a unified Dalit politics, these
Dalits work against the very grain of diversity. Without adequately
accounting for the political condition and the ways in which
electoral politics works, this ranting lot unnecessarily continues
to debate the inescapability of caste and class politics. By unifying
Dalit leaders, it is not guaranteed that the ideal, real Dalits would
get into office. What is the guarantee that a Dalit representative
won't be a corrupt menace tied to his/her political masters, and
what assurances are there about his/her social condition?

And again, the gist of caste is divisions, and for as long as caste
exists the divisions are going to exist—for good or bad. Currently,
Dalits have to deal with both kinds of deeds—good and bad.
The good is to elevate the voice of the downtrodden among
Dalits and the bad that they don't get adequately represented.
However, while they themselves are divided, members of the
Dalit middle class advocate for political unity. By reducing the
political problems to one of unification, these hopeful-to-be-
Brahmin-bourgeoisie-in-Dalit-garb fail the expectations of the
society they claim to belong to.

Crisis of Political Leadership

A Dalit leadership that lacks humility is presently the most
salient crisis in the Dalit movement. Some sections of Dalit

leaders who have gained from the sacrifices—monetary, physical, psychic and spiritual—of the destitute working-class Dalit community have ascended into a class of ungrateful Dalits. Many of them run amok with narcissistic pride and insecurity. They see themselves as rivals and competitors in the liberal political space.

These Dalit leaders have a political agenda that is concerned with the community as well as with self-glorification. Although all claim to work for the Dalit community, their goals are not necessarily the same. Some dream of prime ministerial position, some think of getting a central ministry berth, while a few are happy to get a place in Parliament as nominated members. Their strategies vary depending on their goals and thus the political calculus doesn't fit the requirements of each one's needs. This gives rise to multiple interpretations of the situation and the community interprets it according to their capacities and interest. The Dalit leaders win their followers' support on the kind of leadership traits they offer to the community. The community, on the other hand, is interested in leaders that carry charisma and have a respectable demeanour. The majority of Dalits who are eligible to vote have not witnessed Ambedkar, neither do they know of him through his video speeches or audio recordings. Many know him through the Dalit art, culture and literature that keeps his memory alive. The Ambedkar *gaayan* (singing) party, theatrical and cultural troupes have iconized Ambedkar and also translated his life and works for the semi-literate or illiterate community in rural and urban areas.

Ambedkar is sceptical of the middle class. He is unsure of its potential to bring about revolution. His scientific analysis of the condition argues that the middle class is incapable of producing a 'New World Order' which is 'self-government and self-determination'.[57] Addressing the issue of the power of labour, Ambedkar contends:

Correct leadership, apart from other things, requires idealism and free thought. Idealism is possible for the Aristocracy, though free thought is not. Idealism and free thought are both possible for Labour. But neither idealism nor free thought is possible for the middle-class. The middle class does not possess the liberality of the Aristocracy, which is necessary to welcome and nourish an ideal. It does not possess the hunger for the New Order, which is the hope on which the labouring classes live.[58]

Party workers and local leaders are equally responsible for the non-unification of Dalit political leadership. Many leaders join politics according to their vested interests and commitment to the cause. Some get attracted to the leadership traits of a particular party leader, some want to pay allegiance to Ambedkar's bloodline, some want to follow his revolutionary politics, some believe in the inclusive leadership of all oppressed castes, while some believe in Dalit-centric polity. Such expectations are often dictated by the senior leadership. The executive party decisions do not always represent local realities.

Local constituencies vary demographically and so do the needs of different constituencies with regard to national-level sentiment. Local leaders have to be alert to the needs of their multi-caste and multi-religious constituencies while simultaneously staying committed to the party ideology. They also broker deals with other parties to maintain their presence in their constituencies. Many self-oriented Dalit leaders fail to demonstrate accountability. Due to this, the mistrust among people escalates into antagonism and results in an outward manifestation of rage.

The select few Dalit political leadership, like all other caste political leadership, also has strong class sensibilities. They want to adjust their path towards the corridors of global capitalism. They too aspire to join the ranks of the Dalit bourgeoisie like the

Brahmin, Kshatriya Bania or Shudra bourgeoisie. Their family and friends have no moral bearing to calculate their presence. Like Dalit bureaucrats, Dalit politicians want to put their children in world-class educational institutes. This is not a bad goal, but it gets muddier when such aspirations come at the expense of lower-working-class Dalits. There are enough instances of venality by Dalit politicians—just like other non-Dalit dominant-caste politicians—in the government. In one such case, a minister and an official of the social welfare department of the Maharashtra government tampered with the rules of the foreign studies scholarship to benefit their offspring. This scholarship is primarily aimed at providing opportunities of foreign education to deserving, poor Dalit students. In the wake of greed and nepotism, the Dalit leadership too has lost its ethical compass.

Second-Generation Beneficiaries

The children of the Dalit elite who study overseas are no help to the community either. As they do not experience suffering the same way poor Dalits do, they do not work towards strengthening the movement. A case in point is the child of a senior Dalit bureaucrat who was studying in the US. She had to write a project proposal on social disadvantage. She struggled to find such a community. After much research, she found an indigenous community in Bolivia that fit the bill of a disadvantaged community. Little did she know that the intent of her project had a Dalit component and that her professors wanted to encourage her to study the Dalit population of Bihar. She was so blinded by an a-caste sensibility that she could not identify with the Dalit discourse and neither could she find value in it. Like her dominant-caste Indian friends, she found Dalit issues an over-discussed topic without credible sources. This Dalit child would graduate from one of the better-known universities in the world. Her father, a senior bureaucrat, had dedicated his life to the service of the downtrodden. However, he could not pass on the same values to his offspring. Such Dalit graduates, without their Dalitness, become an enduring burden on the community. In addition to not contributing, they also participate in devaluing the Dalit struggle.

Dalit politicians' children have a different reading of this situation. Due to dynastic politics in India, Dalit politicians nurture their children to take over their inheritance. These politicians who affirm their abiding commitment to Ambedkar do not take even a leaf of wisdom from his life and works. Ambedkar never groomed his children towards dynastic politics. He was a very critical father. He looked at his children without any sense of preferential treatment. For Ambedkar, democratic values were the locus of his politics. This was demonstrated in his political, public and private life.

Dalit Middle-class Attitude to Power

In the midst of dynastic politics, the Dalit leadership has a wonderful opportunity to offer an Ambedkar version of radical politics. Instead, the reservation-hungry, self-serving Dalit politicians want to consolidate their hegemony by providing benefits to their offspring. In dynastic politics, the Dalit community suffers the most, because it is not an individual-centred community with imperial sensibilities. It has a community-oriented approach.

The alternative political diction offered by Kanshiram on Dalit pride is now seeing its end. Mayawati's political leadership that had its roots in idealism seems to be waning in the face of a hypocritical political environment. She unsuccessfully tried to promote Anand Kumar as the second-in-command with a promise that he would never contest elections. Due to the allegations of promoting dynastic politics in the party Kumar stepped down.[59] Mayawati's act can be seen as a way of luring the political

constituency which is enamoured with feudal dynastic realities at
the state as well as national level. With the Congress and major
state-level political parties engaging in dynastic politics, Mayawati
may well have been trying to do the same. However, the political
party she represents scorned the dynastic discourse at the time of
its founding. The Bahujan Samaj Party is a UP-based India-wide
party that has the political pulse of the Dalit community. There is
something vicious about dynastic politics. It makes the oppressed
an oppressor.

Then there are the upwardly mobile Dalits who are second- or
third-generation Dalits, like the bureaucrat's daughter discussed
earlier. They try to misrepresent themselves, and want to perfect
their condition under the shelter of dominant-caste groups. They
speak fluent English and write unending commentaries on social
media by reproducing certain community myths. Although, to
look at the positive side, myths are known as powerful interpreters
that have the ability to change the oppressive position. Arjun
Dangle[60] writes that owing to the lack of rhetorical myths in the
Dalit sphere, there is a lacunae in the Dalit movement. Dangle is
a proponent of accepting the myths from the history and culture
of the Buddhist sphere and some from the Puranas. The rhetoric
needs to be grounded in theoretical myths that would enable a
more accurate understanding of the Dalit condition. However,
the myths that are created by class-conscious Dalits are merely
used to redeem their own position. At times they have no basis
and at worst do not offer new canvas to the struggle.

Such Dalits form groups which are exclusively tied to their own
class networks. Membership to their social, religious or cultural
groups is not open to the Dalit public sphere. Many such closed
groups operate like clandestine organizations with an immense
fear of the state and dominant-caste colleagues as they accept
their subordinate position at the workplace or in the Brahminical
public sphere. Their email groups, WhatsApp groups, and other

communication platforms are resolutely attached to self-serving interests. I was privy to the conversations in one such group of bureaucrats that operates on an anonymous platform. In the online group discussions, even normal conversation took place within prescribed hierarchies. Appellations like 'sir' and 'madam' were used often. These groups of educated so-called well-off Dalits did not concern themselves with breaking the hierarchy which is the root cause of caste. They happily remain within the caste ecology by reproducing the essence of discrimination. They make sure that their power is conveyed to the lower layers of society and not to the upper crust.

However, in an awkward turn, such white-collared salaried employees in the public and private sectors denounced the logic of class-based divisions and instead preferred to act solely under the purview of caste while benefiting from class-based privileges. This has done harm to the entire sociopolitical movement of Dalits. Students and employees benefit from the social movements led by subaltern working-class Dalits. Scholarship, reservations, promotion, discrimination and other affirmative-action-oriented programmes are the outcome of the social movements led by the most vulnerable Dalits. These educated coteries don't flinch before abandoning the dues they owe to the foot soldiers—the toiling masses of their community. Due to the growing divide among the community, there is a downward realization of the collective future. This is perhaps the reason Anand Teltumbde has accused the Dalit middle class to be 'solely responsible' for the degeneration of the Dalit movement today.[61] Arjun Dangle observes that such middle-class Dalits as 'Dalit Brahmins' who do not share the ideas of 'revolutionary movements and struggles' are invested in self 'derogation'. Such Dalits demonstrate their mental impotence towards lived reality of all.[62] In addition, this class, by virtue of its bourgeois attitudes, has come to be, to use Martin Luther King Jr's words, 'unconsciously insensitive to the problems of the masses'.[63] It has frittered away its profound position as a conscious arbiter between the oppressed and the oppressive forces. Instead of advocating change it has lost its radical zeitgeist and moral responsibility.

Dalits cannot and should not fight their battle alone. The reason is obvious. They are fighting against a fiction that is not their creation. They are simply reacting and responding to the boorish structure that emerged from Brahminical arrogance. Since Dalits do not have control over the functioning of caste, they are forcibly incorporated into the system, and become salient actors in it. They either react sharply or assimilate silently; however, the possibility of creating an alternative system to the caste dungeon becomes a distant possibility. They unconditionally submit to the casteist order, adopting its values, morals, standards of speaking, beauty, logos of assimilation, consumption, food and social habits. Their dual image, which is neither true nor original, puts them in an awkward position; they unquestionably buy into Brahminical myths as the ideal characteristics of gaining personhood. However, they are refused by the Brahminical class that still sees the aspiring Dalit middle class as Untouchables. This creates tremendous risk for their social survival and so they develop what E. Franklin Frazier calls a 'considerable self-hatred . . . because of their ambivalence' towards their own group.[64]

Caught in this predicament, the Dalit middle class tries to find avenues to rebel and propel their frustrations through violent and non-violent means. Oftentimes, they utilize working-class Dalits for their protests and rallies. They try to find the most amenable solution that would not risk their economic position in society. A good option but one that is difficult to exercise is to seek out cross-caste and cross-class alliances. What Dalits need is to recognize behavioural tactics of the enemy who enjoys keeping them in a lowly position. A simple tactic to refute casteism is to find allies and sympathizers in the oppressor camp who are willing to work alongside the oppressed under their leadership. A tactical Dalit movement has the potential to blow up the system of hierarchy and difference. It will rescue freedom, equality and fraternity alongside political and economic democracy for all.

However, this does not seem to be happening. The Dalit middle class continues to grow and fragment further, without making any dent in existing caste prejudices.

English-medium Middle-class Dalits

Gaining command over English to produce a newer counterculture is still not in the domain of middle-class Dalits. Many write and rewrite not to produce something but only to respond or react to something. Unable to leave the cauldron of existing Brahminical diction, this group is unable to think beyond the superficiality of the imposed order. Often, it merely performs within caste-centric debates without offering critiques of class and religious inequalities, thereby becoming an apt consumer of the Brahminical plot. Currently, in India, barring a handful of institutionalized and non-institutionalized Dalit intellectuals, there isn't any real effort to produce original thinking. There is no commitment to challenge the dialectical superimpositions of caste and class, gender and sexuality as a conduit of protest. By failing to do this, Dalit knowledge production becomes too narrowly framed.

Partly, this is an outcome of the heavy oppression of the caste system that doesn't allow Dalits to be fully self-confident. Many caste intellectuals prefer putting forward the same thesis and simply rewriting it in new jargon. Another reason may also be the lopsided education system that was made the state governments' responsibility and not the centre's. The state governments enamoured with sub-nationalism put in place ghettoized education models and imparted learning only in regional languages. The poor rural class was exposed to this quality-less education where exposure to the English language was severely restricted, with many beginning to learn it only from eighth grade. This created what commentators have called a 'dual-track education system' where subaltern classes were fed with vernaculars and the middle and upwardly mobile classes with English.[65]

This further added multiple problems to the project of democratizing education and opportunities. Higher education was mostly offered in regional languages, and technical education, owning to its Western roots, had not been written in those languages. Naturally, this gave an upper hand to English-educated middle and upper classes who formed the corpus of Indian elites. They benefited immensely. Meanwhile, regionally educated individuals with late English-medium training were faced with immense challenges to cope with the higher education that was 100 per cent rooted in English culture and came with different methodological patterns of studying. Earlier, in our regional state boards, we passed exams through rote learning. This type of learning concentrated on what John Dewey referred to as 'the quantity of information personally absorbed' as opposed to the 'quality of work done'. The difference between quantity as the individualistic mode and quality as the community mode of learning rarely surfaced, which eventually produced more harms upon the disadvantaged class.[66] However, after twelfth grade, the exam pattern was entirely different wherein emphasis on research and most importantly the English language were valued. Those who came from central or international board English-medium schools automatically adjusted to these education patterns in central and private universities. The subaltern class, however, still spent most of its time discerning the language by burying itself in the English-to-vernacular dictionaries or language-learning apps on smartphones.

Therefore, the cream of English-speaking society which benefited from the independence struggle continued with the privileges it had enjoyed in the pre-Independence era. They occupied important positions in the government sector. After the liberalization of the Indian economy in the1990s, the doors opened for private-sector employment. The middle class was now accessing global culture and acclimatizing to the new avenues of society. The subaltern rural mass, on the other hand, continued to bear the brunt of changes in government policy disfavouring them over private owners with immense wealth. Whatever changes took place, the middle class remained the prime beneficiary alongside the rich aristocratic class.

Sanyal is mistaken in identifying the middle class with a strong pan-Indian identity. During pre-colonial and colonial times, this class was much rooted in its provincial identity, thereby giving rise to Bengali middle-class pride on similar lines as Punjabi and Marathi pride, among others. However, what Sanyal misses is the overwhelming practice of untouchability—the caste factor that singularly determined one's position in the socio-economic order and labour production. The caste system governed the market and it continues to influence market rules in the Indian setting. The privileged class which had contributed to the freedom struggle was the middle class, argues Sanyal. It was already enjoying the comforts of its exploits in the rural and semi-urban economy. It was a propertied class secured in the feudal structure that was primarily responsible for incorporating slavery into its fiefdom. It did not distribute wealth, neither did it create opportunities for the 'lower' castes to occupy positions of power in the economic chain. They also discouraged entrepreneurial activities among this group by confining them to farms and artisanal industry. The generational bondage continued under the rigorous system of bonded labour that was tied to the eternally unpayable loan of the landlord. P. Sainath's extensive reporting has uncovered the existence of such a covert system of feudalism practised openly without any checks.[67] Farmer suicides are an outcome of this enclosed economic relation that is easily implementable on the fertile ground of caste. This propertied landlord class translates into the middle class in the urban-metro-capitalist economy. By ignoring the perspicuous existence of caste in the make-up of class identity, Sanyal reproduces the myth of class sans caste in India.

The primary identity of upper-middle-class Dalits is based on caste followed by class. Though this class may want to try to base itself in class categories first and caste second, the casteist set-up of the economic order does not allow it the freedom to slip into the fluid capitalist chain. The Dalit middle class is surrounded by the upwardly mobile, traditionally well-off dominant castes. The latter have a sizeable influence in the workplace and thereby on its culture. The Dalit middle class, hypnotized by this vision, tries to emulate them in the same lexicon and accents.

In the academic realm too, they happily emulate unoriginal Brahminical thinking. The Brahmin and allied-caste academia has made a career out of a few themes that continue to be theorized endlessly. Post-colonialism, Marxism and continental philosophy are some of the major disciplinary ice-breakers that get purchase in Indian humanities and social sciences research. Clearly, the elite academicians who profited out of fooling the subaltern masses by forcing them to focus on post-colonialism killed the radical subaltern consciousness. Due to the limited accessibility to the theory and methods of this concept, projects like post-colonial studies easily ensured the dominance of 'upper'-caste elites in academic spaces. Dalits have only started to grapple with this question fifty years later.

The field of literature also falls short of originality. Barring a few Dalit feminist and radical Ambedkarite traditions there isn't any attempt to generate new thought. 'Comparative literature' occupies an important place among young Dalit scholars. Almost every literary scholar I meet is invested in comparative English literature. Although it is a profound topic and deserves rightful attention, it is still a bit late to join the game. A decent amount of work has already been done between Dalit literature and African-American literature, and a slight portion covered by anglophone Africa and tidbits of Europe. This is not to say there isn't a turf to explore more.

Dalit knowledge creation is again losing the radical beam wherein it had once birthed a wholesome revolution. Literary activism during the Dalit Panthers era had inspired many regional outfits. In the Telugu region it was journals like *Nalupu* and *Edureet,* in Karnataka it was the Dalit Sangharsh Samiti, in Tamil Nadu, the Panthers are still roaring, in the Hindi belt, BAMCEF-led literary criticism produced heaps of critically sharp, quality literature. Now the Hindi magazine *Dalit Dastak*, *Round Table India* and other print- and web-based platforms in Hindi, English and other regional languages are bringing dynamic attention to the literary nature of Dalit thought. In addition to this, social media platforms utilized by literary and social spheres act as an intervening model to this question. Scores of self-help groups on social media alongside YouTube channels act as independent mediascapes for Dalits across India.

In contrast, comparative English literature continues to be a trap-like zone of limited scholarship within the Anglo world that does not offer universal updates beyond the anglophone countries. This is evident in the Dalit lack of engagement with francophone, lusophone, Arabic, African, European, East Asian,

Latin American and other regional literatures. In all these years, I have met only one Dalit doctoral student who expressed his interest in studying African literature. Many might question the lack of linguistic accessibility. While it may be true to a certain degree, there are enough fiction and non-fiction works translated into English from various languages.

The imaginative locus could expand if Dalits prioritize their identity as a guiding universal condition. If they put themselves into a long and unabated tradition of Dalit livelihood, they might be able to depart from a submissive attitude. The rich tradition and indomitable spirits of their ancestors seldom enter the conceptual and analytical fields. This could effectively happen once Dalits work towards building active solidarity with other oppressed groups in the world.

5

Dalit Capitalism

'Indian capitalism has not arisen out of any social need or development; nor out of any struggle for the ownership of the means of production; not out of any historic battle fought on behalf of the new science and technology. Rather the class which was specially privileged by religion to monopolize wealth . . . earned profit—using inherited wealth . . . if proletariat is divided along the lines of caste and religion, it is difficult to launch a class war and establish a classless society. For this reason, capitalism needs a society riven by religion.'
—Baburao Bagul, 'Dalit Literature Is But a Human Literature'

'The essence of Social Democracy is that there shall be no excluded or exploited classes in the Socialist state; that there shall be no man or woman so poor, ignorant, or black as not to count one . . . I have come to believe that the test of any great movement towards social reform is the Excluded Class.'
—W.E.B. Du Bois, 'Socialism and the Negro Problem'

'We should learn to do business. The high caste in the village will not buy milk from us. In fact, they will not buy anything from us. Undeterred, we should practise business in our locality. We should not allow the village to earn at our expense.'
—B.R. Ambedkar[1]

A Theory of a New *Vanguard* Class?

Now we turn to the emerging concept that holds water in the cushy quarters of the neo-liberal glossary: Dalit Capitalism. The capitalism that we see today is inspired by the industrialized Western models and partially imitates the African-American and Brahmin–Bania styles of trade.[2] This capitalism is inspired by the fact of being an oppressed group that deserves equal participation in the private ownership of public resources by controlling the line of production and manipulating labour value. If these are the measures of capitalism, surely it is not Dalit capitalism. It could be best read as Dalit/capitalism.

DICCI started off as a quasi-formal space for budding Dalit entrepreneurs who had emerged in the shadow of Indian neo-liberalism (the post-1990s liberalization-privatization-globalization era), an additional avenue to break the shackles imposed by traditional (caste) capital.

A somewhat similar trend had appeared across the Atlantic during the late-nineteenth and early-twentieth centuries in the US among the southern African-American population. Heralded and supported by white capital, Booker T. Washington laid the foundation of capitalist enterprise by the marginalized in America. Its influence was so wide and far-reaching that the banker class—the gnomes of the south—came under the control of Black capitalist forces. Such was the might of the emerging Black capital enterprise.

DICCI organized a national conference on SC/ST Entrepreneurs in New Delhi on 29 December 2015 which was attended by Prime Minister Narendra Modi. The organizers clamoured that DICCI's existence indicated that it was ready and excited to enter the global market and draw influences from the epicentre of global capitalism: the United States. As DICCI is an entity catering to marginalized business persons, one of the co-presenters argued that Dalit capitalism was as relevant as nineteenth-century African-American capitalism, and that the chairperson of DICCI, Milind Kamble, could be compared to Booker T. Washington. 'Booker T. Washington is more than a hundred years late in India,' declared a mentor of DICCI, Chandra Bhan Prasad. Referring to the audience that included the Dalit entrepreneurial class, Prasad mentioned the pain of 'becoming' something out of nothing. 'These are the people who have come from a hungry mother's womb' was his poignant cry.

However, when such transcontinental similarities are drawn, one has to contextualize the parading of these gestures. The reference to Booker T. Washington at times does not fall well and indeed may be counter-intuitive. History has divergent accounts to offer to the romanticized acclamations of Black capitalism. The attempt to understand the struggle against caste and racial discrimination in a similar vein has been going on since the nineteenth century. Jotirao Phule (1827–90) had identified with the struggles of African Americans. His resonance with their struggle can be seen in his reference to the 'good peoples of America', alluding to the White abolitionists who were 'self-sacrificing' in the 'cause of Negro Slavery'. It was an epochal moment in the American Reconstruction Era (1865–77), and the Thirteenth Amendment to the Constitution of the United States in 1865 abolished slavery,[3] the Fourteenth Amendment gave equal protection under the law in 1868, while the Fifteenth Amendment guaranteed Black men the right to vote in 1870. This landmark was also a motivation for dominant-caste social reformers in India to see a triad of hope that was inspired by the abolition of American slavery and the British colonial system and the growing awareness among lower-caste groups.

This movement was later continued by B.R. Ambedkar, who went on to become the single biggest stalwart of the Untouchable struggle, making the anti-caste movement an important element

in the twentieth-century global emancipation project. Ambedkar
was a keen observer and admirer of the work of African Americans,
in particular W.E.B. Du Bois. Among Ambedkar's papers is his
widely known correspondence with Du Bois in 1946. At the
time, the National Association for the Advancement of Colored
People (NAACP) under Du Bois's leadership was fighting for the
inclusion of racial rights in the mandate of the United Nations San
Francisco Conference in 1945. Expressing his immense faith in
Du Bois's movement, Ambedkar requested him for a copy of the
NAACP presentation, as he wished to make a similar presentation
to the United Nations for the cause of the Untouchables.[4] The
two giants, Du Bois and Ambedkar, were reading each other and
were known for their political and social revolutionary schemes in
their respective geographies.

Battling over African-American Inspiration

A Dalit in DICCI, expressing loyalty to the ideology of Ambedkar,
refers to the African-American adage of minority-led capitalism
under the leadership of Booker T. Washington by idealizing the
figurehead. On the other hand, Du Bois, who admired Ambedkar,
gives us a sense of the limitations of Washington and his project.
In his magnum opus, *The Souls of the Black Folk* (1903), Du
Bois splendidly churns out his arguments against Washington's
approach. Offering a compelling case, Du Bois critiques the
contemporary leader of the south for his accommodationist pact,
also known as the Atlanta Compromise. This approach tended
to narrowly define the objectives of emancipation, to be achieved
through economic self-sufficiency alone. Surrounded with the
logic of 'work and money', Du Bois found no sense in claiming
the fruits of materialistic gain without paying absolute attention
to human dignity and freedom. According to Du Bois, political
power (right to vote), civil equality and higher education formed

the basis of strengthening the Black struggle. For him, Washington was a pacifist who could not transcend the idea of race and the inequities that follow in its wake.

Washington's act of establishing a vocational training institute (the Tuskegee Institute) to supply labour to the market owned by the White capitalist class and of relinquishing hard-won political and civil rights just to gain access to the market economy was treacherous for Du Bois. He believed that Washington's efforts of turning the Black underpaid artisanal class into a business class was futile if it was unable to create a space for political and social protection. In Washington, Du Bois saw someone who represented the shibboleth of the 'old attitudes of adjustment and submission' allegedly accepting the (civil) 'inferiority of the Negro races'.

Although Du Bois had the 'greatest admiration for Mr Washington and Tuskegee' there were ideological disagreements that led to the rift between the two giants of the era. Writing a eulogy on Washington's death in *The Crisis* (1915), Du Bois appreciated his accomplishments but also wrote about his shortcomings. He asserted that Washington could not 'grasp the growing bond of politics and industry' and a sophisticated understanding that the relations 'between white and black was founded on caste' and not economy.[5] This is the moment cheerleaders of Dalit capitalism need to pay attention to. It is the accepted subordinating level of self that gets recognized and feeds into the casteist ecology. In the Dalit capitalist project, Dalits are not asked to become owners of powerful corporations or industries that are still the monopolies of the dominant castes. For example, profitable businesses of heavy metal industries are yet to find occupancy under Dalit capitalist wings.[6] This rush to strengthen caste-based capitalism would further solidify caste in the neo-liberal autonomy. Doing this would only lead to a 'firmer establishment of color caste in this land' as Du Bois had contended.

Washington was a relatively taller and more respected Black leader of the time, recognized equally by the Black and White elites of America. His demeanour was well known outside the US too. The dispute between Du Bois and Washington led to the separate paths they considered most appropriate for the emancipation of the Black race in America. Du Bois's emphasis lay on higher education for the Black population that could create the 'Talented Tenth, who through their knowledge of modern culture could guide the American Negro into a higher civilization'.[7] Without this base, Du Bois believed the Black population would remain subjugated under White control. Washington's approach was to elevate 'Negro' labour to the status of honourable labour. He believed that the economic foundation laid by Black people would elevate them. It was the first- and second-generation free slaves that he believed deserved proper training to hone their skills bequeathed from 250 years of slavery. In *Industrial Education for the Negro* (1903), Washington expressed surprise over the amount of modern education being given to the 'Negro men and women . . . in literature, in mathematics and in the sciences, with little thought of what had been taking place during the preceding two hundred and fifty years'. He saw

> young men educated in foreign tongues, but few in carpentry
> or in mechanical or architectural drawing. Many were trained
> in Latin, but few as engineers and blacksmiths. Too many were
> taken from the farm and educated, but educated in everything
> but farming.[8]

Thus, he wanted to concentrate on the vocational training of Black people.

Du Bois's fundamental difference with Washington was the interpretation of the higher education sought by Black people. Washington firmly believed that the Black population could acquire and develop intellectual and cultural status on the foundation of industrial training 'coupled with intellectual and moral training', which would in fact yield a way to their freedom. This freedom meant participation in the 'all-powerful business and commercial world'. He quoted Edgar Gardner Murphy, a White southern clergyman who established the Conference on Racial Relations in 1900 and promoted the interests of labour laws and stressed that they were in favour of creating an 'agricultural class, a class of tenants or small land owners' from the Negro race.

Washington formally established National Negro Business League in 1900 with an intent of creating a capitalist class among the Black population in the US. Its aim was to 'promote the commercial and financial development of the Negro'.[9] And thus it was 'resolved to establish an industrial enterprise wherever a possibility presents itself'. Through economic autonomy, Washington hoped to achieve the 'social equality' that was not accorded to the Black population of America.[10] Although the league's interest was to foster a network among Black businesses through 'advertising' it also encouraged entrepreneurship among the Black community. This league had key confidants in the White capitalists in the country. It enjoyed a cordial relationship with the White-dominated Chamber of Commerce, which offered up its office spaces and network of local Black businessmen for league meetings. The White capitalist networks offered their support and cooperation through occasional associations to advance mutual capitalist interests. The National Negro Business League was an important and dear project of Washington's and he headed it till his death in 1915.

Du Bois, on the other hand, wanted the Black population to acquire positions of eminence in arts, literature, academia and other forms of cultural, moral and intellectual endeavours. He wanted them to first acquire higher human dignity that would prevent society from compelling them into subordinate jobs. He laid this out neatly in a survey of the American post-reconstruction era in a widely circulated paper, 'The Economics of Negro Emancipation in the United States' (1911). Du Bois placed emphasis on the Black labour that was systematically disenfranchised and exploited by the American south which found a way through political power, courts, treachery, cheating, wage contracts (which was used as a tool to keep Black labour in check and exploit it under the rubric of law) and notorious legislations to subjugate it.[11] The southern White capital was able to do this 'under the cry of race prejudice' that was already in action in the United States. Du Bois wanted to elevate Black people from the prescribed subservient position on to their deserving larger human capacities. This is similar to the idea of Ambedkar who wanted Untouchables to leave the hamlets that were the site of traditional caste-mandated occupations. In one of his speeches in 1943 to a Marathi-speaking audience, Ambedkar suggested breaking the taboo by adorning new and clean clothes and embracing a style that would offset the aversion imposed on Untouchables by the dominant-caste gaze. A year earlier, in Nagpur, he had appreciated the Untouchable women's conference for breaking away from the dominant castes' depreciating gaze upon Untouchable women by wearing clean clothes with pride.

One way to understand Washington's position is to see the rationale of the White industrial capitalist society which concentrated its interests on creating a labouring class. Washington cut to the chase and spoke for the capitalist class as well as the Black working force. His emphasis on training rather than learning was summed up in the conclusion to his 1904 thesis where he commented that 'as a slave the Negro was worked, and that as a freeman he must learn to work'.[12] Meanwhile, Du Bois was suspicious of the dependence of big businesses on politics and philanthropy that produced a 'sycophantic and cowardly leadership'.[13]

Washington was an influential figure among those Indian middle-class aspirants during the turn of the twentieth century who aimed to carve out a mercantile independence within the established order of subjugation. Washington's writings were translated into various vernaculars in India, signalling the growing appetite amongst the upwardly mobile caste groups.[14]

The ground for contemporary Dalit capitalism is identical to what Washington had proposed for Blacks and what Du Bois vehemently opposed. The vested interest of privileged caste capital can be on the verge of being toppled if does not collaborate with the marginally powerful and demographically active populace. But the projection of DICCI and the likes as the sole proprietor of the modern Dalit project only harms the real Dalitdom that struggles to survive in an extremely unequal market-based society.

Dalit Capitalism?

To begin with, it is important to understand and settle the notion of capitalism and its emergence in modern society. Capitalism is defined by the growth of modernity, colonialism and extensive forms of oppressive mechanisms that are employed to extract maximum labour for minimal wages. The capitalist narratives of the Western world, for example, used the existing social relations that were based on class distinctions to construct inclinations towards capitalism as a central meta-narrative in defining the relations of society. However, these relations were purposefully solidified in order to appropriate the after-effects of material culture brought by modernity.

In the Dalit context, as the book *Defying the Odds*[15] shows, it is the leftovers of traditional industrial scions where, in the absence of any takers, Dalits were called on to take over the unwanted units. Hence, something unwanted and unrelatable to the measures of capitalism is presented as Dalit capitalism. Dalits still have to garner the support of traditional capitalist moguls to fit into the brackets of capitalism. The tribe of Dalit capitalists can be best understood in terms of the various myths propounded by the capitalist world. It is arduously argued that they have vast purchasing power, which is clearly an exaggeration. Relative to their population, they are nowhere close to being called 'influencers' of the capitalist economy. Their contribution is invisible and doesn't matter to the aggressive, casteist Indian capitalist set-up. Dalits do not own any real wealth in India. They are at best rentiers and at worst deprived occupants of the Indian capital. Their participation is severely restricted and manipulated. This new image of Dalit capitalists is a creation of the dominant castes to diffuse the potential risk of Dalit rebellion against capitalism. It is a clever plot to lure the oppressed class into the promises of capitalist dreams.

A comparative research of Dalit capital's influence on the Indian economy along with the household expenditure of the Dalit middle class with those of the dominant castes would reveal telling data. Given their negligible presence and beggarly contribution, the rich Dalits' median income would come out to less than the median income of the non-Dalit middle class in total.[16] So, a rich Dalit is still poor and wretched in the grand scheme of the caste–capital programme. Over a third of Dalits are agricultural labourers with the number of landless increasing in the neo-liberal economy from 65.9 per cent in 1991 to 71 per cent in 2011.[17] The assurance to a majority of Dalits in the neo-liberal economy is clearly out of the purview of the managers of the neo-liberal order.

The rising middle class among Dalits is an outcome of reservation policies, the liberalization of the economy, and growing consciousness. Owing to this, a small percentage of Dalits now have purchasing capacity to own a house, consumer goods, private modes of transportation and other sources of income. These consumption habits of market culture have added a fear of introducing an improvised version of a new Dalit class seduced by the material culture which has the blood of its exploited workers on its hands. This class, with its aspirational attitude, unknowingly stands guard before the frontiers of corruptible consumption that is detrimental to the causes for which they and their forebears have been fighting. If reproduction of the class consensus in the Dalit community is going to be the ultimate aim of caste capitalism, this looms as a quasi-exploitative model. In the hunger for greed and imposition of hard-headed market principles, there is the fear of Dalits dividing the Dalit constituency through capitalism. It threatens to create an alternative under-class for Dalits. There cannot be multiple classes among Dalits if they have to attain a morally credible and strong selfhood. If classes continue to operate within oppressed caste groups, the struggle that has been ongoing and which is fighting to fix caste disorder will then have to refocus its attention on class wars, which is an additional strain on the overly burdened shoulders of Dalit liberation fronts.

The term 'Dalit' is analogous to anti-oppression. The defining trait of the Dalit community is to resist oppression of any form. And capitalism chooses to *continue* oppression. This juxtaposition is unfeasible and the two cannot go hand in hand. Dalit households have been protesting against the capitalistic sensibilities of greed. If someone from the community attempts to galvanize Dalit interests for individual profitability, that person is not well regarded and is even socially ostracized. This form of idiomatic expression testifies to the Dalit's resistance to the nefarious and dissipated life introduced by the dominant-capital-centred culture. There is a mimicry of the pleonexia of the dominant castes who retain their hegemony by oppressing human and natural lives for petty profit.

DICCI's aim is to fight caste with capital—for caste and capitalism cannot coexist, goes the mantra. Capitalism, here, is seen as an egalitarian project that seeks to launch a utopia of mutual gain that relies upon an equitable exchange. Meaning, there will be a moment of Dalit capital forces sitting together and on an equal plane to negotiate with the oppressor. This assertion needs qualification. If understood within a broader global capital mechanism, the résumé of neo-liberal capitalism is not impressive. For it has proven to uproot indigenous lives by replacing them with so-called 'civilized notions of modernism', inaugurating unending chapters of chronic disaster. Caste capitalism's strong belief lies in the fact that capitalism will uproot the heinous and rigid caste system, although it is nostalgically upheld by the beneficiaries of caste. History again mediates to offer an alternative vision, almost as déjà vu to the current exciting possibilities. Lower-caste capital already existed in the nineteenth century. Jotirao Phule's family belonged to the landed propertied class and won lavish contracts from the state. Phule himself was a private contractor and entrepreneur in his later life and owned 200 acres of land in the busy suburbs of Pune. He too failed dismally to amenably navigate through the reconstruction project of caste society—the superstructure of the Indian condition.

Demands for social rights were raised time and again by a handful of upwardly mobile owners of miniscule capital in former Untouchable communities. In the *Gazetteer* of the Bombay Presidency published in 1880 and a report on the Land Revenue Settlement written in 1899 there is evidence of growing entrepreneurial activity among the Mahar (formerly Untouchable) communities of Maharashtra. The Mahars started 'gathering capital as petty contractors and moneylenders . . . manag[ing] their business without any help of high caste clerks'. 'The rise of Mahars will probably be one of the features of social change,' states the Land Revenue Settlement report.[18] A similar situation was occurring in north India among the Chamar (leather worker) capital enterprise which protested against its position in the traditional caste set-up. For the Shudras—the artisanal and landowning castes lower than all others but above Dalits—Sanskritization—a practice of following the rituals of the dominant castes in order to climb up the traditional order—amounted to social change. What it in fact did was reproduce the structure of oppression idealized in Brahminical discourse. Even with the Mahars and Chamars becoming petty capital owners the situation of the community is starkly depressing. While some Mahars and Chamars have achieved wealth in certain regional contexts, the relative outcome of their capitalist experiences is not indicative of the majority of the community because they still have to bear the brunt of the lowest-paying jobs and worst form of atrocities. Even with their newly acquired economic strength, aided by intellectual temerity, they have not been adequately successful in making a dent in the social oppressions they suffer. This is because caste power plays into the actions and reactions they receive from other non-Dalit communities.

Clearly, then, capitalism has not proved to serve the rightful purpose of eradicating social divide, nor did the twentieth-century form of state socialism. That is why Ambedkar's call for a 'modified' version of state socialism remains the order of the day wherein the state takes control of important industries and agriculture to regulate the flow of capital and the surplus produced in the process.

The enclosed warring of non-Dalits and Dalits in the neo-liberal agenda created, ironically enough, a certain kind of benefit to being marginalized, so that one could claim some, if not an equal, share in the global dominance of market finance. To gain tenders, contracts and appropriate funds for capitalist projects hints at the political importance of such projects. The admirers of such projects include government agents as well as private entities who look towards the struggle of the marginalized to offer patronage for creating something new under their rules. It also teases the idealism of a modified form of state socialism whose aim is to subvert total reliance on a state riddled with corruption. DICCI's vision includes the words 'Developing Business Leadership'. In its ten-year history, DICCI has gained access to important monetary portfolios in India where it shares the dais with the National Board of the Ministry of Micro, Small and Medium Enterprises, BFSI (banking, financial services and insurance) Sector Skill Council of India, National Skill Development Council, Confederation of Indian Industries, Affirmative Action Council, Monetary Policy Consultative Committee, Reserve Bank of India (RBI), among others under the policy of affirmative action. Would this gesture of drawing capital from state resources ever qualify as *capitalism* in the neo-liberal form of economic arrangement? Especially if the businesses that are offered to Dalits are predetermined by their caste occupations, viz., the leather business, management of farming and production and manufacturing of caste-centric social economics, would it be correct to declare the caste blindness of capitalism?

Aseem Prakash's study of Dalit capitalism shows that Dalits continue to undergo multilayered exclusion.[19] The economy is situated within dense structures of society. The social mandate decides economic functioning. The community networks that often work in the entrepreneurial chain are not in favour of Dalits. This affects Dalit capital owners doubly: first, due to the lack of Dalits in the network chain they are unable to cross over easily, and second, dominant-caste entrepreneurs use their own networks to keep Dalits from accessing the market. When it comes to taking bank loans and dealing with other state-owned institutions, Dalits have to undergo humiliation only to finally be left with one option: being co-opted by dominant-caste capital. In these partnerships, the dominant-caste person uses his/her influence to command business prospects while doing little work compared to the Dalit. In this transaction too, the 'social relations' that Kancha Ilaiah argued about in his *Post-Hindu India* are absent.[20] Social relations are important to regulate the dominance of caste hegemony in the foundation of capitalism. In the absence of established social relations there is limited scope for empathizing with other caste groups. Due to the lack of conversation with other groups in a commercial exchange, the buyer and the seller, the worker and the owner do not have reasons to establish norms of human relationality, thereby deepening the ignorance of other group. Therefore, in the absence of social endosmosis, capitalism in India finds its immoral ethic. Sharing of space and capital does not allow Dalits to create social queering. A national television reporter once shared his experience of reporting on Dalit capitalists in Gujarat. A Dalit real estate businessman had to 'partner' with a Patel (dominant caste) in order to retain his presence in the market. All the work was done by the Dalit but the name of Patel was used for better marketability. The profits were divided equally. The story doesn't end here. Patel would seldom touch the money given by the Dalit for transactions. He would prefer it to be kept on the table to avoid physical contact with the stash of hard cash. When the journalist pressed Patel further, '*usne* camera *par thoonk diya* [he spit on the camera]' in his Dalit partner's name, informed the journalist. The partnering here meant very little blurring of caste lines. The market effectively worked with and retained the caste structure. Irrespective of the new inventions in the market economy, the caste syndrome continued to be unaffected. The data on the control of capital, for example, says it all.[21]

Table 1: Caste-wise Distribution of Indian Corporate Board Members (2010)

	Caste	Numbers	% to Total
1	Forward caste	8387	92.6
	Of which (a) Brahmin	4037	44.6
	(b) Vaishyas	4167	46.0
	(c) Kshatriya	43	0.5
	(d) Others#	137	1.5
2	Other Backward Classes	346	3.8
3	SC/ST	319	3.5
4	Total (1 to 3)	9052	100.0

Refers forward castes (like Syrian Christians).

Table 2: Caste Diversity (Blau) Index of Indian Companies—Descriptive Statistics (2010)

	Blau – Caste
Mean	0.12
Median	0.00
Maximum	1.00
Minimum	0.00
Std Dev	0.19
Skewness	1.16
Kurtosis	-0.28

Source: Economic & Political Weekly

The distribution of board members according to caste shows that nearly 93 per cent were part of the 'forward' caste members, also known as savarna, comprising 46 per cent Vaishya (Bania) and 44 per cent Brahmin. OBCs and SCs/STs have a meagre 3.8 per cent and 3.5 per cent share respectively (Table 1). This clearly shows that the Indian corporate board consists of a small group of minorities and lacks diversity. Even in mergers and acquisitions (M&A) in the Indian companies a study by Bhalla, Goel, Konduri and Zemel found that larger percentage of M&A took place between persons belonging to similar castes. The study found that during 2000–17 caste similarity increased the possibility of M&A. Where Brahmins had maximum representation in the acquirer firm's board the targeted firm's board (nearly 50 per cent) was Brahmin dominated. Similar patterns were observed in the case of Kshatriyas (30.1 per cent), Vaishyas (52.6 per cent) and Shudras (45.7 per cent).[22]

In various businesses too, Dalits have to face entrenched hostility. This prevents them from occupying strategically important positions in the market. On top of this, due to the hostility, Dalits have to sell their goods at lower margins in order to fit into the market chain. This costs them crucial profits. Working in such adverse conditions puts Dalits in a vulnerable position where their caste identity remains a primary roadblock within the current neo-liberal economy. This unwelcoming hesitation, or to paraphrase, Amartya Sen's idea of 'unfavourable inclusion', plays an important role.[23] The bland promises of the neo-liberal regime seem unable to surmount the caste hegemony. Growing wage gaps and loosening of state control over public resources and public capital put marginalized sections like Dalits at the threshold of insecurity. Neo-liberalism has failed the Dalit enterprise.

Capital Aficionado Ambedkar

Ambedkar, while debating Indian social issues, constantly related them to global suffering. His engagement with the post–First World War scenario about the impact of capital is relatively more critical than his position on nationalism-led sovereignty through India's independence. Among some circles, to support the argumentative logic of capitalism, Ambedkar is read as a free marketeer who foresaw capitalism in the Dalit discourse as something that would challenge the fortified caste structure.[24] This is often challenged by his socialist ideals, where there is a suspicion of the nihilistic tendency of capitalism. In one school of thought, Ambedkar is seen as an early supporter of capitalism. His academic writings on monetary economics and finance and his refusal to include socialism in the preamble to the Constitution, giving way to the people's choice, is taken as an indication of his capitalist bent. However, his radical socialist vision is seen in his proto-constitution drafted on behalf of the All India Scheduled Caste Federation in 1947, entitled 'States and Minorities'.[25]

While working as an executive member in the viceroy's cabinet and a minister in the government, Ambedkar was focused on keeping the priorities of his struggles people-centric—the vulnerable people against capitalist forces. In his call for a modified form of state socialism, written in 'States and Minorities', his emphasis was on economic productivity. He recommended that the state invest in industry and agriculture as state-owned property. For these are the two significant components of the Indian economy—Ambedkar was sceptical about private capital and feared the replication of wealth inequality that was the result of the landownership–caste monopoly in India. Sukhadeo Thorat argues that it was due to the type of formation of a specific state–caste entity during the foundational years of Indian independence where the agenda of economic inequality was bequeathed to the state machinery.[26] 'Millionaire Dalits', whatever their actual worth is, may be a sign of change, but without a dynamic vision for the future, they would remain merely a gaggle of geese.

Dalit capitalism is being seen as a new 'Baniaization', as opposed to and moving away from the 'Sanskritization' model. However, if the Baniaization of Dalit groups indicates an assimilation into a classed society, it is a toxic condition of oppression by the oppressed, very much in the Freirean logic of *Pedagogy of the Oppressed*.[27] Freire argued that once the oppressed capture power, they inherit the tendencies of the oppressor. As Ambedkar observes on the capital nature of Bania capital in his magnum opus *What Congress and Gandhi Have Done to the Untouchables* as:

> The Bania is the worst parasitic class known to history. In him the vice of money-making is unredeemed by culture or conscience. He is like an undertaker who prospers when there is an epidemic. The only difference between the undertaker and the Bania is that the undertaker does not create an epidemic while the Bania does. He does not use his money for productive purposes. He uses it to create poverty and more poverty by lending money for unproductive purposes.[28]

The fact that Banias are a benefactor of the caste system advocates the unquestionable rationality of class suppression combined with caste as a surplus value. Banias in colonial times were the oppressors who contributed to the empire's expansion in the Indian subcontinent, more so than in the African countries. Banias were the middlemen who dealt in the indomitable parlance of advancing one's interests. However, the nationalist history of India overwhelmingly lauds the Bania capitalist class as a benefactor of the nationalist movement, thereby declaring them as supporters of the movement when it was not an altruistic dedication at all. On the contrary, it was to exploit the resources of a newly independent nation on their own terms without external colonial intervention. Vladimir Lenin describes this position as being midway between the radical's and worker's struggle.

What 'Baniaizing' Means in the Dalit Household

Capitalism, that is, the exploitation of the working class, is antithetical to how Dalits understand society. In the Indian context, the exploiters belong to categories which are distinctly caste-marked. The owners of agricultural land or industries—referred to as *maalik*, master—are the neo-Kshatriyas graduating from the lowly Shudra status more prominently in the post-Independence era. The owners of factories and industries are Brahmins and Banias; the managers and accountants who pay their salaries are mostly Banias. The petty mercantile class—convenience-store owners, farm equipment suppliers and so on—are also Bania, known as *komati* sahukar in Maharashtra.[29]

It is this last category of traders, the sahukars, that I came to know well while growing up. They exist in most residential areas, and their fraudulent business practices and exploitation are acknowledged by all. Everyone in the Dalit basti where I grew up is aware of it, but no one dares challenge it. When Dalits run out of their monthly salaries, they end up relying heavily on the pittance the sahukar offers as credit to fill their empty stomachs. The deceit that is practised without remorse is their business ethic founded on casteist normativity. There is no social relation between these two groups; they have traditionally been up against each other. The monetarily exploited groups are also oppressed under caste rules. Thus, the caste–class oppression is intertwined. Owing to the caste and market nexus, Dalits have very little avenues to explore. Such malpractices are proof of what Kancha Ilaiah refers to as the 'Hindu Market'.[30]

A child from a Dalit household tries to avoid visiting a Bania in his shop because it is an uncomfortable encounter—humiliating at best and vulgar at worst. I recall how I would be reluctant to fetch milk from the nearby shop every morning run by an ugly man displaying his half-naked body covered with hair. The odour in his shop was caused either because he had consumed too many nuts or had not bathed. Such encounters encouraged us Dalit children to make fun of him, by referring to him as *paadra* komati (farting grocer) or *chikat* Marwadi (stingy Marwadi/ Bania).

The number of unethical practices these traders execute is incomparable. At least in secular marketplaces, the rightful agency of human rights and market rules come to bear upon it. However, in a traditional economic set-up, there is little shame in indulging in malpractice. For instance, the shopkeepers in my area would sell expired products to illiterate Dalits, who would get chronically sick. If a product was damaged or contaminated by rats, it would be sold out of its packet at a lower rate. If the quality of the product was diminished due to exposure to sun or rain, it would still find its way into our households. These traders would even sell food items that were restricted by the government. The concept of food poisoning didn't exist for them as it should have. Once, the government banned cold drinks of a certain brand due to the poisonous content discovered in them. All retailers were asked to prohibit their sale and withdraw these products. Pouncing upon such a desperate situation, our area's shopkeepers made a deal with the local dealer—instead of sending the drinks back to the warehouse, they proposed to sell them at lower rates.

Towards the end of the Hindu calendar year, these traders would close their shops and go on a pilgrimage to the Tirumala temple of Balaji in Andhra Pradesh. An annual visit to this place is a well-known excursion among their class. More recently, non-Dalit lower castes who have climbed up into the neo-Bania status have also joined the queues. I once asked a local trader who was preparing for the pilgrimage about the importance of such a visit. He explained that he had a contract with the god Balaji that whatever profit he made, he would share

30 per cent with him. He was going to fulfil his promise because Balaji had blessed him with enormous profits that year. When I confronted him, he confessed that the profits could not be made by adhering to fair business practices. Whatever is prescribed in religion clearly applies to people who are not from this trader class. Because they are supposedly the custodians of wealth, they have been given the ordained right to control the economy. Society's wealth is regulated under their guardianship. 'It is us who has made India rich and will preserve its richness for a thousand years to come. Even the Islamic invaders could not make us poor because the wealth was concentrated under our command,' this trader told me. His pact with god appeared to have been premised on a pardon for his corrupt practices and the crimes he had committed in the process of accumulating wealth.

There are also many incidents of child abuse and violence on Dalit women committed with impunity. The Bania seldom visits Dalit houses or invites them into his house. I do not recall being invited by my Bania friends. I had no idea about the internal structures of their houses, except whatever I could look at from the gate or main door. Friends from school would ask me to come to their place but rarely invite me inside. When these friends would walk with me, their parents would see me as a criminal because I was from the Dalit basti. They would tell their children loudly so as to make me also hear to not to get into trouble with the police. The family members of a particular Bania friend would look at me suspiciously each time they encountered me. I had a good bond with this friend, Verma, and he would also visit my basti after tuition. Once, he dared to invite me inside his house. That was the first time I could satisfy my curiosity about the grand place he lived in. There was marble flooring, a huge colour television set connected to cable, a huge drawing room, study room, bedroom, kitchen, guest room, terrace and an extra set of rooms of equal size. I was awed after seeing this well-guarded Bania house. I bid goodbye to my friend with happiness on my face. As I stepped outside, I was suddenly accosted by a person who claimed to work for the Bania. He took me into the interior of a shop inside a hidden room where there was a man there who inquired about my background—where I came from, my school—and then warned me to not visit their place again. He told me he was my friend's uncle. At that time, I could not understand why he was prohibiting me from visiting their place. That was the last time I got together with that friend.

The Significance of Social Relations in Traditional Capital Accumulation

As a child, I recall being fascinated with technological equipment like robots and automatic racing car toys. These were advertised on our black-and-white television. I would sit on the darkened streets late at night to gaze at the clear, expansive sky and imagine the twinkling light of an aeroplane. I would think for hours about the possibilities of such a robot flying above my head. The dreams of having access to robotic technology like automatic toys or drones were as distant and unimaginable as the aeroplane hovering thousands of feet above my city.

Then came a new commercial on Doordarshan, the only nationally owned TV channel that was freely accessible. This commercial advertised the chewing gum Boomer that offered the lucky prize of a walkie-talkie. It immediately caught my attention and I became obsessed with winning it. I had to collect chewing gum wrappers that would have letters which would eventually spell 'Boomer'. This meant buying six chewing gums at least; if I was lucky enough to get all of them in one stroke, voilà, jackpot! One chewing gum cost 1 rupee. Getting 6 rupees all at once was beyond my capacity. Thus, I had to collect 6 rupees over a week and a half. Finally, I succeeded in collecting 6 rupees. I took the 50 paise, 1 rupee and 2 rupees coins to the posh store located in the dominant-caste area. The Dalit area only had cheap, low-quality products owing to their affordability. Thus, the Banias, with their limited capital but strong networks, would have stores in our areas and sell lower-quality items that were not advertised on TV.

Excitedly, I went to the shop and demanded six sticks of chewing gum. I ate two and safely kept the rest in the secret pocket of my backpack, to be eaten over a few days. I was interested in the wrapper. I got O, the next one was O too, the third was B, the fourth, fifth and sixth were all R. I took the wrappers carefully and put them in the most secure pocket of my backpack. On reaching home, I secretively went to the backyard and started connecting the letters. They spelt BOORRR. I had missed it. The excitement of so many days had been in vain. I was disappointed that I would not get to use a walkie-talkie like in the movies. We did not even have a phone line in our house. Thus, our contact numbers often corresponded with a neighbour's number, followed by PP (private party) indicating their names.

I believed having the latest technology in my hand would give me access to those cliques of classmates who owned high-end goods and socialized with each other. There were competitions between them to display expensive new technologies; some even got gifts from relatives who were settled in the US. Inevitably, this coterie often attracted the jealously of fellow schoolmates.

Apart from making me part of their cliques, a walkie-talkie could also help me learn about their lifestyles. I did know then that they had computers in their homes, and cordless phones which they used to communicate with each other. They also had cars and chauffeurs if they wanted to visit the other end of town when our city buses would stop operating. They also knew about Western pop music—Celine Dion, Backstreet Boys, Michael Jackson and the like would play in their CD-Walkmans. For me, all this was alien but fascinating. It offered an escape from the everyday experiences of hopelessness, hunger, pessimism and poverty. I was committed to acquiring such a lifestyle.

But, here I was, lost in hopelessness, almost about to cry with despair about this wild dream of owning a piece of technology to gain access to the elite world. But I was not prepared to give up. Thus, I hoped to test my luck one more time. I would need an M and an E. That was it! So it was a matter of buying two gums. I begged my mother for 2 rupees. She told me that she didn't have a buck. But I knew she always kept 2 rupees in a safe place for milk, tea and sugar in case an unannounced guest knocked on the door. After over an hour of my pleading, she was tired and gave me the 2 rupees, mumbling a prayer to god that no guests visit us. As soon as I wrapped my fingers around the money, I rushed straight to the posh store. I heard my mom call out to me to take care that I did not get injured; we did not have money for hospital bills.

I rushed to the sahukar of the posh area who gave me a gentle smile, acknowledging my persistence. This time, he allowed me to cross my limitations and put my hand in the jar to select the two gums. I was glad and selectively ran my fingers through the jar and picked two. I immediately opened the gums in his presence and saw that I had got B and R. 'Oh, not again,' I yelled. The man warned me not to make a nuisance in front of his shop. He made it clear through his tone that an Untouchable yelling in front of the shop would dissuade goddess Lakshmi. So he loudly insulted me with his crass voice, calling me names. I was angry but had no other option. His shop was the only place in the area that sold Boomer bubble gum.

A week passed and I was waiting for 5 rupees so that I could get five sticks of gum at once and win the game. By heaven's grace, my grandma was visiting over the weekend. While leaving, she handed me 5 rupees. As soon as I got the dust-laden note, I rushed to the shop and purchased five gums. This time too I got everything except M and E. I was heartbroken and couldn't pursue the quest any further.

One of our Dalit neighbours had started his grocery business a year back. He was our favourite when it came to taking credit as he trusted us and accepted delays in payment. His monthly instalment of our repayment worked out to be nominal, but he did not take advantage of our vulnerability, even though he would at times get annoyed and cold-shoulder us. The shop only offered basic conveniences and had a turnover of not more than 100 rupees per day. His customers were daily-wage labourers, servants and maids who worked in rich areas.

I went up to his shop when his son, Ratan, who was my age, was taking care of it. Since the shop was a makeshift one in the vacant space of their house, Ratan was buried in his books. There was a sign displaying a 50 paise candy that would give one free scratching voucher. The winner of the voucher could win prizes like a bicycle and a 21 inch colour television. The photograph of the television hypnotized me, and I was lost in the delightful dream of owning a television that had a remote control. Owning a TV would also allow me to watch the television serials that were discussed and debated during our lunch breaks. These serials were telecast only on expensive private cable networks. If I was lucky enough to win a set, I would be able to laugh at jokes with my friends in school that had references to the previous night's show and learn about new English music videos on MTV.

All these dreams made me restless with excitement. I was on my toes and jumping from one corner to another. The television set was just one scratch away. I had learned from the Boomer experience that I would have to get at least ten candies to hit the jackpot. Two days passed, and I continued trying. When on the third day too I couldn't manage to get 50 paise, I was tired and frustrated. I would spend time hovering around the shop, checking whether anyone else had won my dream TV. To my surprise, except one boy in my neighbourhood, no one bought the candy. I was amazed with people's restraint in the face of such a luring offer. No one seemed to care. Three days in, and I was buying the candy again and losing again. Ratan finally interjected. 'You want that TV, right?' I nodded. He said, 'Listen, I too would love to have it. But I'm not buying candies even though I own the shop. If I want I can keep all the candies for myself and win. As the lottery says, the lucky one gets the TV.' I was baffled by this shopkeeper who was warning me instead of just doing good business. He continued, 'See, with 50 paise no one is going to give you a TV worth 10,000 rupees. Do you really think this is the case? If it was so, I would have got the TV first and the other prizes these candies claim to offer.' This moment came as a rude shock to my unassailable urge. The traditional arena of business capital deals with the accumulation of wealth acquired fraudulently by exploiting working-class communities.[31]

I remember how the young daughter of a Bania died owing to some illness. The entire basti grieved and expressed their support in their hard times. Because the Bania was a migrant, he did not have enough relatives to mourn the death. Many of his Dalit customers offered free labour during the funeral. However, it was reported that the Dalits were not allowed close to the dead body. They were kept at a distance and assigned jobs that did not violate the sacred codes. The Bania's business was closed for one day. The next day, everything was back to normal.

These traders were infamous for the mistreatment of our womenfolk. I would observe them looking and behaving with mal-intent. Owing to monetary difficulties, Dalit women would often request for credit on their ration. Seeing their helplessness, the grocer would want to exploit them triply—through money, caste—free labour—and sex. I often overheard the grocer talking crudely about the women folks of our basti. Once, his teenaged son proudly bragged about having had sexual intercourse with one of the women in our area. He hinted to the person with such obvious epithets that it was difficult to maintain anonymity. The news spread like wildfire; even women in the basti started talking foul about her. She was cornered by the others, who ganged up to humiliate her. This was caste patriarchy in action. However, some of us saw this as a structural problem of the caste ecology. Hence, we shifted the attention to the son of the grocer and his exploitation—economic, sexual, emotional and caste-based.

When we directed our attention to him, the exploitative caste fraternity was united against us. They recruited some of our folks to intimidate us in return. The movement heated up and it became a question of our community's rights. When the issue became decentralized, the immunity of the oppressor increased. In the cacophony of the larger fight against the oppressor, the grocer and his son got protection.

The same thing happens in our struggle against neo-liberal capitalism. The immediate oppressor, who is an agent of the global corporate invasion, gets away, and our entire focus shifts to the owners; even though the managers are also oppressors in their own right.

Capitalism within Casteism within Feudalism

There is a common thread of mistrust which gives rise to lies and deceit in business exchanges among the dominant castes, which also spills over into the capitalist set-up. Indian capitalism is a Brahmin-sanctioned Bania-controlled model of business. There is a nexus of the spiritual and material fields; the line between the sacred divine and exploitative business blurs as we enter the domain of Indian capitalism. The Indian capitalist scene is an unregulated turf of spiritual fiefs where the religiously ordained permission of ownership of wealth by a caste group validates the oppression by the spiritual. It has not matured to the degrees of sophisticated capital mobility across various class/groups that non-Indian societies experience. However, it has been successful in producing similarly harsh effects on the livelihoods of the poor working class that are witnessed in other capitalist societies.

The purpose of a revolutionary idea is to change a structure. Dalit capitalism seems to passively reinvent, or slightly modify, the wheel of capitalist structures. If Dalit capitalism is to take a stride forward, it begs the question: What type of alternative structure does it strive towards? Or is it merely interested in creating the nouveau riche who will be used as a model objet d'art for feeding the voracity of the market-driven economy?

Would Dalits then fall into the grammar of oppression that is the primary fuel of capitalism, or will the genesis of suppression be transformed into self-help—by creating opportunities for lower- and working-class Dalits, thereby redefining the caste–capital nexus, proposing a new theory of monetary (r)evolution? If it is the former, Dalit capitalism tragically succumbs to the hypnotic romance of capitalism that offers limited social autonomy without its entire reliance on corporate capital intervention. If at all the aim is to challenge the caste structure, the aide-mémoire clearly reveals that caste has triumphed over capitalism. Every day, brutal atrocities against marginalized castes hints at the dominance of the sticky caste system in neo-liberal India.

The process of accumulation begins with embracing corrupt and unethical practices. The concepts of redistribution and accountability of earned wealth are not within the realm of caste capitalism. When the Dalits who have despised the dominant-caste usurper their entire lives see their own kind doing the same, it would have difficult consequences. In the traditional caste set-up, Dalits were kept away from dominant-caste spaces; however, when the Dalit capitalist lives in the same area as the dominant castes and indulges in similar ritual practices, he/she would not be easily forgiven for their exploitative status by exploited Dalits.

This move by Dalits is only going to recast the structure of oppression to accommodate it within the domain of accepted institutions. There is little revolutionary forethought for the structural remaking which every oppressed society seeks to eventually achieve. It would be a disguised self-deception to imagine that a peripheral entity placed on the margins can counter the philosophy of traditional oppression.

Capitalism's deceptive embrace will augment the efforts of canonized Dalits who want to operate within the Brahminical system as silent partners. This will eventually redirect the blame on to Dalits, who will yet again be held solely responsible for their suffering. In the words of Du Bois, in the context of the African Americans, this kind of system would 'shift the burden of the Negro problem to the Negro's shoulders and stand aside as critical and rather pessimistic spectators; when in fact the burden belongs to the nation, and the hands of none of us are clean if we bend not our energies to righting these great wrongs'.[32] Constant and tireless efforts are being made to reinvent the wheel of structural dominance.

History has had a significant influence on the formation of Bania capital. It is a historical process which continues to operate in the present. The invention of dominant-caste supremacy was essentially conceived to validate discrimination and subjugation. Very little is known about the origin of Bania capital formation and the exposition of materiality (material accumulation) if examined through the Marxist historical process. The emergence of the Bania is attributed to the positivist notion of the division of society for it to execute effective management of the 'rogue' social forces—the caste groups considered 'lower'. And to 'regulate' society one has to normalize the caste order and the hierarchy it fosters.

In India, however, the socialist, communist, rationalist and anti-capitalist movements are very happily aligned with the cultural hegemonies worshipped by right-wing capitalist forces. The people in radical movements have close social and cultural ties with hegemonic power brokers, such as temple owners, business owners and feudal lords. Their ideologies may be opposing but due to similar caste fraternities there remains a connection among them that works well even in their movements against each other. The cultural capital that the dominant castes possess works in their favour during the negotiation of social movements. If a person from a similar caste and class background is on the opposite end of the movement there is a possibility of conversation among them due to the existing social relations. However, the same struggles initiated by Dalits cannot see the light of day due to the distant social relations operating in a caste society. So, you can belong to a dominant caste and still be a successful communist. However, you cannot expect similar results in the case of Dalit and other radical movements led by Dalits. There is a social silence and a large gap in communication. One often hears this doing the rounds in social movement circles: 'You can be a Brahmin or a Bania and behold any radical ideas, you can still have a mutual dialogue with the oppressor as s/he is part of your network. Being a Dalit, you can only expect humiliation, non-acknowledgement, incarceration and state/caste-sponsored violence.' The nexus of caste and capital can be seen in dominant-caste-led social movements in theatre, literature and art against bourgeois Bania casteism.

The fight against bourgeois nationalism and neo-liberalism has failed in India. Bourgeois nationalism firmly believes in the ownership and rulership of a few elites over the large exploited mass. The bourgeois nationalism that we inherited was inherent to the dialectic materialism with a strong force of caste sentimentality that was translated into landlordship—feudalism by granting lands to certain agrarian castes, thereby ensuring the retention of the caste structure. By the maintenance of caste, kings, Brahmins and Banias all benefited. However, to effect the control of caste, dominance had to be continued upon lower castes, who were the primary recipients of caste hierarchy. And to do that the person closest to the lowest structure but higher in the hierarchy was detailed with the privilege of ownership of land and everything that was present on it—the tiller's toil, the surplus, the pasture and cultivation.

On the other hand, neo-liberalism taps into the existing loosened social structure of a society to make inroads, and validates the position of the oppressive ruling class. This helps neo-liberalism bring the exploiter on its side. It has so far not been able to involve Dalits alongside Muslims and other minorities in its fold. No one is willing to identify the traditional mercantile castes as an important agent in executing the exploitation of the poor and working class in India. Farmer suicides in India are largely due to the caste–capital nexus. Historically, and up to the present, farmers primarily depend on these castes for credit due to inaccessibility to institutional credit, leaving them at the mercy of middlemen.[33] These middlemen exploit farmers and revoke their land possession by transferring the farmer's lands into their own names by tying them to unescapable debt. In addition, the state policies of neo-liberalism allowing foreign capital and International Monetary Fund–dictated policies of extraction of surplus in the agro-industry, manufacturing and large-chain production units have given a free hand to the dominant castes.

The problem of indebtedness is inherited by succeeding generations; the bondage is persistent. In the Marathwada region, for instance, farmer's children are forced to till land because their land ownership is gone. They are discouraged from taking up education because they are tied to the land which was once their ancestral property and is now owned by dominant-caste groups. A fellow law-school classmate described a horrid situation in his village where all the sahukars and patils (landowning feudal castes) owned the land as well as the children of the tiller of the land who were tied to it through bonded labour.

The labouring groups—the working-class subaltern caste groups in India who actually produce the wealth—are put on the margins of the production cycle. There is no adequate opportunity nor are industries remodelled to benefit them. Giving an opportunity to a handful of Dalits and recruiting them as agents of caste-controlled capitalism is a shrewd strategy to keep the rest of the group under duress.

Caste in the Neo-liberal Agenda

Capitalism in the neo-liberal mould has not delivered on much of the promises that had been made; rather, it has added to the death count of most marginalized people in India. The advent of neo-liberal corporate capitalism from the 1980s onwards could not loosen the grip of caste control on the capital market in India. While economic globalization was welcomed, the cultural forms of articulations, viz., expression of self in a free-market context, individual liberalism and cultural identifiers like sexuality, gender and class could not shake off the entrenched casteism. The for-and-against debates on capitalism made little impact on the everyday life of the marginalized as it succumbed to the power dynamics that forged what Teltumbde refers to as 'unholy alliances'.[34]

In a neo-liberal age, the traditionally wealthy and powerful castes have adjusted well to the capitalist exploration in India. By acting as agents of Western and imperialistic exploitative capital, the mercantile castes impose the neo-liberal will upon the working class, oppressed caste groups. In debates against neo-liberalism in India, seldom does anyone refer to tackling the native capitalist forces before attacking Western imperial structures. The debate of the left movements in India squarely points to the Western imperial order as the central problem while remaining blind to the local, everyday caste oppressions carried out within the new capitalist caste market. This is effectively done by borrowing theories and experiences of other oppressed groups in other countries. Their experiences are made to represent the experiences of the oppressed in India. So a Dalit has to feel the pain of the capitalist exploitation of his counterparts in Asia, Africa and North America. The Dalit remains agentless in the left discourse. Ideally, when Dalits are organized against the oppression of landlords, a clear classification of the caste structures within which feudal society operates should be acknowledged at the outset. Instead, caste is obliterated from the imagination of the Dalit and the struggle. Hence, a Dalit suffers for being Dalit but is not allowed to feel his oppression as one. Instead, he is made out as a non-Dalit, non-caste actor, and limited to only his working-class self.

The murder of Dalit agency gives birth to a consciousless Dalit constituency which is unable to act for the social change of its community. Instead, it rallies for the cause of dominant-caste comrades who are doing their job of protecting their community by not naming them and their caste oppression. They put the cauldron into the hands of a phantasmagorical outsider—an imagined one—to which a Dalit never has access. This oppression just remains in the imagination of a Dalit, who rarely experiences it simply as a 'worker'. Even in the left movement, Dalits experience the power of the dominant castes over them.[35] Therefore, a concretized Dalit involvement in the revolutionary project remains unrealized. Dominant-caste leftists have safeguarded their caste brethren from the revolutionary outcomes of oppressed caste–class folks. The left movement without a conscious radical Ambedkarite Dalit involvement is a failed project and a sad episode in India's history in terms of the real liberation of the working class.

Thus, the vision of the crony leftists[36] in India was limited by the understanding of capitalism as theorized by Marx, Lenin and Mao. They blindly rejected the native revolutionaries who lived and understood Indian society's pains far more intensely. In the Marxist framework in India, there is little focus on caste-based capitalist exploitation. Phule and Ambedkar remain ignored and despised figures, and uncomfortable 'ram-baan'[37] for curing India of vested Brahminical polity.

The sahukar who is at the helm of subaltern castes (Dalits and other oppressed castes) exploitation is the first 'class enemy' alongside the Brahmin who came to dictate his terms upon our consciousness. The distance of consciousness from Dalit thraldom through the Brahminical indoctrination of withdrawing human dignity and pride from Dalits impeded the process of articulating our suffering, thereby effectively hampering the revolution. It was Phule who first gave a rebellious framing to subaltern castes' being. He marshalled the consciousness of the collective oppressed, which he fondly termed as 'Bahujan', incorporating pan-Dalit, Shudra, Muslims and women of all castes. Ambedkar then introduced a courageous praxis and put it into the language of human and civil rights. He did not stop there but started to claim political rights as being central to his *dialectical materialism*, largely concerned with the social transformation and material processes.[38] His class-based approach to India's problems is underestimated and a long-missed opportunity. The huge influence of Marx upon the world and thereby upon Ambedkar is evident in the scores of Marxist books to be found in Ambedkar's library.[39]

Ambedkar's simultaneous war on orthodox Hindu dogmas alongside caste-inspired class battle put him in a unique position. He was the living model of a sophisticated thinker and a serious threat to paradoxical Indian society. That is perhaps the reason Ambedkar is the most loved and hated person in India. The sentiment towards Ambedkar—positive or negative—arises out of the desire to either destroy or maintain the status quo.

~

Thus, we come to view Dalit capitalism aggressively anchoring in the global experiences of capital and labour mobility in contemporary times. Dalit capitalism has experiences of imitation (of dominant-caste capitalism) at best and comparative experiences of other oppressed groups (the African Americans) as second-best options to choose from). It has deviated from originating a new theory of capital accumulation and its redistribution mechanism. Economic mobility as a passage for social stabilization, as promised in the Dalit capitalist discourse, needs to be substantiated. So far, it doesn't seem to offer that confidence. On this duality, it seems apposite to reminisce about Baburao Bagul, the founding father of the Dalit and Marathi literary movement. Bagul notes that the Indian version of post-colonial capitalism developed to fight minor battles of the elite classes, who have been widening the class divide by unequal concentration of wealth. The major battles referred to social inequalities. The myth of Indian democracy is, paradoxically, strengthened by the capitalist forms which accommodate social, economic and religious inequality. The legal measures of protection of the marginalized are another form of subversion of the legal ethic where legal doctrines in a capitalist democracy merely postpone the implementation of effective laws. By doing this, the traditional codes of conduct are maintained and thus untouchability remains unattended and untouched. The emergence of capital-directed democracy only produces inequalities of all forms, mainly 'economic, religious and racial', comments Bagul. He continues:

Economic development through capitalism does not necessarily solve social problems. On the contrary, the development of capitalism gives rise to war, colonialism and Fascism, as can be seen from history. It is capitalism which has imposed the utmost number of wars on human life; wars fought to capture colonies and markets . . . to suppress movements and philosophies antagonistic to its ideology. Thus, economic development motivated by profit does not necessarily solve social problems.[40]

Adding a further layer, Bagul compares social movements that failed to produce a programme to solve the problems of untouchability. The economic foundations of society are intimately tied to human suffering. The social structure that is generationally framed and developed responds to the modern techné of power relations. The pain in Dalit thought is not an imaginary one. It is a concretely felt emotion which is not abstract. Thus, the global commentary on suffering evades a certain kind of esoteric particularity which does not necessarily localize the temperament.

The elites in India who populate the market, control the state, and rule the social order legitimize their profligacy by parading themselves as the benefactors of globalization. The larger experiences of the caste-cemented ecology of capitalism is not limited to the economic sphere, it spills over to the social health of people, where the social welfare policy of the state is subverted and instead shifted to the charitable conduits of corporate social responsibility. An institution like DICCI, which is operating under various forms of discrimination, is pushed further to the margins. It doesn't have any purchase to influence the market, let alone the state and society. Thus, Dalit capitalism is the farcical face of an oppressive and exploitative order.

The 'solution' of Dalit capitalism and creating a few millionaires are predicated on the extraneous notions of acquiring wealth without due consideration of the complexity of caste.

By this logic, the emancipatory tradition and ethical values of Dalits—which are essential to liberating them—are crushed. The rich values that outperform the modes of oppression are sidelined. Thus, scholars like Gopal Guru identify the resurgence of Dalit capitalism as the 'spectacle' that produces a false perception to generate 'high-profile consumerist consciousness' among lower-working-class Dalits. This results in forming a 'low-intensity spectacle' that is interested in personal gain over the communal. And thus, Dalit capitalism is seen struggling to gain 'larger visibility and recognition in the real life of the corporate class'.[41]

Dalit capitalism is the romantic idea that capitalism is a solution; it does not acknowledge that capitalism is a problem to begin with and a pernicious system to have. It is ardently sold to the general public with the aid of popular culture and media. A few Dalit figures are repeatedly projected as success stories of capitalism. They are given generous space in the media. Thus, to fit into the caricatures of media presentations, these Dalit capitalists participate in reproducing the myths of 'success stories'. Many aspiring Dalit entrepreneurs and venture capitalists who go to solicit their guidance are given their books or magazine articles profiling them as reference points. On the ground, however, there is no assistance for credit or to establish a start-up for budding entrepreneurs. There are many regional and local Dalit entrepreneur groups which are informally connected with each other and work more effectively than these organized capitalist gangs. By brandishing the image of Dalit success stories, the capitalist framework paints an ideal picture: one day you will also win the lottery and ascend to the top; that is, win the 21 inch colour TV you had dreamt of. Such lies are constantly penetrated into poor neighbourhoods and working-class Dalit shanties. A single Dalit success is taken as a sign of guaranteed success available to all Dalits. Dalits are not only hungry for economic and political emancipation but also for 'identity, meaning and self-worth' as other oppressed and degraded people of the world, Cornel West reminds us.[42]

Dalit capitalism is a smokescreen. There are no guarantees provided by these promoters about the outcome of such a project of Dalit emancipation guided through entrepreneurial development. Will these few successes guarantee the overturning of hegemony and an end of the caste system? The caste system is not only a Hindu religio-social order but a mythical product advanced for material denigration. Capitalism may offer upward mobility to the historically oppressed. The subaltern masses who seldom had purchasing and negotiating power won't be given it en masse. If ever there will be so-called Dalit personalities, they will be attuned to the ideology of mythical progress framed in caste cartography and denuded individuality. An individual is a composite being of communitarian principles where everyone is one, and not one is everyone. This is the value that a powerful community sets closer to its raison d'être. The Dalit community is a model of applying the universalist ethos of care and nurture amidst paucity.

In sincere appreciation of conservative Booker T. Washington's work, many Indians in the early nineteenth century found his position identical to Ambedkar's. Speaking on the floor of the Bombay Legislative Assembly, a representative of Karachi, N.A. Bechar, complimented the works of Ambedkar. He added that just as President Lincoln 'who, by one stroke of the pen, freed the whole of the Negro population from slavery in America and let me hope further that in fullness of time my friend Dr Ambedkar will become for his people Booker T. Washington'.[43] The comparison was slightly misplaced in terms of Ambedkar's socialist endeavours; however, it was closer in terms of Washington's indomitable conviction in uplifting his people by establishing institutions. On the other hand, both Ambedkar's and Du Bois's vision was for the liberation of the toiling masses. Du Bois had said, 'The hope of the future of the Negro race in America and the world lies far more among its workers than among its college graduates', a turnover from his Talented Tenth.[44] Ambedkar, too, was a poor person's politician who marshalled the politics of workers aiming to align the Dalit cause with that of the workers of the world.[45] His efforts hit the caste wall and thus he turned to the caste–class strategies of organizing.

Capitalism is a manufactured system that, in India, works in tandem with the deeply rooted oppression of caste, whether in villages or urban bastis or in the shiny offices of corporate boards in big cities; this nexus plays out to trap the oppressed on the inescapable path to perpetual suffering.

6

Brahmins against Brahminism

'He, whoever has burnt his caste, is my comrade.'

—Kabir

'To My Old Master . . .
I will not bring this letter to a close; you shall hear from me
again unless you let me hear from you. I intend to make use
of you as a weapon with which to assail the system of slavery
— as a means of concentrating public attention on the system,
and deepening the horror of trafficking in the souls and bodies
of men. I shall make use of you as a means of exposing the
character of the American church and clergy — and as a means
of bringing this guilty nation, with yourself, to repentance. In
doing this, I entertain no malice toward you personally. There
is no roof under which you might need for your comfort,
which I would not readily grant. Indeed, I should esteem it a
privilege to set you an example as to how mankind ought to
treat each other.'

—Frederick Douglass, 1848

'[Brahmins] have been the most inveterate enemy of the
servile classes [Shudras and the Untouchables] who together
constitute about 80 per cent of the total Hindu population.
If the common man belonging to the servile classes in India is

242

today so fallen, so degraded, so devoid of hope and ambition, it is entirely due to the Brahmins and their philosophy.'

—Ambedkar, *What Congress and Gandhi Have Done to the Untouchables*

'The brahmins do not talk about caste wherever they are in dominance and make money, but discriminate Parayars in the name of caste wherever they seek to work.'

—Iyothee Thass[1]

A random event invitation popped up on my smartphone. I usually don't bother to read every notification but this one caught my attention. It was eerily titled 'Knapsack Anti-Racism Group'. The description of the meeting invited participants to discuss how to communicate with their families on the topic of racism. Intrigued by this thought, I rushed to the YMCA meeting point in Cambridge, Massachusetts. I was welcomed by a group of diversely colourful but predominantly White women in their twenties. I was slightly late to arrive due to the New England blizzard, and thus walked in in the middle of an ongoing discussion.

A short-haired White woman in her fifties was the co-convener of the meeting along with her Black female colleague of Caribbean descent who seemed to be in her late twenties. A White queer woman in her early twenties who introduced herself as an engineering student narrated a story of racism in her house. 'My mom hired a Mexican construction worker to fix our roof. She was very sensitive about his racial identity. She refused to invite him in the house and told me stories about "these" men.' The narration varied between high and low pitches as she tried to explain her internalized experiences of racism. Her hands rested on the table while she kept her gaze pointed to the ground, avoiding eye contact as she narrated her story. She accused her mother of not giving her the opportunity to think about fellow human beings as human beings and instead profiling a person of Mexican origin.

Then, a lady next to her, another White working woman in her late twenties, stated her racist experiences at a family get-together. 'Whenever we meet for get-togethers there's an agreement in our family to not discuss politics and race. But somehow it simmers under the surface of our regular exchanges. There's someone who accidentally touches the issue and we are doomed to disagree on the questions of American racism.'

One male manager in his twenties commented that he tried to be a radical, but his radicalism did not help him recruit employees. Therefore, he preferred to present his liberal side to candidates. He mentioned this to state that his radical ideas were not acceptable to his White family and White counterparts.

As the event concluded, I realized that it was an event for White folks who would go back to their family reunions for Thanksgiving and come across internalized forms of racism. It was a training session to tackle the 'knapsack of racism' that one carried as a privilege and without conscious acknowledgement.

The meeting's aim was to re-conceptualize the issue of race in day-to-day life. After the event, I did some research about this initiative. I came across a formidable White lady, Peggy McIntosh, who appeared on TV shows, attended news briefings, conducted training programmes everywhere from NASA's Goddard Space Center to the American Society for Engineering Education, the House of Bishops of the Episcopal Church and many more such organizations of power and knowledge by demonstrating how White racism was a privilege that most White people conveniently carry but do not want to see. In her 1988 paper entitled 'White Privilege and Male Privilege',[2] McIntosh identified forty-six blind spots of White privilege—instances where a person's skin colour gave them an undue advantage. 'If these things are true, this is not such a free country,' concluded McIntosh. In an interview, she asserted that we all live in a world that is 'a combination of unearned advantage and unearned disadvantage in life'.[3] Many people on the side of privilege seldom see privilege as it is visible to the naked eye shrouded within the artefacts of material culture. There is a blindfolding when it comes to privilege. It is seen as an exterior element, attributable to the lavish expenditure of only the elite class. It is never personalized, nor looked at as something which one harbours in day-to-day life. One is quick to present oneself in the garb of victimhood when the question of privilege is raised.

On another instance, during the 2016 US presidential elections, I witnessed the racial politics of America first-hand. Almost every discussion and rally mentioned the undertones of race in guiding the American life. Democrats presented themselves as liberals, whereas Republicans held their ground as conservatives. As the primaries were getting closer, I could spot white people—young and old—canvassing for alternatives to the conservative politics of the Republican Party. They were trying to present an image of America to White Americans that was still not that popular. I was told by an organizer friend in the Boston area, Umang, that these White people were committed to the ideology of non-racialism. Their job was to knock the doors of White people and have a conversation about White ignorance that plays a part in forming a conservative consensus. Liberal White people targeted conservative and liberal White voters to educate them about the importance of progressive politics.

In these two instances, I couldn't help but draw similarities with the Indian context. Here, in contrast, the privileged-caste citizens of the Brahminical world seldom talk about or question the notions of privilege when discussing caste—with a few exceptions.[4] The structural issues of class, gender and caste are presented to us without adequate emphasis on recognizing one's own privilege. Therefore, the struggle against an oppressive system simply gets passed on, becomes a problem of the Other. The invisible Others are made responsible for curbing the mayhem in society without accounting for one's personal responsibility in perpetuating it.

Such attitudes are glaringly visible in the anti-caste struggle. Many individuals of the dominant-caste fold come to the Dalit struggle without accounting for their compliance in an unequal system that executes systemic oppression upon Dalits. 'How can I be a casteist if I am working in the movement against caste?' is the usual refrain heard time and again. It is the same as a man declaring himself free of patriarchal sensibilities by virtue of his participation in the women's movement. We all have to acknowledge that we owe a greater debt to oppressed groups than mere symbolic rhetoric. This quest to find the oppressor group's acknowledgement of being complicit in oppression led me to investigate the role of Brahmins in the anti-caste struggle. Did Brahmins ever participate in this struggle? Or did they often choose to sit on the sidelines? Were Brahmins united in their understanding of the Dalit struggle? Or did they have varying or contradicting opinions on the question of caste? These questions directed me to the annals of the anti-caste movement's two most formidable personalities: Phule and Ambedkar. Looking at Phule's and Ambedkar's organizational activities, one can easily spot the participation of Brahmin and non-Dalit individuals who braved the prevalent Brahmin orthodoxy by choosing to denounce it. By chronicling their contribution to the anti-caste struggle in this chapter, I present how knowledge and discourses get shaped by the people who are secondary victims, even as their primary position remains that of oppressor. The Brahmins' acknowledgement of privilege led to their participation in the anti-Brahminic movement. Their contribution to the struggle, however, remains unknown.

On this note, let us look at the Brahmin position in contemporary India, followed by the individual Brahmins who were important participants in the struggle to tear down the caste system. To start with, the progressive, moderate and radical Brahminical class has been historically participating in progressive movements ever since the recorded history of the Buddha. The first contingent of Gautama Buddha's monks were Brahmins. This was one of the first minority groups that accepted the egalitarian ethos of the time by going against their kith and kin. Such Brahmins did not, however, represent the entirety of the heterogeneous Brahmins who differed from oppressive Brahmins. It is widely misunderstood that 'Brahmin' is a homogeneous category. On the contrary, it is hugely divided along approximately 500 sub-castes, class and regional lines. Addressing a conference hosted by the Belgaum District Depressed Classes in 1929, Ambedkar referred to the hegemony of Maharashtrian Brahmins in the political affairs of the state. He placed the Brahmins of other provinces, viz., Gujarat, Punjab and United Provinces, to a lower economic ranking compared to the dominating *peshwas*.[5] The RSS, which remains an unregistered organization, is single-handedly controlled by the Maharashtrian Kharade Brahmins.[6] The Brahmins from other states and sub-castes undergo subordination at the hands of dominant-caste Brahmins,[7] whose suffering does not feature in the popular discourse.

The Control over 'Unspiritual' Wealth

The 85 per cent Elite Brahmin Media

What India consumes today in the form of news is basically Brahmin propaganda. A study by the Centre for the Study of Developing Societies (CSDS) found that in 2008 '[t]op Upper Castes'—the Brahmins—had an 85 per cent share in key media positions, compared to the Scheduled Castes and Scheduled Tribes, which was nil.[8]

As of 2018 too, the media remains a business of Brahmins with their extensive editorial and journalistic control over narratives. A Deshastha (Maharashtrian) Brahmin editor friend once jokingly said to me, 'The media is a monopoly of Tam Brahms [Tamil Brahmins]. Even we are intimidated to enter their fiefdom.' Something similar was echoed by Ambedkar seventy years ago as he found no faith in the Brahmin-run press which he termed the fiefdom of 'Madras Brahmins' that was antagonistic to the Dalit cause. Thus, he decided to launch his own print publications. *Mook Nayak* (Leader of the Voiceless, 1920), *Bahishkrit Bharat* (The Ostracized India, 1927), *Janata* (Masses, 1930) and *Prabuddha Bharat* (Awakened India, 1956) were born to this effect. Additionally, an organization called the Samata Sangh was floated by Ambedkar, and another newspaper, *Samata* (Equality, 1928), was launched with Devrao Vishnu Naik as its editor.

In current times, Robin Jeffery's detailed study of India's print media, entitled *India's Newspaper Revolution* (2009), found no Dalit representation in the newsroom and on the editorial board of 300 media decision-makers. Similarly, *Washington Post* South Asia bureau chief Kenneth Cooper had discovered back in 1996 that over 4000 Indian newspapers published in 100 languages hardly had India's lower castes, mostly Dalits, represented. 'Not one daily newspaper has made speaking on their behalf its role,' Cooper commented, drawing from his experience of reporting from India for over two decades.[9]

Young, dynamic Dalit journalist Sudipto Mondal, who has covered some of the bravest stories in coastal Karnataka and in the aftermath of Rohith Vemula's suicide, found himself surrounded by Brahmin and Bania editors he had to report to and follow the commands of. He had no one in his profession who hailed from his own social background who could understand his issues and support him as a Dalit journalist in the casteist news business. Living a life of caste isolation in the Brahmin media ecology, Mondal took it upon himself to find Dalit journalists. After ten years of searching, he was successful in finding 'eight Dalit journalists in the English media'. Of them, only two have risked 'coming out'. Of the eight, half couldn't survive the casteist environment. Mondal charted out the stages of the pipelining of Indian journalists who carry regressive caste biases from their training at elite journalism schools into their profession. Drawing from his experience of studying and working in elite media spaces, Mondal presents to us a visual that is appallingly undemocratic and backward-thinking. He comments, 'The predominance of the Brahmin in the profession is as old as English journalism in this country. But what's truly distressing is that more than 200 years on, the modern journalism classroom is almost a replica of the typical Indian English newsroom'[10]—à la protected Agrahara.

Like Mondal, I met two Dalit journalists working in mainstream English publications who had found their names listed in Mondal's eight. These two are among the higher ranks and have a massive following. Their writing meets at the cusp of literary attainment and journalistic rigour, a quality not found in many scribblers. These two journalists have unchallenged, academically proven résumés. Despite their qualification and established journalistic credentials, they fear coming out. They are afraid that their writing will be typecast, which will come at a huge cost as it will invite a jaundiced view. The two journalists prefer to be in the mainstream and continue to be acceptable in society and the media industry for their merit. They are 'passing Dalits' who are trying to find their autonomy without anyone's prejudicial thinking. They do not want their writing to be categorized as Dalit writing. They want to be able to write independently like other dominant castes without fear of being judged. These few select

Dalit journalists find themselves surrounded by an establishment that is busy plotting new means to undermine their community. They are afraid, and this is reflected in their thoughts—unless they are totally freed, no radical humanist project will birth from their pens.

On television sets, Sharmas and Pandeys are seen flashing on screens in prime-time programmes. These people offer no clear remedies to the problems of millions that tune in. The TV news industry has now become a way to pass the time than a knowledge-seeking endeavour. There is not a single personality on TV who can claim to have a Dalit background. Dalits feature in TV news panels when Dalits are lynched, raped, murdered and made victims of arson. The value of a Dalit is priced according to the number of dead Dalits. Egregious atrocities that get reported invite Dalit panelists. However, Dalits do not feature in debates on environmental issues, climate change, economic affairs, planning commissions, media analysis, film and television, feminism discussions, LGBTIQA issues, communalism, political commentary or foreign matters; they are not seen offering sociological, economic, political and cultural insight to any particular problem. This has to do with the absence of Dalits in newsrooms. A Dalit perspective to the above areas of discussion would add a layer of sensible reporting. However, there is no urge to gather Dalit opinion on issues of national importance. Currently, there is no known Dalit working as a regularly paid columnist in any English-language newspaper in India except me. It is the result of the widely accepted casteist attitude that Dalits are incapable of thinking for themselves.

Corruption Scandals

The issue of scandals and corruption in India is endemic. The major national scandals are birthed and anchored largely by the dominant-caste groups, but its blame is often flung towards the non-privileged caste groups. The infamous 2G corruption scandal of the UPA-2 government was widely reported. A. Raja, a Dalit lawmaker from Tamil Nadu, was the prime accused in the case. During the widespread allegations, Raja's Dalit identity was often invoked to reinforce his corrupt caste character. Similar targeted accusations have been directed in the past against Mayawati, Lalu Prasad Yadav, Madhu Koda, Shibu Soren and other SC, ST and OBC elected lawmakers. In the same vein, however, the caste of corrupt dominant-caste leaders was never brought up. Their corruption was not seen as a representation of their caste character, only of their individual character. A simple google search of 'corrupt politicians in India' will mostly direct you to SC, ST and OBC leaders.

~

In the Harvard Kennedy School yard, I bump into Indian students who join my table during luncheon hours. After pleasantries and introductions, they inquire about my research. I blurt out, 'I study the caste system.' 'Nice. Do you study caste here (US) or in India?' Deepan, a mid-career bureaucrat, asks. I reply that I study it in both regions. Deepan gets interested and asks more questions but his aim is actually to find out my caste. Ten minutes into the conversation, it is still not established. Deepan gives up; I continue. This is how every conversation between a Dalit and a dominant-caste person goes: the latter wants to establish that India's caste problem is the fault of all Dalits, and I am compelled to defend my community against his accusations. Deepan and his two friends at the table start jumping to conclusions without even beginning to know my opinions. I tease them further. The conversation is, predictably, about lower-caste politicians, reservation, merit and corruption. Without further ado, Deepan

starts lamenting about the corruption of Indian politicians, and
the most obvious name he takes is of Lalu Prasad Yadav. 'Lalu
was a casteist who openly practised casteism. He only promoted
backward-caste bureaucrats. Prior to this it was an unknown
phenomenon. He was hardly educated and was responsible for
all the havoc in the state. A person with little respect for law; had
no educational standards.' I intervened to correct him that Lalu
had a law degree and spoke English pretty well; perhaps he had
missed his deliberations in Parliament. I reminded him that the
promotion of a disproportionate number of Brahmin bureaucrats
was normalized, a fact to which he was completely blinded.
Only when 'lower'-caste OBC bureaucrats were raised to higher
positions was it perceived as a problem.

Lalu's most famous alleged corruption scandal was the fodder
scam, which was originated by his Brahmin predecessor, Jagannath
Mishra. Mishra was booked for five cases in the scam, one of which
was registered by the CBI in 1996. Currently, Mishra is facing
two trials related to the case.[11] Lalu inherited the corrupt system.
However, the media and the entire political spectrum chose to
zero in on the fodder scam placing the entirety of blame on Lalu.
Fellow Indian students at the lunch table found reason after reason
to discredit Lalu's leadership. These are too petty and irrational
to find a mention here. But all of them were oriented towards
confirming the inability of the likes of Lalu Yadav and Mayawati to
run the affairs of state. These Harvard students bluntly overlooked
the morass created by earlier dominant-caste chief ministers. They
did not have any definite party affiliation, but they were united
in one belief and norm: to uphold the dominant-caste political
discourse by berating 'lower'-caste politicians.

The new language of political casteism is corruption.
Corruption is equated with Dalit and lower-caste practices.
This is why the 2011 anti-corruption movement in India was
able to successfully galvanize the otherwise apolitical or 'neutral'

educated urban class. It launched the careers of many dominant-caste wannabe politicians. The corruption of politicians was held as a primary target. Along with the political class, the judiciary was also declared corrupt. Of all the chief justices, only one was targeted by his name and caste:[12] K.G. Balakrishnan, the first Dalit chief justice of India and the former chief of the National Human Rights Commission. Such is the fate of Dalit elites in positions of power. They continue to be haunted by their caste, regardless of their achievements. And it is the visible Dalits who are the first to receive negative attention. They are most unwelcome in liberal spaces of democracy. Thus, we witness baseless accusations and falsified stories being floated against

India's Cabinets Have Always Had Socially Skewed Composition

Columns show percentage share of different social groups in Union Cabinet

■ Upper-middle caste Hindus ■ Muslims ▦ Non-Muslim minorities ▦ SC ■ ST

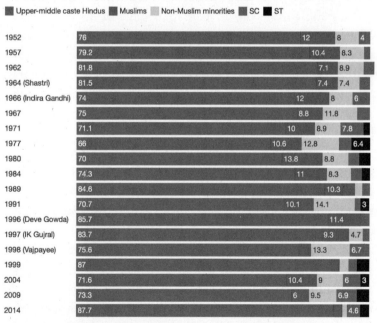

Year	Upper-middle caste Hindus	Muslims	Non-Muslim minorities	SC	ST
1952	76	12	8		4
1957	79.2	10.4	8.3		
1962	81.8	7.1	8.9		
1964 (Shastri)	81.5	7.4	7.4		
1966 (Indira Gandhi)	74	12	8	6	
1967	75	8.8	11.8		
1971	71.1	10	8.9	7.8	
1977	66	10.6	12.8		6.4
1980	70	13.8	8.8		
1984	74.3	11	8.3		
1989	84.6		10.3		
1991	70.7	10.1	14.1		3
1996 (Deve Gowda)	85.7		11.4		
1997 (IK Gujral)	83.7		9.3	4.7	
1998 (Vajpayee)	75.6		13.3	6.7	
1999	87				
2004	71.6	10.4	9	6	3
2009	73.3	6	9.5	6.9	
2014	87.7			4.6	

Upper-middle castes include both forward and OBCs

Source: Mint research based on data compiled by Gilles Verniers at Ashoka University

Dalits in public spheres. Two senior BJP leaders, Dilip Singh Judeo and Bangaru Laxman, were caught on camera accepting cash. However, their individual fates were turned different. Judeo was rehabilitated, fielded in the parliamentary elections, whereas Laxman, the erstwhile president of the BJP, was disowned.[13] What led to such differential treatment? Laxman was a Dalit and Judeo was not. Mind you, Laxman was the BJP's national president.

In the corporate sector, which is disproportionately controlled by dominant castes, all scandals are orchestrated by them. A cursory glance at some of the frauds depicts the reality.[14] Due to this epidemic, India has witnessed the repetition of tragedies. Harshad Mehta,[15] Vijay Mallya[16] and B. Ramalinga Raju[17] are some infamous names that immediately come to mind when we think about corporate scandals. In addition, some large-scale scandals that are still alive in public memory because of the involvement of crores of rupees include the 2010 Commonwealth Games scandal,[18] Sahara scandal,[19] Sharadha scandal,[20] Surya Pharma,[21] Winsome Diamond,[22] IGI Airport GMR DIAL Scam,[23] Mundhra Scandal (known as India's Very First Corruption Scandal),[24] and so on. However, the Jeep scandal of 1948 takes the credit for being the first.[25]

This above list is certainly not exhaustive. The scams by government officials, private individuals and corporations amount to defaults of more than $60 billion. The amount increases as we add the mercantile castes to the list. We have also not taken a serious look at the temple-led corruptions, like the church scandals in the West that have been under scrutiny in recent years. The absolute control over spirituality—temples, rituals and wealth amassed from the torridity of godly guilt—is akin to the medieval-era Vatican extortion from the church's subjects. The Brahmin priests outdo Vatican practices; they control the subaltern public by managing religious rituals.

But while some church reforms have taken place over the centuries, and investigative journalism in the West has exposed such corruptions, Indian temples and their practices remain unquestioned. Although a government body has been established to oversee its functioning, there is very little public scrutiny and media intervention into the business of temple management and organization. Political parties too have shied away from opening up a critical dialogue on the looted wealth of the non-Brahmin public. The institution of the temple continues to be in command of significant wealth and power.

It appears that the dominant castes who have access to caste networks and social capital use them to loot the country without any accountability. The investigative agencies, political class and bureaucracy that complete the nexus work to conveniently let them off the hook.[26] In addition to the corruption by these dominant-caste groups, there are plenty of landed caste groups who are seen as neo-Kshatriyas. Given the extent of their wealth, they might easily jump a rung or two up the ladder to acquire neo-Bania status. A simple google search reveals the large amounts looted by thugs from public sector banks, thereby punishing taxpayers by increasing taxes to recover the looted amount. Reserve Bank of India data revealed that between 2012 and 2017, the 'loan fraud' cases figure went up to 612.6 billion rupees.[27]

In response to these scandals, the government of India pledged to inject $32 billion to bail out the banking sector.[28] The government, which allowed banks to hand over public money to defaulters, is now using the public money to keep the structure of the corrupt sector intact, without solving the deeper problem and using it for social welfare relief programmes for the needy and vulnerable. Taxpayer money is not available to them in the form of loans or credit lending for building small businesses. The fraudulent acts are still not seen as crimes by the court of law but as a matter of civic dispute. Most defaulters are acquitted by the court or are living rich lives as celebrities. Harshad Mehta, known as the 'Baap of Bank Frauds', who was among the first of neo-liberal India's scammers, was out of prison for a long time and even made a comeback as a popular market guru.[29]

In this corruptible morass, we see some judges catching up too. The exposé of the judiciary's involvement in the land allotment case is one such instance. The Karnataka State Judicial Department Employees House Building Cooperative Society offered plots at huge subsidies to the court employees. The nobility of certain dominant-caste judges came to dust when they applied for the plots against the orders of the Supreme Court, and later handed over their 500 times more expensive plots to family members.[30] After surveying the cases of corruption in India, Shekhar Gupta wondered whether those who are supposed to be running the country and are accountable to the citizenry are against the subaltern sections of Indian society.[31]

All the above-mentioned scandals are reported incidents which occur in the public domain. However, in private spheres, unaccounted corruption, non-payment of wages and dues, and harassment of Dalits continues unabated.

Now that we have established that Brahmins are a singular group that largely rules all public aspects of India, let's examine how 'other' Brahmins did in the past in terms of wrestling with ill-gotten caste privileges and take a look at the movements of anti-Brahminism led by progressive Brahmins.

Early Anti-Caste Brahmins

In western India, Swami Chakradhar founded a popular sect known as Mahanubhav. The first written Marathi text, *Lilacharitra*[32] (thirteenth century), which details his incidents and life discourses and forthright instances of Brahmin rebellion against Brahmins and Brahminism—known at the time as *brahmanya* and *brahmnatva*, respectively. It is the text of a society that highlighted progressive Brahmins' rivalries and trysts with orthodox Brahmins.[33]

Chakradhar offered critiques to the order of the day. In the tradition he began, the premium on one's status was not determined by caste. Therefore, his followers and the people around him received flak for practising casteism, including many Brahmins who continued to embrace caste-based stereotypes and prejudices. Chakradhar maintained his anti-caste stand for as long as the person receiving it could take it. But he did not push it too aggressively, at times accommodating for his followers' comfort, rather than hurting them. He rarely forced 'them to radically transgress caste norms outside their small circle'.[34] Owing to his anti-caste activities, his Brahmin followers began to question his caste and debated about his caste background. His piety was acknowledged but his caste remained under question. His followers discussed among themselves: 'Yes, sure, sure. Chakradhar is God. But what is his caste?'[35] Chakradhar proved his Deshastha Brahmin origins without much enthusiasm as he declared his vision of non-caste-conscious society. He subverted the notion of purity attached to caste. He asserted that the one who rejected Brahminical ways of life was 'purer' than anyone else.

During this time, we see an interesting mix of anti-caste reformist movements being embraced by Brahmins. The primary critique of caste came against the more priestly Brahmins who tended to enjoy more privileges and maintained supremacist values. Various incidents in *Lilacharitra* studied by Christian Lee Novetzke takes a look at such anti-orthodox actions. *Lilacharitra* is a text that primarily critiques divisions based on caste, gender and language. Novetzke suggests that around 90 per cent of the lilas feature or centre around a Brahmin figure. Thus, *Lilacharitra* becomes a text providing 'Brahminic critique

of Brahminism . . . that forms its own veritable ethnology of caste
and caste practices'.[36] In the life of Chakradhar, who represented
the reformist tradition, many incidents suggest how he personally
embodied his critique. When he saw a dead dog on the street, he
carried it on his head and disposed of the carcass. As we know,
a carcass is associated with impurity and its removal is a lowly
job designated for Untouchables. He also dined at the homes of
Untouchables, tribals and castes lower in the order.

He ended the tradition of Brahmins asking for alms only from
Brahmins or 'upper'-caste families, and suggested getting alms
from the homes of people belonging to all castes. As the concept
of purity and impurity of cooked food was prevalent, Bhatobas
(a Brahmin caste name) would ask for only uncooked food from
the lower castes and be rude towards them. In Chakradhar's sect,
Mahanubhav, Brahmins were recommended to beg for food not as
Brahmins but as renunciates to dissolve caste barriers. 'You should
beg food from all four castes as Dharma Shastras instruct.'[37] His
directions came at a time when Brahmins would flaunt their
janeu, the sacred thread, to get better alms than non-Brahmins.
From the thirteenth century onwards, the western Maharashtrian
tradition had a rebellious character against Brahminical values,
often led by Brahmins themselves. Much of the Brahmin-led
critique was premised on the duality of self, a paradox of being a
reformer. On the one side the Brahmins were invested in retaining
the Brahmin caste character and at the same time offer critiques
to Brahminism and its practises around caste. Novetzke calls this
'Brahmin double'—which is premised on 'reformist critique'[38] as
opposed to the radical uprooting of such a system. This meant
to work up to a level and then 'retreat[ing] from the critique just
enough to avoid significant trouble'.[39]

As the colonial century dawned upon India, we saw two
prominent anti-caste intellectuals rising against the Brahminical
state to create a caste-diverse coalition in the nineteenth and

twentieth centuries. These were Phule and Ambedkar, and their Brahmin and non-Dalit comrades lent their voice and active support to the anti-caste struggle.

The Brahmin Comrades of Phule and Ambedkar

Jotirao Phule (1827–90) and B.R. Ambedkar (1891–1956) lived during the times of the colonial regime in India. Sometime after it established its dominance in the mid-nineteenth century, the East India Company slightly relaxed caste rules for its own benefit in western India. The erstwhile Peshwa government there—a Brahmin monarchy—used to supplement state resources towards the education of Brahmins. As the East India Company's rule strengthened, it needed administrative support for governance. Thus, it opened up opportunities for English-educated Indians —a product of Macaulay's education policy to create 'Indian[s] in blood and colour, but English in taste, in opinions, in morals and in intellect'. These anglophone Indians, who comfortably became Macaulay's new 'class', had worked in the rural and urban gentry and had the knowledge of Indian society and some of the British as well. These positions were a convenient way for the Company to hire dominant-caste groups in positions of power in order to rein in local working-class dissent. Brahmins were the front runners to apply for these positions. They did not waste time in acquiring the strategic positions that placed them in a mediatory role between the Company's administration and the ruled masses. By virtue of their free access to education, Brahmins single-handedly occupied these positions. A survey during 1886–87 detailed the positions of Indian castes in the administration. Of the 328 Hindus, 211 were Brahmins, 26 Kshatriyas, 37 Prabhus, 38 Vaishyas or Banias, 1 a Shudra and 15 others.[40]

In addition to their traditional religious authority, Brahmins were now armed with additional powers—administrative and

political. This gave little space to lower-caste groups to escape
the thralldom of Brahmin oppression. Brahmins acted as the
handlers of exploitative British governance by paying obeisance
to British authority. In return, they were given a free hand to
retain their supremacy in the hierarchal order. Being loyal agents
of the colonial government, Brahmins worked as per a twofold
strategy: to petition the British to establish a varna-based order;
and use their religious and social authority to partake in quelling
any substantive reform programmes led by non-Brahmins.[41] Due
to this weirdly placed position, the Shudra kings of western India,
especially the descendants of Shivaji Bhosale and social reformers,
had difficulties adjusting to Brahmin diktats. They often clashed
with the Brahmin authorities. This led to a continued animosity
that gradually resulted in the sidelining of Brahmins.

The British also began to feel harassed by the onerous, oft-
repeated demands of Brahmins. Thus, they too chose to selectively
dilute the Brahmin command in their administration by granting
subsidiary positions. In one incident in April 1818, Pratapsinh,
the descendant of Shivaji Bhosale, was granted the status to
rule the small state of Satara. It was recorded by the Bombay
government that the installing of Pratapsinh was 'to establish
among the Mahrattas a counter-poise to the remaining influence
of the former Bramin [sic] government'.[42] The Peshwa rule was
considered treacherous to the principles of the Maratha kingdom
established under the reign of Shivaji Bhosale. Thus, a movement
against Brahmin supremacy was under way in nineteenth-century
western Maharashtra.

In this light we see Jotirao Phule, a Shudra social reformer
who 'pioneered attacks on the religious authority of Brahmins'
to bring attention to the suffering of the lower-caste and
Untouchable citizens.[43] The collapse of the Peshwa Brahmin rule
in the nineteenth century simultaneously brought with it certain
reforms in terms of education. The lower-caste groups could now
get education with the aid of Christian missionaries. Although the

English-medium schools were populated by Brahmins and other dominant-caste groups, a small percentage of 'lower' castes could be seen in the classroom. In these schools, Phule gained proximity to the politics of anti-Brahmin rule. Rosalind O'Hanlon, who closely studied Phule's activism, suggests that the peer groups that were formed in the schools 'enforced a temporary intellectual uniformity on its members'. This helped Phule develop a close circle of friends who would be his confidants and allies in the revolutionary work he was going to undertake.

Jotirao Phule

Phule's team of radicals consisted of both Brahmins and non-Brahmins who were mostly his friends and stood by him till the end, staunchly supporting him in times of adversity. Sadhashiv Ballal Govande, Moro Viththal Walvekar, Vishnu Moreshwar Bhide, Annasaheb Chiplunkar and Govind Joshi among other Brahmins find overwhelming references in Phule's biographical works and social activism. Phule's schoolmate Govande was the son of a poor Brahmin. Phule and Govande got their hands on Thomas Paine's *Rights of Man* in 1848, the same year Phule was to open the first of many schools for girls in Pune. Paine's *Age of Reason* had influenced Phule and his friends to get a candid sense of the order of the Christian church and its flirtation with political power. Due to this, Krishnaji Arjun Keluskar, Phule's close Brahmin friend, observed that Phule did not opt for conversion to Christianity when Christian conversion was rife amongst lower-caste groups across India. Along with Paine, Phule and Govande drew inspiration from the lives of Shivaji and George Washington.[44] Govande ended up writing a Marathi biography of George Washington in 1892 chronicling the freedom fighter's life.[45] Phule was inspired by the American abolitionist movement. Upon reading *Uncle Tom's Cabin*, he commented that anyone who had read the book 'will have to cry with shame in public'.[46]

The book made a remarkable impact on Phule to analogously put caste in the framework of race.

Phule laid a path for dominant-caste progressives to participate in the anti-caste struggle. According to Daniel Immerwahr, the dedication of Phule's book *Gulamgiri* (1873) attempted to invoke solidarity among dominant-caste forces. By suggesting that White people were the good people of the United States who were instrumental in freeing slaves, Phule exhorted his countrymen to draw inspiration and similarly free oppressed-caste groups from 'Brahmin thralldom'. This effort partly succeeded. The dedication was:

To THE GOOD PEOPLE OF THE UNITED STATES AS A TOKEN OF ADMIRIATION FOR THEIR SUBLIME DISINTERESTED AND SELF SACRIFICING DEVOTION IN THE CAUSE OF Negro Slavery; and with an earnest desire, that my countrymen may take their noble example as their guide in the emancipation of their Sudra Brethren from the trammels of Brahman thralldom.

Brahmins against Brahminism

Balshastri Jambhekar was an editor of *Durpan*, western India's first Anglo-vernacular weekly. Jambhekar was the first Brahmin professor of mathematics and astronomy at Elphinstone College in western India. Along with Govind Vitthal or Bhau Mahajan (1815–90), who was another prominent editor, Jambhekar ran reformist Marathi newspapers like *Prabhakar*, *Dhumketu* and *Dyana-Darshan*. Jambhekar and Mahajan were educated pioneers in British-governed western Maharashtra who launched remarkable journals and newspapers to advocate social reforms and widow remarriage. This duo stood strong against the orthodox values of Hinduism and its appalling practices. The vernacular press and English newspapers played an important role in intellectually shaping young educated radicals.

Prabhakar took an active stand against rigid caste practices, provoking regular debates on the privileges of Brahmins and the lowly status of women and backward castes. One of its chief contributors was 'Lokhitvaadi' (people's welfarist) Gopal Hari Deshmukh. Deshmukh took serious objections to contemporary Brahmins who had made it a business of single-caste dominance. He referred to his contemporaries as 'stupid Brahmins of the present' who curtailed reformist traditions and made rigid strictures against inter-caste marriage. He noted:

> Now, some of our Brahmans have become rich; others spend their time in pursuit of good food given for nothing, or waiting to see who will give out daksina. Although they know the Vedas off by heart, they are the enemies of its true meaning. I hesitate to call them learned at all, because a man who just repeats the words without understanding the meaning is of no more value than an animal making noises to itself.[47]

Early Marathi reformers took inspiration from the European scientific temper and looked up to innovations in science and reason, 'steam and watch' (industrialization), and the legal system. Social reformers educated in Elphinstone College started the Marathi Dnyan Prasarak Sabha (Marathi Society for the Spread of Knowledge) in 1848. The society noticeably took a stand against religious orthodoxy, which it blamed for creating differences between human beings and thereby giving rise to the caste system. It acknowledged that owing to such a divisive system the country was in a shambles.

> Our political power has been destroyed, our wealth has gone, our institutions have decayed, our trade is worth nothing, our ancient learning has been ruined, the incentive for individual education has disappeared, ignorance has increased, our once glorious cities have vanished, and our peasantry has become impoverished.[48]

Dadoba Pandurang Tarkhadar, a lower-varna Vaishya and contemporary of Phule, was a director of the Normal Class at Elphinstone College. He started a religious reform group called Paramhansa Sabha in 1848, a secret society to break the caste system, along with Ramchandra Balkrishna Jayakar, a Brahmin assistant commissioner in the customs department, as its president. Dadoba Pandurang saw hypocrisy in the religious texts and the unquestionable positions that Brahmins acquired. The societies he formed had discarded the caste system and the supremacy of Brahmins alongside the superstitious practices of magic and daily ritual, proclaiming, 'The religion of mankind is one. The whole of human kind is one caste.'[49] Phule was pleased with Jayakar's efforts and grew to like him so fondly that he dedicated his 1869 ballad written in praise of Shivaji, *A Ballad of Shivaji*, to Jayakar 'as a Mark of Profound Respect and a Testimony of Sincere Affection'.[50]

All of these contemporaries of Phule were noted names who participated in challenging their own social positions and the systems of hierarchies they operated under. Phule adopted a Brahmin widow's son prior to his death and even bequeathed his property to the adopted child, Yashwant, who was sheltered at an orphanage run by the Phule couple. The issue of Brahmin widows was a contentious one and no progressive Brahmin took as bold a step as Phule to challenge this system in western India. When Phule decided to start the first school for Dalit and Muslim women in Pune, he was generously assisted by his schoolmate Govande, who was by then working in the government along with Sadashiv Hate who helped him run the school. The school began at a Brahmin's house in Budhwar Peth at Tatyarao Bhide's Bhide Wada.[51]

Phule's move to start the school was in direct opposition to the Brahmins' absolute control over education. The Hindu College of Pune, also known as Poona Sanskrit College, which had been started in 1821 by Chaplin, then British commissioner to India,[52] under the patronage of Brahmin Peshwa Bajirao II's

Dakshina Fund was open for 'Brahmins only'.[53] Under such dire circumstances and living in the belly of the beast, Phule marshalled a social reform path, and was generously and ardently supported by his Brahmin friends and admirers.

During this time, amidst the strong protest and community pressure from Brahmins, Phule and his wife Savitribai were evicted by Phule's father, Govindrao Phule, from his house.[54] The school was then closed for a brief time. Meanwhile, Jotirao and his friends were educating their wives. Keshav Shivram Bhavalkar (Joshi), a Brahmin government teacher at the Marathi School and a member of the Paramhansa Sabha, along with Sakharam Yashwant Paranjpe and Sadashiv Govande, had begun teaching Savitribai Phule and Saraswatibai Govande in 1848. In addition, it is reported that Savitribai had also taken formal teacher's training at the American mission's Ms Farar's Institution in Ahmednagar and in the Normal School under Ms Mitchell in Pune.[55] This group of women then became teachers and was tasked to teach girls.

Sometime later, in improved circumstances, the school was reopened in Peeth Joon Ganj at a place provided by Govande as no one else was willing to offer their properties. Govande also chimed in by providing slates and a subscription of 2 rupees mensem (per month). Vishunpant Thatte, a Brahmin teacher, assisted in teaching as student enrolment was increasing. Moro Walvekar and Deorao Thosar assisted in the logistical demands of the school by preparing and sending circulars to different people. Major Thomas Candy, the principal of the Poona Sanskrit College, supplied books. Phule's physical instructors and comrades Lauji Rangraoot Mang and Ranba Mahar helped in enrolling more students of both sexes.[56] Seeing the success of this effort, Phule decided to start another girls' school. With the help of Annasaheb Chiplunkar, a Brahmin, another school was started with Savitribai Phule as headmistress and Vishnupant Moreshwar and Vitthal

Bhaskar serving as co-teachers on 3 July 1851 at Chiplunkar's property in Budhwar Peth. The school now required a management committee as its scope was expanding. Phule inducted his friends in this intensely path-breaking movement as this time too it received great opposition from society.

When Phule fell ill, he organized his Brahmin friends under the Society for Increasing Education amongst Mahars, Mangs and Others with Govande as its president, Walvekar as secretary and Paranjpe as treasurer—all of them Brahmins.[57] The society dedicated its efforts to recruit more Mahar and Mang students. It organized lectures to propagate the benefits of education. Annasaheb Chiplunkar gave passionate speeches promulgating the importance of women's education by supporting the cause of the Phule couple. He also launched an attack against the Dakshina Fund and the supremacy of Sanskrit, which was a powerhouse of Brahmin control. Annasaheb Chiplunkar got a petition signed by noticeable personalities against the Brahmin control of the fund. The money from the Dakshina Fund was meant for Brahmins as a religious gift fund. Taking objection to this, some of the progressive Brahmins took the lead and decided to divert half the amount towards the cause of education. This created a fuss between the orthodox and progressive Brahmins. The progressive Brahmins stood up to the orthodox ones and won the battle. Major Candy granted 75 rupees a month towards the maintenance of schools.[58]

Phule decided to institutionalize his most important movement, the Satyashodhak Samaj (truth-seekers society), a fiery social reformist organization that focused on the oppressed and subaltern masses. It aimed at eradicating the menace of caste and Brahmin-directed superstitious ideology. Phule's biographer Dhananjay Keer described the Samaj as 'the first institution to launch a social movement in modern India'.[59] Arguably, it focused on liberating the oppressed masses through education and social movements. It did not place the onus on Brahmins as other reformist Brahmin-led movements of the time did. The Brahmo Samaj, Prarthana Samaj and later Arya Samaj believed in the sacredness of the Gita, which Phule viewed as merely a political treatise designed to keep the oppressed masses within the shackles of the religious order.

Phule had serious problems with 'god-ism', wherein irrational demands of religion were forced upon the peasantry by Brahmins. The Samaj, which was by now a formidable movement in western India, began creating ripples by its direct actions. It shook the Brahmin orthodoxy and simultaneously openly challenged the Hinduized reformism of other groups. Its work was peasant-centric, along with other social reform projects like widow remarriage, abolition of child marriage, abolition of untouchability, spread of education, opening of centres for prevention of infanticide, creating incentives for the free education of poor students, including scholarships, and open opposition of the Brahmin order. To carry out this work, Phule was hugely assisted by his notable Brahmin friends, Vinayak Bapuji Bhandarkar, Vinayak Bapuji Dengle and Sitaram Sukharam Datar. Taking inspiration from the success of the movement, several other Brahmins of repute too started contributing to the movement either via financial assistance or through direct participation.

While almost all the names that find mention in the pioneering work of Jotirao were Brahmins, his affection for Brahmins was certainly not blind. Phule was critical even of his Brahmin friends who were part of the movement and its organizations. At times, he would chide them for presenting mistaken views about the Shudras and Ati-Shudras ('Untouchables').[60] Phule was of the opinion that Brahmins alone were the group responsible for the suffering of the 'lower' castes. His writings and advocacy were centred against Brahmins by calling them cheats, hypocrites and treacherous, among other names, denouncing the sanctity of their religion as fraudulent. This view attracted negative attention and led to personal attacks on Phule. Phule survived, and so did his work.

B.R. Ambedkar

Let us now turn to Ambedkar's movement. Early on, Ambedkar had strongly emphasized that his fight was an agitation against the Brahminical values that treated one class of people higher over the other simply by virtue of one's birth. The Brahminical class is not limited to creating differences only but it also is 'resolved to the belief that the upper–lower castes are birth based', wrote Ambedkar in a *Bahishkrit Bharat* editorial (1 July 1927). Ambedkar led the ceremonial burning of the *Manusmriti*—a second-century CE text that he referred to as the 'book of the philosophy of the brahminism' that prescribed the worst forms of injunctions against Untouchables. It is reported that the burning of the *Manusmriti* was a suggestion made by Ambedkar's Brahmin comrade, Sahasrabuddhe.[61] Like Sahasrabuddhe, there is a list of impressive Brahmin and 'upper'-caste individuals who rallied behind Ambedkar and chose him as their ideal leader.

Ambedkar's non-Dalit comrades are profiled in an important collection by Yogiraj Bagul, a historian of Ambedkar's movement from Maharashtra.[62] This book documents the contributions of eleven non-Dalit, mostly Brahmin, followers of Ambedkar. Bagul's efforts to bring out these stories intend to recognize the voices of Ambedkarites who are not so well known in anti-caste groups as well as orthodox caste circles.

Ambedkar was involved with Brahmins from an early period in his life, despite the bitter experiences he had had at their hands. He worked with the Brahmin and other dominant-caste progressives who made contributions to his movement. Ambedkar's Brahmin comrades walked shoulder to shoulder with him and contributed via physical presence, intellect and money. Some Brahmins rose to become Ambedkar's close confidants, assuming charge of important roles in the movement. In addition to Brahmins, the Chandraseniya Kayastha Prabhu caste, also known as CKPs, relatively higher up in the caste hierarchy, alongside members of the Bhandari caste and other 'upper-caste' individuals also notably participated in Ambedkar's movement.

Young Ambedkar and Non-Untouchables

Ambedkar's early influences were his teachers, who taught him directly and indirectly. One of them was his schoolteacher, Krishna Arjun Keluskar. Although Keluskar did not formally teach him, he noticed the potential of young Ambedkar, who was a regular visitor to the garden in south Mumbai, keeping up with his reading habits. Ambedkar, one of the two Untouchable (school) graduates in the province, was publicly felicitated by Keluskar who was an assistant teacher at Wilson High School. Ambedkar the bookworm was given access to Keluskar's private library where he could explore various texts and manuscripts of his interest.[63]

Ambedkar was gifted a book on the Buddha written by Keluskar, *Life of Gautama Buddha*, as a matriculation gift. Keluskar also recommended to the maharaja of Baroda, Sayajirao Gaikwad (1863–1939), to assist in Ambedkar's further education. To substantiate his plea, Keluskar was able to get recommendations from Sir Narayan Chandavarkar so that Ambedkar could pursue his BA at Elphinstone College, Mumbai.

Of a progressive leaning, Maharaja Gaikwad had a policy of offering scholarship to encourage education among the Untouchable castes. One possible reason for his progressivism could be the humiliating casteist experiences his family had had to endure. The Gaikwads were considered inferior in the kingly caste hierarchies of the Marathas. Pratapsinh Bhosale, a descendant of Shivaji, considered the Gaikwads and Holkars inferior and impure Marathas who could not claim the role of Kshatriyas. Pratapsinh noted in his diary about the Gaikwads:

I discussed with the Resident the acts of treachery that the Gayakavad has committed upon the Maratha caste in leading certain people astray by offering them a reward for contracting marriage alliances. The Gayakavad is a kunbi; he has led the people of our caste into wrong, and polluted the caste. He holds authority in his own caste, and has no reason to force himself into our caste [sic].

Pratapsinh further added: 'The Gayakavad of Baroda, as a mere kunbi, has offered some people of the Maratha caste the inducement of money and led them into betrayal and pollution.'[64] Perhaps due to this, Gaikwad's bent towards progressive politics could be traced to his personal interest in the lives of 'lower'-caste reformers. When Jotirao Phule had a paralysis attack, Gaikwad had immediately sent financial assistance. He also helped Phule publish the guiding manifesto *Sarvajanik Satya-Dharma Pustaka* which Phule acknowledged in one of his poems.[65] Jotirao had a personal affection for Gaikwad and vice versa. The mutual affection developed over the years when young Sayajirao visited Poona in 1881 after his installation as a prince in the kingdom. Following this, in the year 1883, Jotirao paid a visit to the maharaja in Baroda to read from his new book, *Cultivator's Whipcord*, which exposed peasant exploitation at the hands of Brahmins. In 1885, both had the opportunity to connect in Poona again when Jotirao and his comrades organized a function in honour of the maharaja. The maharaja recommended bestowing the title of 'Booker T. Washington' upon Jotirao Phule in 1888.[66] Thus, he had the opportunity to meet and witness the formidable struggles led by both Jotirao and Ambedkar.

~

During his civil rights activities, Ambedkar gained as many friends as adversaries among dominant-caste Hindus. The Shudras in Maharashtra were particularly fond of Ambedkar's efforts and Maharaja Gaikwad was his sincere admirer. He not only inducted Ambedkar into his administration but also patronized some reformation programmes, only to be halted by pressure from the Brahmin orthodoxy. Maharaja Gaikwad also presided over the Depressed Classes Mission Society of India's conference held during 23–24 March 1918 in Mumbai. The relationship between Ambedkar and Gaikwad lasted for a few decades. At the Round Table Conference in 1930 in London, Gaikwad called on Ambedkar to join him and a Brahmin knight, Sir Annepu Patro, for a dinner hosted at Hyde Park Hotel. The *New York Times* found this worthy of a headline. Running the report under the title 'Prince and Outcast at Dinner in London End Age-Old Barrier; Gaekwar of Baroda Is Host to "Untouchable" and Knight of High Hindu Caste', it was 'one of the biggest pieces of news coming out of the conference'.[67]

Krishna Arjun Keluskar was Ambedkar's reference point during his early scholar–activist days in the 1920s and 1930s. Scott R. Stroud has analysed how Keluskar introduced John Dewey to Ambedkar.[68] *Ethics*, Dewey and Tufts's magisterial work of over 618 pages published in 1908,[69] determined Ambedkar's early entry into the Deweyean philosophy of pragmatism accompanied by Tufts's anthropology that took a normative approach to morality and ethics. Dewey and Tufts's explain the nature of ethics as a morally defined position in the framework of customary action. This philosophy was matured and advanced by Ambedkar.

After returning to India from America, Ambedkar had to face adverse situations in Baroda.[70] For help, he turned to Keluskar, who recommended Ambedkar to the position of principal at Sydenham College, Mumbai. However, Ambedkar was denied the post because of his Untouchable status. Instead, a professorship was offered to him at Elphinstone College. Ambedkar politely refused the offer, and chose instead to 'dedicate himself to a life of service to his people' as he 'did not want to take up any job in future that would hinder his social work'.[71]

Ambedkar's rainbow followers

Ambedkar's strategy included involving progressive Brahmins who were interested in the cause of Untouchables and Brahmin reform. Thus, one of the first institutions established by Ambedkar, Bahishkrit Hitakarini Sabha (1924)[72]—the Depressed Classes Institute—had Brahmin members of noted distinction. Dr C.H. Setalvad, a liberal party member and a Gujarati Brahmin judge, was inducted as the president, Meyer Nissim and G.K. Nariman were vice presidents with a Parsi background, the Maratha members were solicitors Dr R.P. Paranjpye, Dr V.P. Chavan and B.G. Kher. However, the management of the Sabha was under the control of Untouchables—Ambedkar was the chairman of the committee and S.N. Shivtarkar was the Chambhar-caste secretary and N.T. Jadhav the Mahar-caste treasurer.

In the inter-caste dining initiative, Ambedkar's non-Dalit colleagues excitedly took the lead in throwing grand dinner parties at their respective homes. One such event was organized at Sahasrabuddhe's house which received the attention of press. It was also printed in the fifth edition of the *Samata* newsletter on 24 August 1928. The news item carried the names of participants and their respective sub-castes to indicate the diversity of representation in the radical inter-caste dining efforts. Of the twenty-two participants, people from diverse castes such as CKPs, Mahars, Chambhars, Bhandaris, Matangs, Malis, Marathas, Shimpis, Govardhan Brahmins, Andhrapradeshiya Brahmins and Vankar-Meghwals were reported. Such efforts were frequently undertaken at the houses of members of the Samaj Samata Sangh (Social Equality League).[73] With these caste rainbow experiments, Ambedkar proved his organizational maturity.

Every biographer of Ambedkar shows how caste Hindus and Brahmins were Ambedkar's close associates and leading some of his movement's activities. His biographer Keer notes that Ambedkar's Brahmin colleagues were at the forefront on many occasions. The labour unions, educational institutes, newspapers, Independent Labour Party and various subcommittees that Ambedkar presided over had his Brahmin comrades' impressive participation.

Brahminaction

Along with their solidarity, many Brahmins identified with Ambedkar's struggle and were radical Ambedkarites. One name that prominently comes to the fore is Gangadhar Nilkanth Sahasrabuddhe, a Chitpavan Brahmin who steadfastly stood by Ambedkar's side. Sahasrabuddhe was a labour union organizer in the Mumbai area who fiercely advocated against the orthodox practices of Hinduism.

The historic Mahad conference in 1927, the Kolaba District Depressed Classes Conference, was presided over by Ambedkar, although in the preparatory meetings Ambedkar had refused to do so, and had requested to search for a person of stature who had contributed to the Dalit movement. But the people in the Kolaba region of Mumbai wanted Ambedkar to preside over the conference. Ambedkar still did not budge. It was Sahasrabuddhe who succeeded in convincing him to preside over the historic conference that paved the way for launching a radical Dalit movement under Ambedkar's leadership.

Sahasrabuddhe was also the proponent of Ambedkar's ceremonious burning of the *Manusmriti*. The second resolution at the conference, the *dafan vidhi* (ritual burying) of the *Manusmriti*, was proposed by Sahasrabuddhe, seconded by P.N. Rajbhoj and supported by Shriyut Thorat.[74] Sahasrabuddhe stood by Ambedkar's side and led the procession along with six Dalit sages. This event brought Ambedkar into the national limelight and became a bone of contention with orthodox and conservative Brahminical Hindu groups.

During this conference, Sahasrabuddhe appealed to the touchable castes in his speech.

> If the touchable castes feel that Untouchables should love them then the initial steps have to be taken by the touchables. The touchables need to create a confidence among Untouchables that the former are convinced about their love towards the latter. In order to gain the trust of Untouchables, the touchable castes have only one option: whatever obstacles are created in the development of Untouchables need to be eradicated.[75]

This simple and straightforward statement put the onus of the caste system on the touchable castes. Sahasrabuddhe was a forthright radical who saw the paradox of those belonging to the touchable castes who expressed sympathy with the Dalit cause, but on the other hand did not actively participate in the struggle. Sahasrabuddhe also edited Ambedkar's journal, *Janata*, for fifteen years. He made rallying calls for Ambedkar's inclusion in the 1942 viceroy's cabinet. Through his widely read editorials, he challenged the British government for denying Dalit members their fair share in the cabinet. In the *Janata* edition of 9 August 1941, Sahasrabuddhe penned an article titled 'Ingrezaanchi Dhokebaazi' (Betrayal of the British).[76] In the article, he made it clear that like Hindus and Muslims, Untouchables were also a separate political entity which was agreed upon by the British in the Round Table Conference, 1930. And denying Untouchables their rights was thus hypocritical. In the next editorial on 16 August 1941 Sahasrabuddhe challenged the Hindu Mahasabha, the Muslim League and the British government for collectively denying Untouchables their rights. Sahasrabuddhe's widely read editorials evoked a strong public response. Yogiraj Bagul argues that it was to the credit of

Sahasrabuddhe that many protest rallies and conferences were organized in various regions of western India. Shantabai Chavan presided over the All India Dalit Women Conference in Mumbai on 20 October 1941 which passed a first resolution condemning the British government for injustice against Dalits.[77] Dalit and non-Dalit leaders in the movement regularly facilitated the dialogues in 1941 up until 1942 when the British government had to finally give in and induct Ambedkar into the interim government as a labour member. Sahasrabuddhe's organizing around this issue had produced formidable momentum in the public. Various conferences that were hosted during this time had singularly denounced the hypocrisy of the British government. The Dalit leadership called it out loudly and Sahasrabuddhe amplified those voices to a higher pitch.

During the early years of the Depressed Classes Institute, various programmes were undertaken under its auspices. However, of these, education, culture and economic conditions were identified as the three components that aimed to target the improvement of the Untouchable condition. On the economic front, there was not much success; still, Sahasrabuddhe managed to pull together three cooperatives to help the Sabha's activities. Due to his radical activities, Sahasrabuddhe gained the title of 'Ambedkari Brahman' (Ambedkarite Brahmin).[78]

Another surprising Ambedkar ally was Shridharpant Tilak, the son of conservative Bal Gangadharpant Tilak. Shridharpant actively participated in Ambedkar's social activities. Ambedkar presided over the Conference of Depressed Class Students in Poona on 2 October 1927 and Shridharpant Tilak was one of the three speakers alongside P.N. Rajbhoj and Solanki.[79] After the conference, Shridharpant hosted a tea party in Ambedkar's honour at his residence, Gaikwad Wada, in Narayan Peth, Maharashtra.

Continuing with this tradition, Shridharpant threw his house open to host a choir of Untouchable boy singers for inter-dining to support the initiative of the Samaj Samata Sangh that was housed at Gaikwad Wada. By inviting them, he defied all opposition from the community, particularly the Brahmin trustees of the Kesari-Maratha Trust. His residence, Lokmanya Nivas, was decorated with a board that said 'Chaturvarnya Vidhwansak Samiti' (Chaturvarna Annihilation Committee). This invited the wrath of his relatives and his Brahmin social circle. Shridharpant was put under tremendous pressure and unremitting humiliations were hurled at him even in *Kesari*, the newspaper that had been started by his father.

Owing to the mounting pressure from the orthodox Brahmin community and the conservative circle of the Kesari-Maratha Trust which dragged Shridharpant to court for seven years, Shridharpant cut his life short on 25 May 1928 by jumping under the Mumbai–Pune express train. Ambedkar blamed the caste Hindu orthodoxy of the *Kesari* circle for this incident; Shridharpant referred to them as 'a gang of rascals'.[80] He wrote a final letter addressed to Ambedkar before committing suicide. A copy was published in *Samata* on 29 June 1928. It reads:

Before the letter reaches your hand, the news of [my] leaving the world would have [reached] your ears. In order to advance the work of your 'Samaj-Samata-Sangh' educated and social reformist youth need to be attracted to the movement. I am extremely delighted to see your persistent efforts in this and I am confident that god will bless you with success. If the Maharashtrian youth take this cause, then the problem of untouchability will be resolved in merely 5 years. To convey the grievances of my depressed classes brothers to god Krishna, I am going ahead. Please convey my regards to friends. With regards, Sincerely.

Yours truly,
Shridhar Balwant Tilak
25/5/28[81]

Upon learning of the death of Shridharpant Tilak, Ambedkar passed a resolution at the Jalgaon Conference on 26 May 1928 acknowledging his contributions.[82] He also mourned

Shridharpant's death in his editorial: 'I was expecting great amount of karma from Shridharpant; now he is dead.' Ambedkar had grown closer to him after the latter's engagement with the Samaj Samata Sangh increased. Shridharpant had in no time become part of Ambedkar's friends' circle.[83] He made a point of paying a visit to Ambedkar whenever he travelled to Mumbai, and if Ambedkar was in Pune, he would try to get Ambedkar to come to his house in Gaikwad Wada. Shridharpant's and his sibling Rambhau Tilak's fight with the trustees of the Kesari-Maratha Trust blew up. Both siblings were known for their liberal views and social reformist outlook. In the legal fight between the Kesari-Maratha Trust trustees and the Tilak brothers, the latter had insisted on hiring Ambedkar as a lawyer. However, Ambedkar had to turn down the offer owing to the circumstances.

Labour leader N.M. Joshi, a Brahmin, was a sincere admirer of Ambedkar before the latter shot to prominence. Ambedkar was a student in the mathematics class taught by Joshi at Elphinstone High School. Over the years, as Ambedkar scaled heights, both Joshi and Ambedkar met with each other on numerous occasions to build solidarities. Joshi's Samaj Seva Sangh attracted progressive caste Hindus to the organization. It was here that Ambedkar got to meet other progressives who eventually joined his movement. When Ambedkar went to the Round Table Conferences, Joshi was sitting in the hall as a labour representative. His work as a labour organizer and Ambedkar's as a labour minister had forged amicable partnerships between them. Ambedkar pushed for the inclusion of Dalit leadership in the Indian delegation for the International Workers' Conference. This proposal was received with hesitation from the labour organizers, accusing Ambedkar for creating divisions in the working class. Joshi defended Ambedkar's proposal and counterposed a question to the 'radical-orthodox' Brahmins in the labour movement about the lack of Brahmin efforts to include Dalits in the international delegation. 'You all have worked for so long in the movement, why didn't you germinate the Dalit leadership? As a matter of fact, Dalit workers form a sizeable corpus [of the movement]. Thus, the question remains, is Ambedkar casteist or are we casteist for excluding Dalits?'[84] Joshi accepted that it was a failure of the labour movement to foster a caste-inclusive environment.

Another trusted confidant of Ambedkar's who was given the responsibility of caring for his most valuable possessions—books—was S.S. Rege. Rege was appointed librarian of the People's Education Society (PES) in 1946. He was Ambedkar's go-to person in keeping track of the books housed in Mumbai at Rajgruha, his residence, and Siddharth College, where Ambedkar had donated some of his collection. Ambedkar's love for books is well documented by various individuals who knew him closely. Nanakchand Rattu described the bibliophile Ambedkar who had once remarked that he would shoot a person if he dared snatch his valuable books.

Rege hailed from an educated Gaud Saraswat Brahmin family from Vengurle village in the Sindhudurg district of western Maharashtra. Rege was trained as a librarian. Through his brother-in-law, Dattatreya V. Pradhan, secretary of the newly formed Independent Labour Party and a member of the executive council of Samaj Samata Sangh, Rege came in contact with Ambedkar. He became an important person of contact at the institutional level in Ambedkar's public life. Alongside his job as a librarian, he was also called upon by Ambedkar to discuss the appointment of various faculty members at Siddharth College. Rege was elevated to the position of vice president of the PES. During his final years, when Ambedkar was anxiously trying to complete *The Buddha and His Dhamma*, Rege became a frequent point of contact in Mumbai. He would be asked to visit Thacker's publishing house in Kolkata to get proofs or to send relevant books to Delhi. Rege holds a respectable name in Ambedkar's biography as an institution builder. A highly regarded individual, he continued to advise the Dalit masses after Ambedkar's death through the PES until he passed away in 2004. There are various testimonies and stories written in reference to Rege as someone who stood tall in continuing Ambedkar's legacy.

Another important name which has not received the recognition it rightfully deserves is Devrao Vishnu Naik, a radical Ambedkarite and editor of two revolutionary journals: *Brahman-Brahmanetar* (Brahmins and non-Brahmins) and *Samata*. Naik was born into a Govardhan Brahmin family, a 'lower' sub-caste among Brahmins. Naik had experienced the disfavour of Brahminism in his personal life: A rich moneylender Chitpavan Brahmin had harassed his farmer family, and the orthodox Brahmin fraternity did not treat his sub-caste with equal respect. Naik thus decided to work for the social cause of anti-caste-discrimination. He was aware of Ambedkar's work through newspapers and the fact that his Bahishkrit Hitakarini Sabha had non-Dalit office-bearers.

In order to disseminate Ambedkar's and his anti-caste organizations' efforts among the Brahmin audience, Naik launched the first Brahmin-centric anti-caste newspaper, *Brahman-Brahmanetar*, on 1 August 1925. Ambedkar's meetings, rallies and his movement's activities were widely reported in this paper. Naik not only propagated Ambedkar's views to the Brahmin community but also participated in movements alongside Ambedkar. In the Mahad conference and post-Mahad protests against the violence committed by Hindus upon Untouchables, Naik took on a leading role.[85] He was appointed the vice president of the Samaj Samata Sangh. Naik's prominence grew and thus he was included in Ambedkar's inner circles, accompanying him to marches, conferences and rallies. He was deputed to address the rally at a conference organized by the Depressed Classes Association in Solapur under the presidentship of Ambedkar, who was unable to travel there. Naik was sent to convey his written message to the gathering. He was also inducted in Ambedkar's delegation to meet M.K. Gandhi on 14 August 1931 alongside leading activists and leaders like Bhaurao Gaikwad, Sitaram Shivtarkar, Bhaskarrao Kadrekar, Ganpatbuwa Jadhav, Amrutrao Rankhambe and P.G. Kanekar.

Naik's work with Ambedkar became well-known across Dalit circles. Thus, his house, which was close to Dadar station in Mumbai, became a reference point for Dalit activists coming to the city. As the work of the Samaj Samata Sangh increased, there emerged a need for a newspaper. Thus, Ambedkar launched *Samata,* a fortnightly journal, with Naik as its editor. Having the responsibility of running two newspapers, Naik eventually stopped publishing *Brahman-Brahmanetar* and concentrated on *Samata,* which was attracting more attention due to its wider coverage of Dalit activities. Naik also edited *Janata,* which was rechristened from *Bahishkrit Bharat* on 24 November 1930. Ambedkar's representation and memoranda to various committees including the Round Table Conferences was published in booklet form and distributed by Naik.

Naik was a bitter critic of Brahmins and Brahminical leadership in the national freedom movement. Taking a jibe at Bal Gangadhar Tilak and his followers' commitment to freedom sans Dalit freedom, Naik affirmed that it was due to the conservative orthodox religion that gave vested powers to Brahmins. Naik's commitment to the movement was acknowledged by Ambedkar in laudatory terms: 'You've immersed yourself into [the] community's struggle, emotions and their aspirations so much that your birth that unlike us was not as an untouchable, is the only difference between you and us.'[86] Eventually, Naik, like most other Brahmins, parted ways with Ambedkar when Ambedkar decided to carry out the struggle under the banner of the newly formed All India Scheduled Caste Federation (AISCF) in 1942.

Many Brahmin and 'upper'-caste comrades of Ambedkar started leaving him after Ambedkar decided to dissolve the Independent Labour Party to form the All India Scheduled Caste Federation. The progressive Brahmins had felt comfortable working within the Labour Party politics and became uncomfortable in the caste-focused organization. While a select few Brahmins' commitment to the anti-caste movement remained uncompromising, a few non-Dalit and Brahmin comrades distanced themselves after Ambedkar gave important portfolios to Dalits in the AISCF, and not to non-Dalits—a practice he had implemented in the earlier organizations. Despite this, Ambedkar remained closely connected with his non-Dalit Brahmin and dominant-caste comrades who had grown under the tradition of the Ambedkar-led Dalit revolution.

Another reason Yogiraj Bagul offers for the growing distance between his Brahmin followers. First, the physical distance of Ambedkar wherein Ambedkar had to leave Mumbai for Delhi to assume charge of the labour portfolio in the viceroy's cabinet, thus limiting the regular interactions he had in Mumbai. Many non-Brahmin leaders also approached Ambedkar to get rid of Brahmins from his organization so that they could put their support behind it.[87] However, Ambedkar remained steadfast and retained his position. Barring a few exceptions, not many Brahmins feature in the movements from the late 1940s till Ambedkar's death in 1956.

Despite the Hindu presence within Ambedkar's movement, the Brahmin orthodoxy prevailed through a complex web of lies, sabotage and virulent attacks. In an interview to the *New York Times* in 1930 from London, Ambedkar spoke about the activities undertaken by the Samaj Samata Sangh. 'The movement,' he said, 'is growing very slowly, but it is growing. The liberals who have joined us have gone beyond the point of seeming self-conscious when accepting the hospitality of an "untouchable" host, but they suffer estrangement from orthodox members of their own caste. That is the chief obstacle to [their] progress.'[88]

Brahminescape

So what is happening now with the Brahmins who are intimately attached to the caste system and drawing its benefits? Brahmins in India are squarely responsible for the ongoing chaos of the disordered caste society. It is by the silence, and at times by diverting the conversation from the focus on Brahminical casteism that Brahmins retain their dominant position in an oppressive society. This is why the caste issue is overwhelmingly seen as a Dalit issue. Oftentimes, caste is seen as something Dalit-related. If you talk about caste today, it is often the Dalit figure that comes to mind as caste is associated with someone who suffers and for whom there is affirmative action. However, caste is also about inherited privilege and dominance that is unaccounted for. This picture of the beneficiaries of casteism is not presented to the world. It is as much an issue for Brahmins and other castes as much as it is for Dalits, as the system would not exist with a single caste—the caste system is relational.

Caste cartography also needs further attention. Currently, the caste order is presented in the graded hierarchical system with one's occupation determining one's caste. This map, however, is an incomplete and unjust description of the caste system. Along with the description of jobs, the demographic representation of each caste group needs to be done in comparison to the ratio of the population and its representation in positions of power. This snapshot would give a clearer picture of the outside and inside world of the caste system and its actualized form in operation. It will also expose to the world how banal and pathological this ecology of caste is.

As racism manifests in various forms, casteism also functions in the faulty education system—formal, informal and religious.

Everywhere you turn, you will see groupism being injected into the minds of the gullible masses. Even without knowing the justness of 'merit' in the face of discrimination, children are thrown naked into the market of hatred. Langston Hughes elegantly handles this issue in *The Ways of White Folks* (1933).[89] A targeted attack on the prejudicial racism that manifests in our minds and the societal pressure we carry as Black or White people is meticulously drawn in the lives of the protagonists of the short stories in the collection. The idea of radical, progressive, liberal and conservative, educated and uneducated, cultured and uncultured White man and woman is put to question. *The Ways of White Folks* chronicles the stories of racialized America and hits hard on the genteel apperception of the profiled bodies. Similarly, the protagonists in Dalit writing have put across episodic narratives of the violence committed on Dalit bodies by the progressive, liberal, conservative and orthodox men and women of the Brahminical class overseen by the minority priestly Brahmins.

The caste disorder is a product of what Nietzsche calls 'priestly aristocracy',[90] a 'priestly caste' that values the retention of purity.[91] It is the super-dominance of the priestly class over the common affairs of civic society. With the ascendancy of the priestly aristocracy, 'antithetical values' become 'deepened, sharpened, and internalized'.[92] It is an unhealthy recourse from the beginning, wherein 'mankind is ill to the effects of priestly naïveté'. Referring to the Brahmin priestly class, Nietzsche suggests that 'Brahma is used in a shape of [a] glass knob and a *fixed idea*' (emphasis added). He further suggests that everything with the priests becomes dangerous, that they are the 'most evil enemies' who transcend from the affective stage to the visceral reactions of hatred, 'arrogance, revenge, acuteness, profligacy, love, lust to rule, virtue'. Nietzsche goes on to justify his proposition of priests being the evil. 'It is because,' he observes, 'of their impotence that in them hatred grows to monstrous and uncanny proportions, to the most spiritual and poisonous kind of hatred. The truly great haters in world history have always been priests; likewise the most ingenious haters; other kinds of spirit hardly come into consideration when compared with the spirit of priestly vengefulness.'

The capacity of priests to take 'spiritual revenge' is the most concerning fallout of the priestly super-dominance. Nietzsche further observes that due to the unchallenged position of the priestly aristocracy, it does not limit itself to the spiritual domain but engages in extreme subversion as well. By subverting the hegemonic discourse of the governing aristocracy, the priestly class offers its own interpretation of the nature of society. So, whatever was perceived and decided as evil by the priests could now be accepted as the new normal sanctioned under the religious order. In the Indian Hindu context, the consumption of beef and the supremacy of Brahmins are some of the glaring examples.

If closely examined, it would appear that Brahmins themselves are suffering from the caste system but do not want to acknowledge that the caste system is governed by elite Brahmins who control their minds and spirituality. Although they do not suffer on the same scale as Dalits and other backward castes, in the quest to prove their superiority Brahmins have suppressed expressing their personal discomfort with the caste system. They are divided in their ranking of hierarchy. The sub-castes of Brahmins practise strict endogamy. Poor Brahmins are often ignored and made outcasts by fellow dominant Brahmins. A friend in the US narrated a story of a Brahmin male who posted his profile on a marriage website. He indicated his caste, sub-caste, *gotra* and all the minute details relevant to Indian 'arranged' marriages—which is a euphemism for strict caste marriages. As soon as he did so, the majority of people who contacted him were Brahmins from his sub-caste. For the first hits, almost all of them were related to his sub-caste. Even people from higher sub-castes did not contact him.

Liberal Brahmins' Passive Anger

I have noticed a trend of liberal Brahmins often lamenting about their angst against the Brahmin community as a whole. In their critiques, they endlessly refer to orthodox family members or vegetarianism being the primary obstacles in creating a diverse society. However, in this hue and cry, they conveniently forget to attack the caste system in its entirety. Instead, they decry the existence of superiority and inferiority in the caste system. Little do they realize that similar experiences of 'upper' and 'lower' have been tormenting the Dalits and Adivasis who bear the burden of all caste groups in Hinduism. The Brahmin dilemma in the sub-caste dictum in this case is that of degradation to one sub-level and nothing more than that. Thus, they prefer to tackle the issue in an accommodationist fashion. This becomes dangerous as they do not utter a word of defiance against caste as a system of segregation. And this caste-mongering class continues to depress other caste folks whom they enjoy having under their command.

There is a thin line of difference between Brahmins and Brahminism. Many Brahmins discussed above in the context of the twentieth-century anti-caste movement consciously chose to differ from the traditional path of Brahminism. They gave up the path at their own cost, aligning with the Dalit cause as their own cause. They identified themselves with oppressed-caste groups and attacked the orthodox Brahmin cult.

As a consequence, they underwent ostracization and excommunication. Yet, they followed the rightful course of action. They were courageous and saw humanity in each human, wrong in the wrong actions and love in the most uncertain places. Such Brahmins are well regarded in Dalit annals and the recollections of struggles. Many who have dedicated their lives to the cause of emancipation of Dalits occupy positions of respect. Of these Brahmins, however, very few qualify as revolutionary radicals. In their liberal abolitionist purview, they practised harmony. Yet, they remained unsuccessful in creating any dent of note in the Brahminical system they benefited from. Brahminism and the caste system offer an easy pass and a privilege of security. Many used this cultural capital to cut through the caste system to align with Dalits, while some used this to work within the liberal framework by offering limited support. However, one aspect remained unfulfilled and that was to create a huge momentum amongst their own-caste people to launch an anti-Brahminism movement. Many liberal Brahmins chose to marshal their cause by staying within the system. Their efforts did not always endanger the security of their position while their relatives and caste kin continued to benefit from the same system that they were fighting against.

The existence of casteism has to be attributed to the Brahmin groups who reap the benefits of it. Brahmins from all quarters—moderate, liberal, conservative and extremists—uphold the glory of having a Brahminical order. Although some among them loathe this, they cannot be found to have genuine interest to eradicate the order. Seldom can a Brahmin be seen on national television condemning the Brahminical order and denouncing it. Instead, distracting euphemisms are deployed to sideline the burning issues of Brahmin domination and Brahmin violence. It is difficult to spot Brahmins acknowledging their share of responsibility in creating and being part of the problem. When issues of accountability arise, blame is shared with other non-Brahmin groups. Barring some lone voices here and there, the Brahmin community overall does not have the courage or dedication to address the pathology of caste. The Brahmin groups who are working in liberal projects or radical movements do not go back to their caste constituency to educate their caste brethren. A Brahmin friend once told me that he'd rather die than convince his Brahmin relatives. 'I gave up on these casteist Brahmins,' claimed the liberal Brahmin. He even severed contact with his Brahmin family. He told me that the issue of caste was presented to him through the bipolar perspective of merit and demerit. Anything related to the productivity of one's capability was defined as caste. He had been forced to think about the merit and demerit of a human being based on one's caste.

Difference in caste society is presented as a consequence of merit and demerit. A person who is different, that is, different from the Brahminical social and cultural order, most often belonging to a non-Brahmin caste, is first made to feel different. This difference is a callous form of declaring the inability of the Other. Thus, the differentiated being lives within a mendacious propaganda. The differences are first forced upon the person as a forewarning about the unequal relationships at play. The unequal terms of a relationship are ways to channel the oppressor group's insecurities to enforce a destabilizing inferiority upon the Other. The Other, having no adequate space or voice to air grievances, is forced to fall in line with the standards of the oppressive Brahminical order.

~

Casteism is the longest-thriving pathology known to mankind. Conjuring differences between human beings out of thin air and claiming they are based on birth, and then ascribing them a certain social status, is a testament to seriously compromised mental and social health. A child is taught to be different from others. The question of one's differences is emphasized so strongly that the child follows it without necessarily making critical inquiries. The child is mentored by the entire family to harbour the feeling of otherness towards Others who are most likely inferior or lower in the socio-economic ladder. The prejudicial attitudes that a child is brought up with prepares it to be harmful towards Others, natural innocence ruthlessly taken away by the oppressive minds in the family. Later, as time passes, when the child becomes an adult, he or she is told—misleadingly—by society that differences don't exist.

Therefore, the adult is now in a dilemma: how to now believe that everyone is equal irrespective of the differences? However, the same adult seldom questions or challenges these foolish differentiations and changing narratives—how the Other is different and not supposed to be mingled with, and is yet 'equal'. The Other that the child was never allowed to play with is now deemed his equal. This leads to bewilderment at the Other receiving state benefits. This is how caste numbs one's consciousness—it is true for both the oppressor and the oppressed.

The markers of difference that are ingrained into a child's thinking early on are later outwardly replaced by the narrative of equality, although they remain deeply relevant in the understanding of society. However, in all this mind make-up, the oppressed group is not given adequate representation to define its characteristics and experiences. The differences, for the Dalit, are and remain very real. It is the lived experience of humiliation and being stripped of humanhood. These experiences, emerging from a different lived reality, ought to be brought to light and openly presented. The differences that exist for all the multiple caste identities ought to be given their due value in the mainstream narrative. In Indian society, the unfortunate reality is that barely anyone truly exists outside their caste. But the false idea of an a-caste, 'normal', 'neutral' identity dominates mainstream discourse—which is actually a thinly veiled ideal of Brahmin identity that everyone is supposed to aspire to. Inevitably, amidst this narrative, it is the Dalit who is forced to feel the burden of being 'different', even though everyone is already different by their respective castes. But, because the Dalit's experience finds no space for expression, and is, moreover, looked down upon due to being at the lowest position in the order, he is branded 'different'. Thus, the Dalit aspires to be someone apart from a Dalit. That is the reason we see many Dalits converting to other religions to get away from the oppressor's gaze. Even after trying to rescue oneself from the label of the Other, the Dalit remains caught in the labyrinth of refusal. The Dalit tries to deal with his/her denigration by completely transforming himself/herself into another being—by reinventing a new identity, this time refusing to adhere to any ancestral and historical relations to the 'despised' Dalit identity. The insistent and relentless Brahminical casteism strips one's identity and wipes out the glorious past and historical connection of Dalits to their ancestral chord. The Dalit lives in the miasma of Brahminical devaluation. The differences are markers of hatred, pain and suffering.

Whatever is the outcome of the ongoing anti-caste war, it is the Brahmin's responsibility to keep it alive. By retaining their hegemony, Brahmins are silent co-conspirators of this slow caste-cide.

Brahminescapeism

A professor friend belonging to a Brahmin caste once inquired about my comments on Brahmins being the singular responsible entities for caste violence. It is the Shudras and Kshatriyas that commit violence on Dalits on a day-to-day basis, said the learned professor. Banias are not even in the field, let alone Brahmins, was his retort. He argued that in the rural economy the Shudras owned Dalit labour, which enabled them to commit unaccounted violence upon subjugated bodies. The professor also cited such incidents. 'Brahmins are nowhere close to these avenues of feudal, class-oriented violence,' he commented. 'Brahmins in fact live the hermetical life of closure. The Agraharas are not bound with these harsh incidences of violence.' By this logic, he claimed that Brahmins eschewed direct confrontation with other castes and had retained their own identity without violent interactions with other caste groups. Empirically, the professor's argument has a valid purchase. In a closed agrarian economy—which is dominated by the feudal caste system—Dalit lives get brutally assaulted. Bondage to landlords is perpetuated for generations, and no possibility of freedom is granted to Dalit labourers and their children. Generation after generation, this is how Dalits get tyrannized.

The source of power that Shudras and other caste groups derive is from the organized power of religion. The Brahmins' control of the religious order that grants downward contempt towards the lower castes is primarily responsible for the Dalit condition. Shudras act within the religious context. Anything beyond the Brahminical zone does not offer the same power play. For example, a Kshatriya does not hold power as an upper-caste person beyond the religious domain. If a Kshatriya migrates out of the religion, s/he will be exposed to the equality that exists outside it. He will be a person devoid of caste standards, that is, an equal human being and no longer an upper-caste person. Similarly, people in the 'upper'-caste column have gained this status by being within the order of Brahminical Hindu religion. Thus, the source of religion brings with it unquestioned power and influence. This is then used against the 'lower'-caste folks who do not have an escape from this violence because they are also conditioned to the caste order. This system of caste is maintained by the Brahmins who occupy the highest place in the order. Their position is unquestioned and remains unchallenged. Their control over the spiritual realm is the first and last reason for the existence of the caste order. Brahmins can, in fact, use their influence to condemn caste-ordained violence. They can also issue warrants against other 'upper'-caste touchable groups who are waging violence against the Dalits. Their power and strength in the religious system benefits their own position and the positions of the people beneath them.

Many Brahmins I come across in the liberal democratic space tell me that they do not believe in caste. They condemn or mock the caste system. Their dissociation comes out of guilt. However, disagreeing with it is not enough to make the caste system wither away. Their action is central to the desired results. Merely not believing in the system is not going to solve the problems created by their ancestors and benefiting their kin. We need 'cultural suicide bomber Brahmins' who are willing to self-immolate and blow themselves up *culturally* to make a voluble notice and impact on the world. An act by a Brahmin—the 'superior'—would certainly send a powerful signal to other 'upper'-caste groups. In his monumental speech, 'What Path to Salvation' (1936), Ambedkar throws open the challenge to caste Hindus to be brave foot soldiers in revolting against the caste system and taking the bullets. He says there is a need to wage a war to emancipate Dalits from the caste system. Drawing an analogy with the American Civil War, Ambedkar hints at the Whites who 'killed thousands of whites who defended the slavery of the Negro people, and also sacrificed their own blood for this cause'. If Brahmin reformers are unwilling to follow the model of White Americans who fought against other Whites to liberate Black people, the struggle of Brahmins is mere rhetoric that 'propose[s] to fight till the last Untouchable dies'.[93]

No other group has done as much harm to Indian civilization as Brahmins, either by partaking in the execution of Brahminical dominance or by remaining silent. Many Brahmins who are confronting the question of privilege and oppression have to confront the primary enemy that lies within their immediate family circles. Their Facebook family group conversations or WhatsApp groups are often laden with heated exchanges. I have noticed that Brahmins who become part of the anti-caste struggle always undergo spiritual, soul-searching moments. They often report their victories in family conversations on the issues of caste, reservation, Dalit politics and OBC movements. Those with victories within their families need to go one step ahead and beyond their comfortable inner circles. Their conscious efforts to reach out to the communities or social clubs they operate in would produce significant results. It would also make them undergo the process of experiencing the struggle of inconvenience. However, a large number of liberal, progressive and radical Brahmins fear ostracization from family members and community groups at the outset so they prefer working in clandestine fashion. They operate secretly, trying to support the movement in whichever way they can but their invisible presence does not create much energy or a critical impact. They want to work with impunity and immunity; however, working for the oppressed masses can draw negative attention and even attacks. One has to be brave and committed to the cause irrespective of the consequences, as the socially committed forefathers and foremothers of the Brahmins and non-Dalit 'upper castes' did in the nineteenth and twentieth centuries. They not only challenged the shallowness of the caste system as a theoretical exercise but also fought against the oppression that was wrought on Untouchables and other 'lower'-caste groups. It was a difficult struggle; they were made unwelcome in their social circles and always had to work towards building trust with the Dalit constituency. In the work against Brahminism, many Brahmins and individual allied-caste reformers had to pay a huge price.

Many progressive Brahmins narrate to me their sob stories about being alienated from their community and friends because of their anti-caste work. Some lament about superior-caste Brahmins looking down upon lower sub-caste Brahmins. Caste violence occurs even among the Brahmin varna; however, it doesn't get reported. A Saraswat Brahmin friend of mine from Ahmednagar married a Deshastha Brahmin and they had to elope in order to get married—they were barred from seeing their parents for over six years. They are victims of the caste system and they know it, but they fear creating a bigger rebellion. Caste rebellion is anticipated and expected only from Shudra and Untouchable caste groups. The anti-caste Brahminic vision is absent from the imagination of Brahmins and other dominant castes. Many Brahmins remain subjects of such a system without realizing their participation in perpetuating it, possibly losing the support of relatives.

Despite the recorded tradition of Brahmin participation in the anti-caste struggle, Brahmin progenies have disowned their progressive ancestors. Had they followed their ancestors' path, the struggle against casteism would certainly have produced a multi-caste cultural outlook. This is one of the reasons that Brahmin leaders of the anti-caste struggle remain unknown and are effectively muted in history. Their life's inspirational work is kept away from the current generation. Owing to this, we lack progressive Brahmin groups taking an active stand against caste as their primary motive. There are no 'Brahmins against Brahminism' social, cultural, intellectual or social media groups existing in India, unlike the young peer groups of various caste folks during Phule's time. Such an initiative could result in encouraging the formation of groups like Kshatriyas against Brahminism, Banias against Brahminism and Shudras against Brahminism across India and abroad. In an elite institution like Harvard the dormitories of Harvard college students proudly display the posters and artwork of the Black Lives Matter campaign alongside LGBTIQA and other minority groups of the USA. Dialogues around race in the dorms and on the campus is encouraged making it a norm for students to be sensitive to the race question. In India, however, dormitories remain segregated along caste lines and personal choices like food and sexuality is heavily policed. Dorms become a space to promote hatred, humiliation and fear to Dalit students instead of becoming a collaborative space of diverse ideas confronting the caste problem. One hardly notices dominant-caste students advocating for social change and becoming the banner holder of the annihilation of caste movement. Sensitization of Dalit lives and problems relating to caste is not in the purview of the university administration and neither in the student groups. A Dalit student lives life in isolation without him/her being acknowledged and appreciated let alone supported by the dominant-caste students on campus.

Many Brahmin academics who have advanced their careers by writing and researching Dalit experiences and the intellectual histories of Ambedkar and non-Brahmin movements can be amply found in all geographies and disciplines. Unlike their predecessors, these Brahmin scholars have restricted themselves to producing knowledge—à la the Manu-prescribed Brahmin vocation. But they have not actively invested in producing another generation of Dalit scholars. Material investment in the lives of Dalits remains at a far end. Established professors and advisers based in overseas educational and research institutes do not have Dalit graduate students. And like these Brahmin professors who either patronize or humiliate Dalits, dominant-caste Indian students more often than not come with a Brahmin saviour mode. The production of pedagogy is restricted within the Brahminical mould. Brahmin academics eloquently describe the life of Untouchables and 'lower' castes, making very little effort in exposing their own caste groups by offering a candid insider view. They are willing to be allies but not comrades putting themselves at the front in the anti-caste war. Being an ally is akin to volunteerism, where one can dodge responsibility and take a day off. Meanwhile, comradeship is a bond of trust that is developed through personal, social and economic sacrifices. The struggle then becomes a common cause and not the *Other's* cause. Nowadays, dominant-caste allies are happy to be passive raconteurs who would at best tweet or send a like on Facebook, but they are unwilling to do the real work. They have not put a critical lens upon themselves and asked, as N.M. Joshi did, 'Why were we not able to produce Dalit leadership. Whose fault is it?'[94] The time for self-realization remains open-ended.

editorial supervision of Richa Burman and the intellectual push of Ranjana Sengupta, who loved this idea since the beginning and managed to bring out more stories from an otherwise extremely reserved person to support the thesis. Richa carefully handled the work with gentle care and a compassionate touch without compromising the scholarly standards of the book.

Shreya Chakravertty for the copy edits. Shreya Gupta for pulling off an excellent cover.

Lastly, gratitude to my large joint family, who kept me engaged with love. This book is published on my father's birthday. He would have been proud to hold a copy of this book.

Notes

Introduction

1. As per the population break-up of dominant castes, OBCs, Dalits, Adivasis, Muslims and other religious minorities including Dalit Christians and Dalit Muslims. Dalits alone exceed 320 million according to one estimate that includes Dalits of various religions. Anand Teltumbde, *Dalits: Past, Present and Future* (New Delhi: Routledge, 2018), p. 3. Also see Anand Teltumbde, 'State, Market and Development of Dalits', in Gopal Guru, ed., *Atrophy in Dalit Politics* (New Delhi: Vikas Adhyayan Kendra, 2005), p.80.
2. Department of Planning, Government of Punjab, 'Survey for BPL Families', pp. 3–4, http://www.pbplanning.gov.in/pdf/BPL16-3-07.pdf
3. World Bank, 'Maharashtra Poverty, Growth and Inequality', http://documents.worldbank.org/curated/en/806671504171811149/pdf/119254-BRI-P157572-Maharashtra-Poverty.pdf
4. Sarah Buckwalter, 'Just Another Rape Story', *Times of India,* 29 October 2006, https://timesofindia.indiatimes.com/india/Just-another-rape-story/articleshow/222682.cms; for a detailed analysis of this ghastly incident see Anand Teltumbde, *Khairlanji: A Strange and Bitter Crop* (Delhi: Navayana, 2008).
5. Data sourced from the National Crime Records Bureau in Hillary Mayell, 'India's "Untouchables" Face Violence, Discrimination', *National Geographic,* 2 June 2003, https://news.nationalgeographic.com/news/2003/06/indias-untouchables-face-violence-discrimination

6.   Amit Thorat and Omkar Joshi, 'The Continuing Practice of Untouchability in India: Patterns and Mitigating Influences', University of Maryland, https://ihds.umd.edu/sites/ihds.umd.edu/files/publications/papers/ThoratJoshi3.pdf

7.   Ritwika Mitra, 'Untouchability Still Prevails in over 640 Tamil Nadu Villages', *New Indian Express,* 30 April 2019, http://www.newindianexpress.com/states/tamil-nadu/2019/apr/30/untouchability-still-prevails-in-over-640-tn-villages-1970871.html

8.   B.R. Ambedkar, 'Caste in India: Their Mechanism, Genesis and Development', in Vasant Moon, ed., *Dr Babasaheb Ambedkar: Writings and Speeches,* Vol. 1 (Bombay: Education Department, Government of Maharashtra, 1979), p. 6.

9.   Harvard Divinity School, 'Shining a Light on America's "Spiritual Blackout"', 4 December 2017, https://hds.harvard.edu/news/2017/12/04/west-spiritual-blackout#

10. B.R. Ambedkar, 'Annihilation of Caste', in Vasant Moon, ed., *Dr Babasaheb Ambedkar: Writings and Speeches,* Vol. 1 (Bombay: Education Department, Government of Maharashtra, 1979).

11. Martin Heidegger, *Being and Time,* trans. John Macquarrie and Edward Robinson (New York: Harper Perennial, 2008).

12. Kancha Ilaiah, *Why I Am Not a Hindu: A Sudra Critique of Hindutva Philosophy, Culture and Political Economy* (Kolkata: Samya, [1996] 2005).

13. Kancha Ilaiah, *Buffalo Nationalism: A Critique of Spiritual Fascism* (Calcutta: Samya, 2004).

14. Kathir Vincent, 'They Killed My Husband, Saying, "How Dare You Love, You Pallar Son-of-a-Bitch?"', Huffington Post, 12 May 2016, https://www.huffingtonpost.in/kathir-vincent/they-killed-my-husband-sa_b_9900086.html

15. Syed Akbar, 'A Love Affair and Murder That Shook Telangana', *Times of India,* 20 September 2018, http://timesofindia.indiatimes.com/articleshow/65879291.cms?utm_source=contentofinterest&utm_medium=text&utm_campaign=cppst

16. Praveen Donthi, 'How Caste Shaped the Experience of Rohith Vemula and Other Students At the University of Hyderabad',

Caravan, 23 August 2016, https://caravanmagazine.in/vantage/caste-shaped-experience-rohith-vemula-students-university-hyderabad; for another detailed account of the incident, see Sudipto Mondal, 'Rohith Vemula: An Unfinished Portrait', *Hindustan Times*, https://www.hindustantimes.com/static/rohith-vemula-an-unfinished-portrait

17. Nitin B., 'A "Stooge" Being Rewarded by His BJP Masters: Hyd Uni Students Slam Award to VC Appa Rao', *News Minute,* 3 January 2017, https://www.thenewsminute.com/article/stooge-being-rewarded-his-bjp-masters-hyd-uni-students-slam-award-vc-appa-rao-55184

18. Anupama Rao, 'Stigma and Labour: Remembering Dalit Marxism', *India Seminar,* https://www.india-seminar.com/2012/633/633_anupama_rao.htm

19. Balmurli Natrajan, 'From Jati to Samaj', *India Seminar,* http://www.india-seminar.com/2012/633/633_balmurli_natrajan.htm

20. Anupama Rao, ' Stigma and Labour'.

21. *DW*, 'Caste Dynamics Behind Sexual Violence in India', https://www.dw.com/en/caste-dynamics-behind-sexual-violence-in-india/a-43732012

Chapter 1: Being a Dalit

1. Yashwant Manohar, 'Ultimatum', trans. Charudatta Bhagwat, in Arjun Dangle, ed., *Poisoned Bread* (Hyderabad: 2009, 2016), p. 18.

2. *Namdeo Dhasal—Poet of the Underworld, Poems 1972–2006*, Dilip Chitre trans. (New Delhi: Navayana, 2007).

3. K. Stalin, *India Untouched*, YouTube, https://www.youtube.com/watch?v=Injodpo3T1o, accessed 22 April 2019.

4. Dhrubo Jyoti, 'Caste Broke Our Hearts and Love Cannot Put Them Back Together', Buzzfeed, 28 February 2018, https://www.buzzfeed.com/dhrubojyoti/will-you-buy-me-a-pair-of-shorts?utm_term=.iblv2XD3E#.jv0rPX2VE

5. Cornel West, *Race Matters* (Boston: Beacon Press, 1993), p. 19.

6. Bryan Stevenson, *Just Mercy: A Story of Justice and Redemption* (New York: Spiegel & Grau, 2015).

7. Rahul Singh, 'Criminal Justice in the Shadow of Caste: Study on Discrimination against Dalit and Adivasi Prisoners and Victims of

Police Excesses', National Dalit Movement for Justice, National Campaign on Dalit Human Rights, 2018.

8. Namdeo Dhasal, *Ambedkarite Movement and Socialist, Communist*, fourth edition (Mumbai: Shabda, 2015), p. 13.

9. Toni Morrison interview, https://www.youtube.com/ watch?v=5afmnSqFP5Y

10. This was observed by American anthropologist Gerald Berreman during his fieldwork in the 1950s in north India. Gerald D. Berreman, 'Caste in India and the United States', *American Journal of Sociology* 66.2 (September 1960): 124.

11. Sigmund Freud, *Jokes and Their Relation to the Unconscious*, trans. James Strachey (New York: Penguin, 1905, 1974).

12. Sigmund Freud, *Humour*, 1927, https://www.scribd.com/ doc/34515345/Sigmund-Freud-Humor-1927

13. Freud, *Jokes and Their Relation to the Unconscious*, trans. James Strachey, pp. 79–87.

14. Ngugi wa Thiong'o, *Decolonising the Mind: The Politics of Language in African Literature* (London: James Currey, 1986), also available on http://www.swaraj.org/ngugi.htm

15. Being Indian, 'I Am Offended', https://www.youtube.com/ watch?v=swozBbWMzNQ&t=90s

16. Barbara Joshi, ed., *Untouchable! Voices of the Dalit Liberation Movement* (London: Zed Books, 1986), p. 146.

17. Ibid, p. 87.

18. Gangadhar Pantawane, 'Evolving a New Identity: The Development of a Dalit Culture' in Barbara Joshi, ed., *Untouchable! Voices of the Dalit Liberation Movement.*

19. D.R. Nagaraj, *The Flaming Feet and Other Essays: The Dalit Movement in India* (Ranikhet: Permanent Black, 2010), pp. 94–95, 109.

20. Omprakash Valmiki, *Joothan: A Dalit's Life*, sixth reprint (Kolkata: Samaya, 2018), p. 72.

21. Edward Said, *Orientalism* (New York: Vintage [1979], 1994).

22. Jean-Paul Sartre, *Being and Nothingness: A Phenomenological Essay on Ontology*, trans. Hazel E. Barnes, (New York: Washington Square Press, 1992).

23. Ibid, p. 301.

24. Plato, *Republic*, trans. C.D.C. Reeve (Indianapolis: Hackett Publishing Company), p. 166.

Chapter 2: Neo-Dalit Rising

1. *Economic Times,* 'My Gotra Is Dattatreya, I Am a Kashmiri Brahmin: Rahul Gandhi in Pushkar', 27 November 2018, http://economictimes.indiatimes.com/articleshow/66820708.cms?utm_source=contentofinterest&utm_medium=text&utm_campaign=cppst

2. Amrutha Vasireddy, 'ISRO Directors Perform Special Pujas At Tirumala Temple', *Times of India,* 31 August 2017, https://timesofindia.indiatimes.com/city/amaravati/isro-directors-perform-special-pujas-at-tirumala-temple/articleshow/60306457.cms; News 18, 'Sack ISRO Chief for Taking Mars Mission Replica to Tirupati: Rationalists', 6 November 2013, https://www.news18.com/news/india/sack-isro-chief-for-taking-mars-mission-replica-to-tirupati-rationalists-649179.html

3. G.S. Guha, 'Religion in India's Army', *Hinduism Today,* https://www.hinduismtoday.com/modules/smartsection/item.php?itemid=1421

4. Ashutosh Sharma, '"Jai Mata Di": Priest Anoints Nirmala Sitharaman As New Defence Minister', *National Herald,* 8 September 2017, https://www.nationalheraldindia.com/national/jai-mata-di-priests-anoint-nirmala-sitharaman-as-new-defence-minister

5. http://www.facenfacts.com/NewsDetails/43663/indian-space-scientists-too-believe-in-superstitions!.htm

6. Alok Prasanna Kumar, 'The Curious Case of Justice Karnan and Its Implications for Higher Judiciary', *Hindustan Times,* 9 March 2017, https://www.hindustantimes.com/india-news/the-curious-case-of-justice-karnan-and-its-implications-for-higher-judiciary/story-nDgSk7GbYVaJSYyTMpNgQK.html

7. Other marginalized groups also hold the Constitution as a vehicle that would secure their rights, cf. Rohit De, *People's Constitution: The Everyday Life of Law in the Indian Republic* (Princeton: Princeton University Press, 2018).

8. *Surya Narayan Chaudhary and Etc. v. State of Rajasthan,* 29 September 1988, *AIR 1989* Raj 99. Indiankanoon.org/doc/942155

9. E. Kulke, 'Integration, Alienation and Rejection: The Status of Untouchables' in S.D. Pillai, ed., *Aspects of Changing India* (Mumbai: Popular Prakashan, 1983).

10. Dhananjay Keer, *Dr Ambedkar: Life and Mission* (Bombay: Popular Prakashan, 2016), p. 449. Rajya Sabha, Andhra State Bill, 2 September 1953.

11. BAWS, Constitution (Fourth Amendment) Bill, 1954, Parliamentary Debates, Vol. 15 (Mumbai: Government of Maharashtra,), p. 949.

12. Ibid.

13. Ibid, p. 949.

14. Ibid.

15. USA, for example, granted civil rights to its oppressed minority a hundred years after declaring the formation of the Union.

16. Sukhadeo Thorat, 'Political Economy of Caste Discrimination and Atrocities: Why Does Caste Discrimination Persist Despite Law?', in *The Radical in Ambedkar: Critical Reflections,* Suraj Yengde and Anand Teltumbde, eds, (New Delhi: Penguin Random House India, 2018), pp. 255–80.

17. 'The Land Conundrum', *Economic & Political Weekly* 53.42 (20 October 2018).

18. Martin Luther King Jr, 'Letter for Birmingham Jail' in Cornel West, ed., *The Radical King* (Boston: Beacon Press, 2015), p. 135.

19. Ibid.

20. B.R. Ambedkar, *Annihilation of Caste* (1936).

21. The caste system was brought upon the Indian people by the foreigners who identified themselves as 'Aryas', coming to India around 2000 BC. The system, akin to the caste system, was produced by Aryans or by the natives who were inspired by Aryans. G.S. Ghurye, *Caste and Race in India* (Bombay: Popular Prakashan, 1932 [2004]), pp. 117–18.

22. Rahi Gaikwad, 'Dalit Youth Killed for Keeping Ambedkar Song as Ringtone', *The Hindu,* 22 May 2015, https://www.thehindu.com/news/national/other-states/dalit-youth-killed-for-ambedkar-song-ringtone/article7232259.ece

23. Hillary Mayell, 'India's "Untouchables" Face Violence, Discrimination', *National Geographic,* 2 June 2003.
    This was the statistic sixteen years ago. Now, with growing Hindu nationalism, which is inter alia Chaturvarna nationalism, crimes against Dalits have increased exponentially. Between 2006 and 2016, as many as 4,22,799 crimes were committed against Dalits alone. Alison Saldhanha and Chaitanya Mallapur, 'Over Decade, Crime Rate Against Dalits Up 25%, Caste Pending Investigation

Up 99%', IndiaSpend, 4 April 2018, http://www.indiaspend. com/cover-story/over-a-decade-crime-rate-against-dalits-rose-by-746-746

24. Ravi Kaushal, 'Gujarat: 4 Wedding Processions of Dalits Attacked in a Week, CM Silent', Newsclick, 13 May 2019, https://www. newsclick.in/Gujarat-Dalits-Wedding-Procession-Attacked

25. B.R. Ambedkar, *Pakistan, or the Partition of India,* and *Revolution and Counter Revolution,* in *Dr Babasaheb Ambedkar: Writings and Speeches,* Vol. 8 (Bombay: Education Department, Government of Maharashtra), pp. 30–31.

Chapter 3: The Many Shades of Dalits

1. Chandraiah Gopani, 'New Dalit Movements: An Ambedkarite Perspective', in Suraj Yengde and Anand Teltumbde, eds, *The Radical in Ambedkar: Critical Reflections* (New Delhi: Penguin Random House India, 2018), pp. 181–200.

2. B.R. Ambedkar, 'Caste in India: Their Mechanisms, Genesis and Development', *Indian Antiquary* 41 (May 1917).

3. http://socialjustice.nic.in/UserView/index?mid=76750

4. He categorized them as 'reluctant chamchas, initiated chamchas, aspiring chamchas, helpless chamchas, party-wise chamchas, ignorant chamchas, enlightened chamchas, chamchas of the chamchas, and chamchas abroad'. Kanshiram, *Chamcha Age: An Era of the Stooges* (Delhi: Siddarth Books, 2015 [1982]).

5. 'Malcolm X: The House Negro and the Field Negro', https:// www.youtube.com/watch?v=7kf7fujM4ag

6. E. Franklin Frazier, *Black Bourgeoisie* (New York: Free Press, 1957).

7. The Round Table Conference recognized Untouchables as a separate category alongside the religious minorities, Sikhs, Christians and Muslims. It was due to Gandhi's stubborn stance that the separate electorates were snatched away. It made them dependent on a representative contesting the election from a general constituency, which would be invariably heavily dominated by the majority Hindu groups where Untouchables could not expect to win.

8. B.R. Ambedkar, 'Caste in India: Their Mechanism, Genesis and Development', *Dr Babasaheb Ambedkar: Writings and Speeches,* Vol. 1 (Bombay: Education Department, Government of Maharashtra, 1979), pp. 3–22.

9.   See Chapter 5 for a detailed discussion on capitalism.

10. *India Today*, 'Why the 200-year-old Koregaon Bhima Battle Triggered Caste Clashes in Maharashtra', 2 January 2018.

11. I am grateful to Anand Teltumbde for directing me to explore this new category and offering examples in this regard. This chapter benefited from his critical comments.

12. Sukhadeo Thorat and Paul Attewell, 'The Legacy of Social Exclusion: A Correspondence Study of Job Discrimination in India', *Economic & Political Weekly* 42.41 (13 October 2007): 4141–45.

13. S. Madheswaran and Paul Attewell, 'Caste Discrimination in the Indian Urban Labour Market: Evidence from the National Sample Survey', *Economic & Political Weekly* 42.41 (13 October 2007): 4146–53.

14. Praveen Donthi, 'From Shadows to the Stars: The Defiant Politics of Rohith Vemula and the Ambedkar Students Association', *Caravan*, 30 April 2016, https://caravanmagazine.in/reportage/from-shadows-to-the-stars-rohith-vemula

15. Rituparna Chatterjee, 'Dalit MPhil Student from JNU, Who Complained of Inequality in Facebook Post, Found Hanging', Huffington Post, https://www.huffingtonpost.in/2017/03/13/dalit-mphil-student-from-jnu-who-complained-of-inequality-in-fa_a_21885438

16. Abhinav Malhotra, 'Dalit Student Commits Suicide at IIT-Kanpur Hostel Room', *Times of India,* 18 April 2018, http://timesofindia.indiatimes.com/articleshow/63821132.cms?utm_source=contentofinterest&utm_medium=text&utm_campaign=cppst

17. The Moolnivasi (original inhabitants) concept approaches the issue of caste oppression through the Aryan Theory.

18. Vivek Kumar, 'Different Shades of Dalit Mobilization', in T.K. Oommen, ed., *Social Movements I: Issues and Identities* (New Delhi: Oxford University Press, 2010), pp. 116–36.

19. Sharankumar Limbale, *The Dalit Brahmin and Other Stories* (Hyderabad: Orient BlackSwan, 2018).

20. Urmila Pawar and Meenakshi Moon, *We Also Made History: Women in the Ambedkarite Movement* (New Delhi: Zubaan, 2014), p. 294.

21. Ibid, p. 295.

22. Ibid, p. 296.

23. Mohandas Naimisharay, *Veerangana Jhalkari Bai* (New Delhi: Radhakrishan Prakashan, 2006).

24. For more on this see Badri Narayan, *Women Heroes and Dalit Assertion in North India: Culture, Identity and Politics* (New Delhi: Sage, 2006), p. 126; Chapter 5, 'Jhalkari Bai and the Koris of Bundelkhand'.

25. Roja Singh, *Spotted Goddess: Dalit Women's Agency, Narratives on Caste and Gender Violence* (LIT Verlag Münster: Munster, 2018).

26. Pawar and Moon, *We Also Made History: Women in the Ambedkarite Movement*, p. 10.

27. I am grateful to Beena Pallical and Lakshmannan for drawing attention to this detail.

28. Guru Gopal, 'Dalit Women Talk Differently', *Economic & Political Weekly* (14–21 October 1995): pp. 2548–50.

29. https://www.marxists.org/archive/marx/works/download/pdf/origin_family.pdf

30. Baby Kamble, *Prisons We Broke*, trans. Maya Pandit (New Delhi: Orient BlackSwan,), p. 118.

31. Mahesh Deokar, 'A New Era of Awakening, Neo-Buddhists and the Academic Study of Pali', *Biblio*, April–June 2018, pp. 14–15.

Chapter 4: The Dalit Middle Class

1. Sanjeev Sanyal, *The Indian Renaissance: India's Rise after a Thousand Years of Decline* (New Delhi: Penguin Books, 2015), pp. 95–96.

2. Gyanendra Pandey, 'The Drive for a Monolingual Order: Segregation and Democracy in Our Time', *South Asia: Journal of South Asian Studies*, 40.1 (2017): 71–86.

3. Rakesh Kochhar, 'A Global Middle Class Is More Promise than Reality', Pew Global, http://www.pewglobal.org/2015/07/08/a-global-middle-class-is-more-promise-than-reality

4. Gurram Srinivas, *Dalit Middle Class: Mobility, Identity and Politics of Caste* (Jaipur: Rawat Publications, 2016); Nandu Ram, *The Mobile Scheduled Castes: Rise of a New Middle Class* (Delhi: Hindustan Publishing Corporation, 1988).

5. Srinivas, *Dalit Middle Class*, p. 40.

6. Pavan K. Verma, *The New Indian Middle Class: The Challenge of 2014 and Beyond* (Noida: HarperCollins, 2015), p. 6.

7. Subodh Verma, 'Economic Gap between Upper Castes and Dalits Persists', *Times of India*, https://timesofindia.indiatimes.com/india/Economic-gap-between-upper-castes-and-dalits-persists/articleshow/46914577.cms

8. Verma, *The New Indian Middle Class*, p. 9.

9. Anuradha Banerjee, Firdaus Rizvi, Sukhadeo Thorat and Vinod K. Mishra, 'Caste and Religion Matters in Access Urban Rental Housing Market', *Economic & Political Weekly*, 50.26 (27 June 2015).

10. Surinder Jodhka and Aseem Prakash, *The Indian Middle Class* (New Delhi: Oxford University Press, 2016), pp. 114–15.

11. Srinivas, *Dalit Middle Class*, and Ram, *The Mobile Scheduled Castes*.

12. Sanyal, *The Indian Renaissance*.

13. E. Franklin Frazier, *Black Bourgeoisie: The Rise of a New Middle Class in the United States* (New York: Free Press, 1997 [1957]), p. 20.

14. Gyanendra Pandey, 'Can There Be a Subaltern Middle Class? Notes on African American and Dalit History', *Public Culture* 21.2 (2009): 321–42.

15. Ibid, p. 79.

16. Sudha Pai, *Dalit Assertion* (New Delhi: Oxford University Press, 2014), p. 116.

17. All India Depressed Classes Conference, Nagpur, 1942, *Report of the proceedings of the Third Session of the All India Depressed Classes Conference, held at Nagpur on 18 and 19 July, 1942 ; the All India Depressed Classes Women's Conference held at Nagpur on 20 July 1942; the Samata Sainik Dal Conference held at Nagpur on 20 July 1942* (Delhi : Gautam Book Centre, 2009).

18. Ambedkar, BAWS, 2009, p. 29.

19. I am grateful to Sukhadeo Thorat for offering critical comments and suggesting further changes which are incorporated here.

20. Srinivas, *Dalit Middle Class*, pp. 149–150.

21. Kancha Ilaiah, 'The Bhopal Declaration', *The Hindu*, 30 January 2002.

22. Pai, *Dalit Assertion*, p. 125.

23. This was reported in a WhatsApp group of elite Indian university graduate Dalits in January 2019.

24. Anand Teltumbde, *Republic of Caste: Thinking Equality in the Time of Neoliberal Hindutva* (New Delhi: Navayana, 2018).

25. Pratap C. Aggarwal, *Halfway to Equality* (New Delhi: Manohar, 1983).

26. Jurgen Harbermas, *The Structural Transformation of the Public Sphere* (Cambridge, MA: MIT Press, 1991), p. 89. Habermas goes on describe the emergence of the public sphere where public opinion was articulated to emphasize the distinctions between state and society. Locating the notion of 'opinion' in modern European thinking, Harbermas surveys the distinction of public opinion from persuasion to the legal doctrine of state by exploring the ideas of Plato, Kant, Hegel, Rousseau, Locke, Montesquieu and Marx. His analysis framed the 'public opinion' as an emergence of certain ethical values.

27. Alison Saldhana and Chaitanya Mallapur, 'Over Decade, Crime Rate Against Dalits Up 25%, Cases Pending Investigation Up 99%', IndiaSpend, http://www.indiaspend.com/cover-story/over-a-decade-crime-rate-against-dalits-rose-by-746-746.

28. For more on this, see 'Below Poverty Line', https://data.gov.in/catalog/below-poverty-line-india

29. Subodh Varma, 'Enrol and Dropout, Education Is a One-way Street for Dalits', *Times of India,* 24 January 2016, https://timesofindia.indiatimes.com/home/sunday-times/deep-focus/Enrol-and-dropout-education-is-a-one-way-street-for-dalits/articleshow/50701654.cms

30. 'House Ownership Status of SC Households', http://secc.gov.in/categorywiseHouseOwnershipStatusReport?reportType=SC%20Category#

31. Ibid.

32. 'Excluded SC Households', http://secc.gov.in/categorywiseExclusionReport?reportType=SC%20Category#; Excluded ST Households, http://secc.gov.in/categorywiseExclusionReport?reportType=ST%20Category#

33. Pratap Mahim Singh, 'Census Counts Just 4% SC, ST families with a Member in a Govt Job', *Indian Express,* 14 July 2015.

34. Socio-economic and Caste Census 2011, Income Source of SC Households, available at http://secc.gov.in/categorywiseIncomeSourceReport?reportType=SC%20Category#

35. Roshan Kishore, 'Locating Caste in India's Farm Economy', LiveMint, 11 December 2015, http://www.livemint.com/Opinion/myrJLTnIfiNVSaJF8ovdRJ/Locating-caste-in-Indias-farm-economy.html

36. Varma, 'Enrol and Dropout, Education Is a One-way Street for Dalits', *Times of India,* 24 January 2016.

37. 'Representation of SC/ST/OBC officers in Government', Press Information Bureau, Government of India, Ministry of Personnel, Public Grievances and Pensions, http://pib.nic.in/newsite/PrintRelease.aspx?relid=132395

38. Maneesh Chhibber, 'For Last Six Years, No Scheduled Caste Judge Sent to Supreme Court', *Indian Express,* http://indianexpress.com/article/india/india-news-india/for-last-six-years-no-scheduled-caste-judge-sent-to-supreme-court-shortage-pending-cases-2825216

39. Ibid.

40. *Outlook,* 'All in the Family', 19 September 2016, https://www.outlookindia.com/magazine/story/all-in-the-family/297828

41. *Times of India,* 2 February 1999 report, quoted in Rana Mulchand, *Reservations in India: Myths and Realities* (New Delhi: Concept Publishing House, 2008).

42. Government of India, Ministry of Law and Justice, Lok Sabha Unstarred Question No. 4551, http://164.100.47.190/loksabhaquestions/annex/10/AU4551.pdf

43. Quoted in A.G. Noorani, *Constitutional Questions and Citizens' Rights: An Omnibus Comprising Constitutional Questions in India and Citizens' Rights, Judges and State Accountability* (New Delhi: Oxford University Press, 2006).

44. P.G. Ambedkar, 'Parliamentarians Write to PM Modi Against Scrapping Dalit and Adivasi Plan", Newclick, 13 February 2017, https://www.newsclick.in/parliamentarians-write-pm-modi-against-scrapping-dalit-and-adivasi-plan

45. N. Paul Divakar, 'The 2017 Budget Is Taking SC/ST Welfare Backwards', Wire, 2 February 2017, https://thewire.in/rights/budget-2017-sc-st-welfare

46. Manual scavenging was outlawed in 1993 in the Employment of Manual Scavengers and Construction of Dry Latrines (Prohibition) Act, 1993 and further in 2013 under the Prohibition of Employment as Manual Scavengers and Their Rehabilitation Act, 2013.

47. Quoted in Bharat Dogra, Roopam Singh, 'Budget Justice for Dalit and Adivasis', *Mainstream* 52.28 (5 July 2014), http://www.mainstreamweekly.net/article5045.html

48. *Times of India*, 'Rs 744cr Dalit Fund Diverted for Games', https://timesofindia.indiatimes.com/city/delhi/Rs-744cr-dalit-fund-diverted-for-Games/articleshow/6173912.cms

49. Hannah Gardner, 'India raids fund for poor to pay for Commonwealth Games', *National*, https://www.thenational.ae/world/asia/india-raids-fund-for-poor-to-pay-for-commonwealth-games-1.559996

50. Ajmal V., 'Dalit orgs unhappy with SC/ST Budget allocation', *Deccan Herald*, 4 February 2019, https://www.deccanherald.com/national/does-union-budget-2019-benefit-716614.html

51. N. Paul Divakar, 'The 2017 Budget Is Taking SC/ST Welfare Backwards', Wire, 2 February 2017, https://thewire.in/105147/budget-2017-sc-st-welfare

52. Sharankumar Limbale, *The Outcaste Akkarmashi*, Santosh Bhoomkar, tr. (New Delhi: Oxford University Press, 2003), p. 103.

53. Ibid, p. 104.

54. Ibid, p. 107.

55. Srinivas, *Dalit Middle Class*, p. 39.

56. The Indian social reform movements, led predominantly by Brahmins and other dominant castes, regulated the structure of struggle.

57. B.R. Ambedkar, 'Why Indian Labour Is Determined to Win the War': Dr B.R. Ambedkar's Broadcast from Bombay Station of All India Radio', *Dr Babasaheb Ambedkar: Writings and Speeches*, Vol. 10, pp. 39–40.

58. Ibid, p. 43.

59. Shailvee Sharda, 'Mayawati's Brother Steps Down As Party National Vice President', *Times of India*, https://timesofindia.indiatimes.com/city/lucknow/mayawatis-brother-steps-down-as-party-national-vice-president/articleshow/64338752.cms

60. Arjun Dangle, ed., 'Introduction', *Poisoned Bread* (New Delhi: Orient BlackSwan, 2009), pp. xix–liv.

61. Anand Teltumbde, 'Bridging the Unholy Rift', in B.R. Ambedkar, *India and Communism*, Introduction by Anand Teltumbde (Delhi: LeftWord Books, 2017), p. 11.

62. Dangle, ed., 'Introduction', *Poisoned Bread*, pp. xxxvi.

63. Martin Luther King Jr, 'Letter for Birmingham Jail' in Cornel
     West, ed., *The Radical King* (Boston: Beacon Press, 2015), p. 137.
64. Frazier, *Black Bourgeoisie.*
65. Sanyal, *The Indian Renaissance,* p. 88.
66. John Dewey, The School and Society (Chicago: University of
     Chicago Press, 1956), p. 16.
67. P. Sainath, *Everybody Loves a Good Drought* (New Delhi: Penguin,
     1996).

Chapter 5: Dalit Capitalism

1. As reminisced from the memories of Baby Kamble.
2. While the Bania caste is part of Hindu society, for the discussion
    pertaining to how the trading classes in India are perceived by and
    behave with Dalits, the term in this book may include the non-
    Hindu merchant classes, such as, Jains, Parsis, Muslims, and so on.
3. Although the amendment stated that it abolished slavery, it added
    extra provisions to continue to place in servitude former slaves by
    adding the exception of being convicted. This led to mass incarceration
    of the Black population, which continues up until today. Cf. Ava
    DuVernay, *13th*, Netflix, 2016; the Thirteenth Amendment read:
    'Neither slavery nor involuntary servitude, except as a punishment
    for crime whereof the party shall have been duly convicted, shall exist
    within the United States, or any place subject to their jurisdiction.'
4. 'Letter from B.R. Ambedkar to W.E.B. Du Bois, ca. July 1946',
    Special Collections and University Archives, University of
    Massachusetts Amherst Libraries, http://credo.library.umass.edu/
    view/full/mums312-b109-i132
5. Caste was a prevalent term used in twentieth-century America to
    describe the 'Negro-White' relations of the American south.
6. Here are the top ten steel companies and their non-Dalit owners.
    Abhishek Jha, 'Top Ten Steel Companies in India 2018', BizVibe,
    19 April 2018, https://www.bizvibe.com/blog/top-10-steel-
    companies-in-india
7. W.E.B. Du Bois, *Dusk of Dawn: An Essay Toward an Autobiography
    of a Race Concept* (New Brunswick: Transaction Publishers, 1984),
    p. 70; W.E.B. Du Bois Papers, 'Du Bois the Activist Life', http://
    scua.library.umass.edu/exhibits/dubois/page6.htm

8.   Booker T. Washington, 'The Fruits of Industrial Training',
     Atlantic, October 1903, https://www.theatlantic.com/magazine/
     archive/1903/10/the-fruits-of-industrial-training/531030
9.   National Negro League, http://lcweb2.loc.gov:8081/ammem/
     amrlhtml/dtnegbus.html
10. Joseph Bernardo, 'National Negro Business League (1900–)',
     Black, 26 November 2008, https://www.blackpast.org/african-
     american-history/national-negro-business-league
11. W.E.B. Du Bois, 'The Economics of Negro Emancipation in
     the United States', *Sociological Review* 4.3 (October 1911):
     303–13.
12. Booker T. Washington, *Working with the Hands: Being a Sequel
     to 'Up from Slavery', Covering the Author's Experiences in Industrial
     Training at Tuskegee* (New York: Doubleday, Page and Company,
     1904), p. 16.
13. W.E.B. Du Bois, *In the Battle for Peace: The Story of My 83rd
     Birthday* (New York: Oxford University Press, 2007), p. 52.
14. Nico Slate, *Colored Cosmopolitanism* (Cambridge, MA: Harvard
     University Press, 2012), p. 23.
15. Devesh Kapur, D. Shyam Babu and Chandra Bhan Prasad, *Defying
     the Odds: The Rise of Dalit Entrepreneurs* (New Delhi: Random
     House, 2014).
16. Subodh Verma, 'Economic Gap between Upper Castes
     and Dalits Persists', *Times of India,* 14 April 2015,
     http://timesofindia.indiatimes.com/articleshow/46914577.
     cms?utm_source=contentofinterest&utm_medium=text&utm_
     campaign=cppst
17. Harry Stevens, 'Dalit Farmers May Fail to Benefit from Agricultural
     Sops Announced by Govt', *Hindustan Times,* 13 February 2018,
     https://www.hindustantimes.com/india-news/dalit-farmers-may-
     fail-to-benefit-from-agricultural-sops-announced-by-govt/story-
     jd3JzyY6qxRgq8adu0hwdK.html
18. Quoted in Eleanor Zelliot, *From Untouchable to Dalit: Essays on
     the Ambedkar Movements* (New Delhi: Manohar), p. 63.
19. Aseem Prakash, *Dalit Capital: State, Markets and Civil Society in
     Urban India* (New Delhi: Routledge Publications, 2015).
20. Kancha Ilaiah, *Post-Hindu India: A Discourse in Dalit-Bahujan,
     Socio-Spiritual and Scientific Revolution* (New Delhi: Sage, 2009).

21. D. Ajit, Han Donker, Ravi Saxena, 'Corporate Boards in India Blocked by Caste?', *Economic & Political Weekly*, 47.31 (11 August 2012): 39–43.

22. Manaswini Bhalla, Manisha V.S.K. Teja Goel, Konduri and Michelle Zemel, 'Firms of a Feather Merge Together: Information Flows, Familiarity Bias and M&A Outcomes', https://www.isid.ac.in/~epu/acegd2018/papers/KrishnaTeja.pdf

23. Amartya Sen, *Social Exclusion: Concept, Application and Scrutiny* (Manila: Asian Development Bank, 2000), https://www.adb.org/sites/default/files/publication/29778/social-exclusion.pdf

24. Balakrishna Chandrasekaran, 'Ambedkar: The Forgotten Free Market Economist', *Swarajya,* 13 September 2014, https://swarajyamag.com/economy/ambedkar-the-forgotten-free-market-economist

25. B.R. Ambedkar, 'States and Minorities: What Are Their Rights and How to Secure Them in the Constitution of Free India (1947)', in *Dr Babasaheb Ambedkar: Writings and Speeches,* Vol. 1 (Bombay: Education Department, Government of India 2014 [1979]), pp. 381–452.

26. Sukhadeo Thorat, 'B.R. Ambedkar's Thought on Economic Development' in Manu Bhagavan and Anne Feldhaus, *Claiming Power from Below Dalits and the Subaltern Question in India* (New Delhi: OUP, 2009).

27. Paolo Freire, *Pedagogy of the Oppressed* (New York: Penguin, 1996).

28. B.R. Ambedkar, *What Congress and Gandhi Have Done to the Untouchables* (Bombay: Thacker & Co., 1946), p. 230.

29. The mentioned exploiters, either owners, managers or employers, could be labelled as bourgeoisie. All the power-holders are in the position of the exploitation matrix of owner–worker, in which the worker is 'reduced to selling their labour power in order to live'. The reduction from human value to labour is an anti-humanistic agenda. The same anti-human norm is followed in the Indian caste system where reduction of human value to sub-standard caste labour is advocated (cf. Karl Marx and Friedrich Engels, *The Manifesto of the Communist Party*).

30. Kancha Ilaiah, *Why I Am Not a Hindu: A Sudra Critique of Hindutva Philosophy, Culture and Political Economy* (Kolkata: Samaya, 1995).

31. Jotirao Phule had discussed this in *Cultivator's Whipcord* wherein productive working-class communities like farmers get tricked by Brahmins under the garb of spiritual solace. Phule had warned the Shudra communities against being tricked by such brutal practices of the Brahmins. Jotirao Phule, *Cultivator's Whipcord: Collected Works of Mahatma Jotirao Phule* (Bombay: Education Dept., Govt. of Maharashtra, 2002).

32. W.E.B. Du Bois, *The Souls of the Black Folk* (New York: Simon & Schuster, 2009 [1903]), p. 60.

33. 'The Land Conundrum', *Economic & Political Weekly*, 53.42 (October 2018), p. 7.

34. Anand Teltumbde, 'Introduction', *India and Communism* (New Delhi: LeftWord, 2017).

35. Sujatha Gidla describes this in the story of her uncle, Satyam, a doyen of the communist movement in Andhra Pradesh, who was constantly reminded by his dominant-caste comrades about his caste position. Sujatha Gidla, *Ants Among Elephants: An Untouchable Family and the Making of Modern India* (New York: Farrar, Straus and Giroux, 2018).

36. Crony leftists in India are representative of the socio-economic nexus created by caste (cultural) capital. The representatives in the state and non-state within the broader caste-leftism have given rise to this cronyism.

37. An antidote to all ills, prominently cited in popular public verse; lit., 'Ram's arrow', which is considered the most powerful weapon against forces of evil.

38. Ambedkar's dialectic materialism emphasized the social lived reality of the oppressed mediated through the non-material experiences which were rooted in the religio-political philosophical sanctions, in addition to the material ones.

39. I visited his private collection of books donated to Milind College, Aurangabad, and Siddharth College, Mumbai. Nanakchand Rattu, Ambedkar's private secretary, reported that among Ambedkar's unfinished work was *Das Kapital* by Karl Marx, which he had begun as a chapter to be included in *Buddha and Karl Marx* with 'rough notes' and pointers to be 'enlarged later on'. Rattu adds, 'In fact, he [Ambedkar] attached more importance to this chapter by elaborating it with

his thought-provoking ideas.' Nanak Chand Rattu, *Last Few Years of Dr Ambedkar* (New Delhi: Amrit Publishing House, 1997), p. 62.

40. Baburao Bagul, 'Dalit Literature Is but a Human Literature', in Arjun Dangle, ed., *Poisoned Bread* (New Delhi: Orient BlackSwan, 2010), p. 291.

41. Gopal Guru, 'Rise of the "Dalit Millionaires": A Low Intensity Spectacle', *Economic & Political Weekly* 47.50, 15 December 2012, pp. 42, 49.

42. Cornel West, *Race Matters* (Boston: Beacon Press, 1993), p. 15.

43. Quoted in Khairmode Changdev, *Dr Babasaheb Ambedkar— Charitra*, Vol. 2 (Pune: Sugawa Prakashan, [1958] 2003) third edition, p. 26.

44. Adolph L. Reed Jr, *W.E.B. Du Bois and American Political Thought: Fabianism and the Color Line* (New York: Oxford University Press, 1997), p. 69.

45. He had requested union leader N.M. Joshi to consider the case of sending Dalit labourers to international labour meetings to develop contacts with other masses (Chapter 6).

Chapter 6: Brahmins against Brahminism

1. Gajendran Ayyathurai, 'Foundations of Anti-caste Consciousness: Pandit Iyothee Thass, Tamil Buddhism, and the Marginalized in South India', Columbia University PhD thesis, 2011, p. 62.

2. Peggy McIntosh, 'White Privilege and Male Privilege: A Personal Account of Coming to See Correspondences Through Work in Women's Studies', http://www.collegeart.org/pdf/diversity/white-privilege-and-male-privilege.pdf

3. Joshua Rothman, 'The Origins of "Privilege"', *New Yorker*, 12 May 2014, https://www.newyorker.com/books/page-turner/the-origins-of-privilege

4. Namit Arora, in *The Lottery of Birth: On Inherited Social Inequalities* (New Delhi: Three Essays, 2017), goes on a self-reflective confessional journey identifying the invisibilized markers of privilege that give dominant castes an upper hand. For instance, attending English-medium schools, being born into families that live in areas catering to the needs of children's well-being, such as sports, having role models, and also things that most of

these children take for granted, like 'access to a library, coaching classes' (p. 7).

5.   Social Conference of the Belgaum District Depressed Classes, Belgaum (23 March 1929), in *Babasaheb Ambedkar: Writings & Speeches*, Vol. 18 (1), pp. 159.

6.   Kumar Ketkar, 'Bhima-Koregaon Has Made the RSS's Social Engineering Boomerang', Print, 8 January 2018, https://theprint.in/opinion/bhima-koregaon-rss-boomerang/27194

7.   Ibid.

8.   Rana Mulchand, *Reservation in India: Myths and Realities* (New Delhi: Concept Publishing House, 2008).

9.   Kenneth J. Cooper, 'India's Majority Lower Castes Are Minor Voice in Newspapers', *Washington Post*, 5 September 1996, https://www.washingtonpost.com/archive/politics/1996/09/05/indias-majority-lower-castes-are-minor-voice-in-newspapers/4acb79e3-13d6-4084-b1d9-b09c6ed4f963/?utm_term=.3c8b7b282afa

10. Sudipto Mondal, 'Indian Media Wants Dalit News but Not Dalit reporters', Al Jazeera, 2 June 2017, https://www.aljazeera.com/indepth/opinion/2017/05/indian-media-dalit-news-dalit-reporters-170523194045529.html

11. Bedanti Saran, 'Jagannath Mishra Surrenders, Sent to Jail in Fodder Scam', *Hindustan Times,* 6 February 2018, https://www.msn.com/en-in/news/newsindia/jagannath-mishra-surrenders-sent-to-jail-in-fodder-scam/ar-BBIKIGk

12. Shekhar Gupta, 'National Interest: The Caste of Corruption', *Indian Express,* 24 December 2011, https://indianexpress.com/article/opinion/columns/national-interest-the-caste-of-corruption

13. Ibid.

14. The list is courtesy of journalisteye.com. '90% of Corrupt Money Is with Upper Castes', http://journalisteye.com/2016/09/27/90-of-corrupt-money-is-with-upper-castes

15. Edward A. Gargan, 'Huge Financial Scandal Shakes Indian Politics', *New York Times*, https://www.nytimes.com/1992/06/09/business/huge-financial-scandal-shakes-indian-politics.html

16. Michael Hodlen, 'UK Court Orders Indian Tycoon Mallya to Be Extradited on Fraud Charges', Reuters, 10 December 2018, https://www.reuters.com/article/us-india-mallya-britain/uk-court-orders-indian-tycoon-mallya-to-be-extradited-on-fraud-charges-idUSKBN1O91DE

17. BBC News, 'India Satyam Computers: B Ramalinga Raju jailed for fraud', 9, April 2015, https://www.bbc.com/news/world-asia-india-32229847

18. Ashutosh Kumar Mishra, '3.8 Malpractice in the 2010 Delhi Commonwealth Games and the Renovation of Shivaji Stadium', https://www.transparency.org/files/content/feature/3.8_MalpracticeIn2010DelhiGames_Mishra_GCRSport.pdf

19. *Hindustan Times*, 'Sahara Scandal: 4-year Chain of Events That Lead to Subrata Roy's Arrest', 1 March 2014, https://www.hindustantimes.com/india/sahara-scandal-4-year-chain-of-events-that-lead-to-subrata-roy-s-arrest/story-gDfYTWadLXecqtkw08xNQJ.html

20. Rediff News, 'The Saradha Chit Fund Scam', 7 January 2015, http://www.rediff.com/news/special/explained-the-saradha-chit-fund-scam/20150107.htm, accessed 10 December 2017.

21. Ambika Sharma, 'Surya Pharma Owes Rs 3,200 cr to Banks', *Tribune*, 1 July 2016, http://www.tribuneindia.com/news/business/surya-pharma-owes-rs-3-200-cr-to-banks/259318.html, accessed 10 December 2017.

22. Budan Gulam Shaikh, 'Winsome, Lose Some: Jatin Mehta and the Great Rs 7,000 Crore Diamond Heist', Wire, https://thewire.in/126904/the-great-rs-7000-crore-diamond-heist, accessed 12 December 2017.

23. *Indian Express*, 'Delhi Airport Scam: GMR-led DIAL Gains Rs 3,415 cr', 18 August 2012.

24. Subramanian Samanth, 'Long View: India's Very First Corruption Scandal', *New York Times*, 9 May 2012.

25. *Outlook*, 'Scamstory', 13 August 1997, https://www.outlookindia.com/magazine/story/scamstory/204016

26. Ritu Sarin, 'CBI Put It In Writing: "Inform Us Discreetly . . . Detention of (Vijay Mallya) Not Required"', *Indian Express*, 18 September 2018, https://indianexpress.com/article/india/cbi-put-it-in-writing-inform-us-discreetly-detention-of-vijay-mallya-is-not-required-5361515

27. Aditi Shah and Devidutta Tripathy, 'Unpublished Data Show India's Fraud Problems Extend Far Beyond Punjab National Bank', *The Wire*, https://thewire.in/banking/unpublished-rbi-data-shows-bank-loan-frauds-extend-way-beyond-pnb

28. Anto Antony, Shruti Srivastava and Siddharth Singh, 'India to Inject $32 Billion Into State Banks to Boost Loan Growth', Bloomberg, 24 October 2017, https://www.bloomberg.com/news/articles/2017-10-24/india-to-inject-32-billion-to-bolster-capital-at-state-banks

29. Pallavi Prasad, 'Harshad Mehta: The Baap of Bank Frauds Before Nirav Modi', Quint, https://www.thequint.com/news/politics/bjp-it-cell-now-frankensteins-monster-says-man-who-founded-it

30. Sudipto Mondal, 'Plot Allotment Row Casts Shadow on New CJI', *Hindustan Times*, https://www.hindustantimes.com/india/plot-allotment-row-casts-shadow-on-new-cji/story-a2uexS7zkPQU2M21LvuW2N.html

31. Shekhar Gupta, 'Are Leaders from "Lower" Castes and Subaltern Groups More Corrupt?', Print, https://theprint.in/national-interest/leaders-lower-castes-subaltern-groups-corrupt/24339/

32. The specificity of thirteenth-century Marathi, Novetzke argues, takes a 'vernacular turn' that improvises its rendition into more 'idioms, conventions of script and usage'. Christian Lee Novetzke, 'The Brahmin Double: The Brahminical Construction of Anti-Brahminism and Anti-caste Sentiment in the Religious Cultures of Precolonial Maharashtra', *South Asian History and Culture* 2.2, p. 233.

33. I am grateful to Anand Venkatkrishnan for pointing me to this literature.

34. Christian Lee Novetzke, *The Quotidian Revolution: Vernacularization, Religion, and the Premodern Public Sphere in India* (New York: Columbia University Press, 2016), p. 152.

35. Ibid, p. 154.

36. Novetzke, *The Quotidian Revolution*, pp. 132–33.

37. Ibid, p. 144.

38. Christian Lee Novetzke, 'The Brahmin Double: the Brahminical Construction of Anti-Brahminism and Anti-caste Sentiment in the Religious Cultures of Precolonial Maharashtra', *South Asian History and Culture* 2.2, p. 233.

39. Ibid, p. 240.

40. Anil Seal, *The Emergence of Indian Nationalism: Competition and Collaboration in the Later Nineteenth Century*, (Cambridge:

Cambridge University Press, 1968), p. 118, in Rosalind O'Hanlon, *Caste, Conflict and Ideology: Mahatma Jotirao Phule and Low Caste Protest in Nineteenth-Century Western India* (Cambridge: Cambridge University Press, 1985), p. 7 fn 4.

41. O'Hanlon, *Caste, Conflict and Ideology*, see chapter 2, 'From Warrior Tradition to Nineteenth-Century Politics'.

42. Ibid, pp. 27–28.

43. O'Hanlon, *Caste, Conflict and Ideology*.

44. The maharaja of Baroda, Sayajirao Gaikwad, had visited the US during the 1893 Columbian Exposition. Having been impressed with the education system, he brought back some educators and librarians to oversee the curriculum for students in Baroda. Thus, many students who were educated in Gujarati, Marathi or English were exposed to the American social, historical system. For more, see Daniel Immerwahr 'Caste or Colony? Indianizing Race in the United States', *Modern Intellectual History* 4.2 (2007): 275–301.

45. O'Hanlon, *Caste, Conflict and Ideology*, p. 110, fn 10.

46. Jotirao Phule, *Selected Writings of Jotirao Phule*, ed. G.P. Deshpande (Delhi: LeftWord Books, 2002), p. 222.

47. *Prabhakar* (Marathi), 11 June 1848, reprinted in *Dnyanodaya*, 15 June 1848, cited in Rosalind O'Hanlon, *Caste, Conflict and Ideology*, pp. 93–94.

48. O'Hanlon, *Caste, Conflict and Ideology*, p. 95.

49. Ibid, pp. 99–100. The Paramhansa Sabha's views of point 3 and 6 is reproduced here.

50. Jotirao Phule, 'Life of Shivaji in Poetical Metre' (1869), in *Mahatma Jyotiba Phule*, Dhananjay Keer, SG. Malshe, Y.D. Phadke, eds (Bombay: Mahatma Phule Samagra Vangmay, 2006, Maharashtra Rajya Sahitya ani Sanskruti Mandal), p. 67.

51. The Phules were generously assisted by their Muslim compatriots Fatima Sheikh and her brother Usman Sheikh. However, in *The Collected Works of Mahatma Phule* published by the Maharashtra government there is no reference to the Sheikh siblings. Some information regarding this can be found in Susie Tharu and K. Lalitha, *Women Writing in India: 600 B.C. to the Present, Vol.1* (New York: The Feminist Press, 1991), p. 162. Another important woman that remains hugely influential on the Phules is Sagunabai Kshirsagar who mentored them since childhood on the

importance of education. Braj Raj Mani and Pamela Sardar, *The Forgotten Liberator: The Life and Struggle of Savitribai Phule* (New Delhi: Mountain Peak, 2008).

52. Hari Narke, *On Savitribai Phule: Dnyanjyoti Savitribai Phule, Savitribai Phule First Memorial Lecture, 2008* (Mumbai: NCERT, 2009); O'Hanlon, *Caste, Conflict and Ideology*, p. 118.

53. Dhananjay Keer, *Mahatma Jotirao Phule: Father of the Indian Social Revolution* (Mumbai: Popular Prakashan, 1964, 2013) p. 48.

54. Ibid, p. 34.

55. Ibid, pp. 26–27.

56. Ibid, pp. 28–29.

57. O'Hanlon, *Caste, Conflict and Ideology*, p. 119.

58. Keer, *Mahatma Jotirao Phule*, p. 39.

59. Ibid, p. 131.

60. O'Hanlon, *Caste, Conflict and Ideology*, pp. 119–20.

61. Yogiraj Bagul, *Dr Babasaheb Ambedkar Aani Tyanche Dalittetar Sahakari, Bhaag-1* (Mumbai: Granthali, second edition, 2015).

62. Ibid. I am grateful to Milind Awasarmol for lending me a copy of this book.

63. Keer, *Dr Ambedkar: Life and Mission* (Bombay: Popular Prakashan, [1954] third edition, 2005), pp. 19–20.

64. Rosalind O'Hanlon, *Caste, Conflict and Ideology*, pp. 38–39.

65. Keer, *Mahatma Jotirao Phule*, pp. 242, 268.

66. Ibid, p. 240.

67. Charles A. Selden, 'Prince and Outcast at Dinner in London End Age-Old Barrier; Gaekwar of Baroda Is Host to "Untouchable" and Knight of High Hindu Caste', *New York Times*, 30 November 1930.

68. Scott R. Stroud, 'The Influence of John Dewey and James Tufts' Ethics on Ambedkar's Quest for Social Justice,' in Pradeep Aglave, ed, *The Relevance of Dr Ambedkar: Today and Tomorrow* (Nagpur: Nagpur University, 2017), pp. 33–54.

69. John Dewey and J.H. Tufts, *Ethics* (New York: H. Holt & Company, 1908).

70. Ambedkar describes the horrible experiences he had to endure that made him weep uncontrollably upon witnessing the humiliations he received at his workplace in addition to the enormous difficulties

he had to face to find lodging by the caste Hindu, Christian and Parsi residents of Baroda. For more, see B.R. Ambedkar 'Waiting for a Visa', in Vasant Moon, ed, *Dr Babasaheb Ambedkar: Writings and Speeches,* Vol. 12 (Bombay: Education Department, Government of Maharashtra, 1993), pp. 661–91. Also, in Nanakchand Rattu, ed., *Reminiscences and Remembrances of Dr B.R. Ambedkar* (Delhi: Falcon Books, 1995), pp. 12–18. In spite of this experience, Ambedkar stayed in affable contact with his long-time friend and dormitory mate from Columbia University Naval Bhathena. Ambedkar also tutored two Parsi students and had a stint at Batliboi's Accountancy Training Institute teaching mercantile law in 1925. Cf. Prabodhan Pol, 'Dr Ambedkaranche Sahakari: Naval Bhathena', *Anveekshan,* January–March 2018, pp. 28–32, https://www.academia.edu/38833819/Ambedkar

71. Keer, *Dr Babasaheb Ambedkar: Life and Mission*, p.66.
72. To work for the cause of Untouchables, Ambedkar chose to launch a social movement. Thus after several deliberations, Bahishkrit Hitakarini Sabha was formed on 20 July 1924; Ibid, pp. 54–55. Also see Ramchandra Kshirsagar, *Dalit Movement in India and Its Leaders, 1857–1956* (New Delhi: M.D. Publications, 1994), p. 82.
73. Started by Ambedkar in 1927.
74. Bagul, *Dr Babasaheb Ambedkar Aani Tyanche Dalittetar Sahakari, Bhaag-1*, p. 131.
75. Ibid, p. 127, author's translation from Marathi to English.
76. Ibid, p. 142.
77. Ibid, p. 143.
78. Ibid, p. 125.
79. Keer, *Dr Ambedkar: Life and Mission,* pp. 93–94.
80. Shatrugahn Jadhav, *Shreedharpant Tilak Aur Babasaheb Dr Ambedkar* (New Delhi: Samyak Prakashan, 2012), p. 36.
81. *Samata,* 29 June 1928, author's translation from Marathi to English, also reproduced in Jadhav, *Shreedharpant Tilak Aur Babasaheb Dr Ambedkar*, p. 108, author's translation from Marathi to English.
82. Jadhav, *Shreedharpant Tilak Aur Babasaheb Dr Ambedkar*, p. 106.
83. Ibid, p. 91.
84. Bagul, *Dr Babasaheb Ambedkar Aani Tyanche Dalittetar Sahakari, Bhaag-1*, pp. 38–39. Author's translation.

85. During the Mahad agitation, two Satyashodhak Maratha youth, Keshavrao Jedhe and Dinkarrao Jawalkar, supported the movement; however they maintained that no Brahmin should be involved. Ambedkar disagreed and called them out in *Bahishkrit Bharat*. 'I disagree with the proposition of Jedhe–Jawalkar who asked to keep Brahmins away from the satyagraha. We are not against Brahmins. We believe our fight is against Brahminism, the people who embrace Brahminism are our enemies.' Jadhav, *Shreedharpant Tilak Aur Babasaheb Dr Ambedkar*, pp. 93–94, author's translation.

86. Bagul, *Dr Babasaheb Ambedkar Aani Tyanche Dalittetar Sahakari, Bhaag-1*, p. 62. Author's translation.

87. Bagul, *Dr Babasaheb Ambedkar Aani Tyanche Dalittetar Sahakari, Bhaag-1*, p. 51.

88. Charles A. Sheldon, 'Prince and Outcast at Dinner in London End Age-Old Barrier; Gaekwar of Baroda Is Host to "Untouchable" and Knight of High Hindu Caste', *New York Times*, 30 November 1930.

89. Langston Hughes, *The Ways of White Folks* (New York: Vintage [1933] 1990).

90. Friedrich Nietzsche, *On the Genealogy of Morals and Ecce Homo*, trans. Walter Kaufmann and R.J. Hollingdale (New York: Vintage, 1989), p. 32.

91. Christa Davis Acampora, *Nietzsche's On the Genealogy of Morals* (Lanham, MD: Rowman and Littlefield Publishers, Inc., 2006), p. 346.

92. Friedrich Nietzsche, *On the Genealogy of Morals and Ecce Homo*, trans. Walter Kaufmann and R.J. Hollingdale (New York: Vintage, 1989), pp. 32–33 for all the following quotes by Nietzsche.

93. B.R. Ambedkar, 'What Path to Salvation', Speech delivered by Ambedkar to the Bombay Presidency Mahar Conference, 31 May 1936, Bombay, translated by Vasant Moon, http://www.columbia.edu/itc/mealac/pritchett/00ambedkar/txt_ambedkar_salvation.html, accessed 21 November 2018.

94. Bagul, *Dr Babasaheb Ambedkar Aani Tyanche Dalittetar Sahakari, Bhaag-1*, p. 39. Author's translation.